RELIGION WITHOUT TRANSCENDENCE?

CLAREMONT STUDIES IN THE PHILOSOPHY OF RELIGION

General Editors: **D. Z. Phillips**, Rush Rhees Research Professor,
University of Wales, Swansea and Danforth Professor of the
Philosophy of Religion, the Claremont Graduate School,
California; **Timothy Tessin**, Lecturer in Philosophy, University of
Wales, Swansea

At a time when discussions of religion are becoming increasingly
specialized and determined by religious affiliations, it is
important to maintain a forum for philosophical discussion which
transcends the allegiances of belief and unbelief. This series
affords an opportunity for philosophers of widely differing
persuasions to explore central issues in the philosophy of religion.

Titles include:

Stephen T. Davis (*editor*)
PHILOSOPHY AND THEOLOGICAL DISCOURSE

D. Z. Phillips (*editor*)
CAN RELIGION BE EXPLAINED AWAY?

RELIGION AND MORALITY

D. Z. Phillips and Timothy Tessin (*editors*)
RELIGION WITHOUT TRANSCENDENCE?

Timothy Tessin and Mario von der Ruhr (*editors*)
PHILOSOPHY AND THE GRAMMAR OF RELIGIOUS BELIEF

Religion without Transcendence?

Edited by

D. Z. Phillips

Rush Rhees Research Professor, University of Wales, Swansea
and
Danforth Professor of the Philosophy of Religion
The Claremont Graduate School, California

and

Timothy Tessin

Lecturer in Philosophy
University of Wales, Swansea

First published in Great Britain 1997 by
MACMILLAN PRESS LTD
Houndmills, Basingstoke, Hampshire RG21 6XS and London
Companies and representatives throughout the world

A catalogue record for this book is available from the British Library.

ISBN 0–333–71765–1

First published in the United States of America 1997 by
ST. MARTIN'S PRESS, INC.,
Scholarly and Reference Division,
175 Fifth Avenue, New York, N.Y. 10010

ISBN 0–312–17630–9

Library of Congress Cataloging-in-Publication Data
Religion without transcendence? / edited by D.Z. Phillips and Timothy
Tessin.
p. cm. — (Claremont studies in the philosophy of religion)
Includes bibliographical references and index.
ISBN 0–312–17630–9
1. Religion—Philosophy. 2. Transcendence (Philosophy)
I. Phillips, D. Z. (Dewi Zephaniah) II. Tessin, Timothy.
III. Series.
BL51.R3486 1997
210—dc21   97–13671
                                                                         CIP

This book is printed on paper suitable for recycling and made from fully managed and
sustained forest sources.

10 9   8   7   6   5   4   3   2   1
06 05 04 03 02 01 00 99 98 97

Printed in Great Britain by
The Ipswich Book Company Ltd
Ipswich, Suffolk

Contents

Acknowledgements

The symposia published here are the products of the 1996 Claremont Conference on the Philosophy of Religion held at the Claremont Graduate School.

I am grateful to the contributors to the collection, not only for participating in the conference, but for their generous support of the fund which contributes to the holding of future conferences. I am indebted to Helen Baldwin and Jackie Huntzinger, secretaries to the Department of Philosophy at Swansea and the Religion Program at Claremont respectively, for their administrative assistance, and to those graduate students at Claremont who helped, in various ways, to make the conference run smoothly. I am particularly grateful to my research assistant, Keith Lane, for preparing the typescript of 'Voices in Discussion' and other material. I also gratefully acknowledge the financial support for the conference provided by the Claremont Graduate School, Pomona College and Claremont McKenna College.

As further evidence of the co-operation between Claremont and Swansea, I welcome Timothy Tessin as co-editor of the series.

D. Z. P.
Claremont/Swansea
Swansea 1997

Notes on the Contributors

Barry Allen teaches philosophy at McMaster University in Hamilton, Ontario, Canada. He is the author of *Truth in Philosophy* and assistant editor of the journal *Common Knowledge*.

Marina Barabas is Assistant Professor of Philosophy at Charles University, Prague. She has also taught at King's College, London and at the University of Massachusetts, Boston. Her work is mainly in moral and political philosophy, and ancient philosophy.

Joseph Augustine Di Noia O.P. is Executive Director of the Secretariat for Doctrine and Pastoral Practices of the National Conference of Catholic Bishops. He is also Professor of Theology in the Pontifical Faculty of the Dominican House of Studies and Adjunct Professor in the American campus of the John Paul II Institute for Marriage and Family Studies, both in Washington DC. He is the author of *Diversity of Religions: A Christian Perspective* and co-author of the forthcoming, *The Love That Never Ends: A Key to the Catechism of the Catholic Church* and *Veritatis Splendor and the Renewal of Moral Theology*. He is editor in chief of *The Thomist*.

Stephen Grover is Assistant Professor of Philosophy at Queen's College in the City University of New York and formerly a Fellow of All Souls College, Oxford. He has published papers in the philosophy of religion and is engaged on a book on Leibniz and the best of all possible worlds.

John Hick is Emeritus Danforth Professor at the Claremont Graduate School and a Fellow of the Institute for Advanced Research in the Humanities at the University of Birmingham, England. His publications include *Philosophy of Religion; Evil and the God of Love; Death and Eternal Life; God and the Universe of Faiths; An Interpretation of Religion* (Gifford Lectures 1986–7); *Disputed Questions in Theology and the Philosophy of Religion; The Metaphor of God Incarnate; A Christian Theology of Religion*.

Michael Hodges is Professor of Philosophy at Vanderbilt University. He is the author of *Transcendence and Wittgenstein's Tractatus* and of numerous articles. He is working with John Lachs on a book on Wittgenstein and Santayana.

Gareth Moore O.P. is Prior of the Dominican Community of Froidmont, Rixensart, Belgium and former tutor in Old Testament and Philosophy at Blackfriars, Oxford. He is the author of *Believing in God: A Philosophical Essay* and *The Body in Context: Sex and Catholicism.*

D. Z. Phillips is Danforth Professor of the Philosophy of Religion at the Claremont Graduate School and Rush Rhees Research Professor, University of Wales, Swansea. He is the author of *The Concept of Prayer; Faith and Philosophical Enquiry; Death and Immortality; Moral Practices* (with H. O. Mounce); *Sense and Delusion* (with Ilham Dilman); *Athronyddu am Grefydd; Religion Without Explanation; Dramâu Gwenlyn Parry; Through a Darkening Glass; Belief, Change and Forms of Life; R. S. Thomas: Poet of the Hidden God; Faith After Foundationalism; From Fantasy to Faith; Interventions in Ethics; Wittgenstein and Religion; Writers of Wales: J. R. Jones;* and *Introducing Philosophy.* He is editor of Swansea Studies in Philosophy, co-editor of Claremont Studies in the Philosophy of Religion and editor of the journal *Philosophical Investigations.*

William L. Rowe is Professor of Philosophy at Purdue University. He is the author of *Religious Symbols and God; The Cosmological Argument; Philosophy of Religion; Thomas Reid on Freedom and Morality.* He has held a Guggenheim Fellowship, has been a Fellow at the National Humanities Centre and is a past president of the Central Division of the American Philosophical Association.

Richard Schacht is Professor of Philosophy and Jubilee Professor of Liberal Arts and Sciences at the University of Illinois at Urbana-Champaign, where he has taught since 1967. He is the author of *Hegel And After; Nietzsche* and most recently *The Future of Alienation* and *Making Sense of Nietzsche.* He is the current Executive Director of the North American Nietzsche Society. His interests centre on issues relating to human nature, value theory, social theory, and related developments in European philosophy.

Ninian Smart is J. F. Rowny Professor of Comparative Religion at the University of California Santa Barbara and was founding professor of the Department of Religious Studies in the University of Lancaster, England, which pioneered modern studies in religion in the UK. He is is the author of many books of which he prefers *Reasons and Faiths: The Religious Experience; Doctrine and Argument in Indian Philosophy; The Science of Religion; The Dimensions of the Sacred; The World's Religions.*

Timothy Tessin is Lecturer in Philosophy, University of Wales, Swansea. He is co-editor of *Philosophy and the Grammar of Religious Belief,* and, from this volume, of the series Claremont Studies in the Philosophy of Religion. He is associate editor of the journal *Philosophical Investigations* in which he has also published articles.

Michael Weston is Lecturer in Philosophy at the University of Essex. He is the author of *Morality and the Self* and *Kierkegaard and Modern Continental Philosophy,* and of papers on the philosophy of religion, moral philosophy and the philosophy of literature.

1

Introduction: Appropriating 'Transcendence'

D. Z. Phillips

We cannot take for granted our ability to appropriate the word 'transcendence' in our common discourse, if only because we may not have a common discourse for this concept. Words may slide, slip and lose their hold, so that a time may come when it is better to let them go lest further damage is caused. There is an irony in a situation in which intellectuals think of themselves as the guardians of sense. What if the perilous state of the concept of transcendence has to do, in part, at least, with what we, as intellectuals, have made of it? It is not my intention, in this introduction, to answer that question one way or another, but one cannot read the papers in this collection without being confronted by it.

In the opening symposium, Barry Allen argues that an ontological conception of transcendence, static, absolute, and complete, is a world well lost. This does not mean that such an ontology ever existed. It is a philosophical chimera which has been exposed in the attack on metaphysics so characteristic of analytic philosophy in the twentieth century. To yearn after Reality and Truth is to yearn for something unreal – 'a view from Nowhere'.

In the same symposium, however, Timothy Tessin asks whether religious realities or truths, or, indeed, *any* concern with reality or truth, *must* share the same fate as Reality and Truth conceived metaphysically. If the metaphysical notions are abandoned, may this not clear the way for a clear appreciation and reappropriation of concepts of transcendence, including, perhaps, how such a concept may appear in religion?

1

For John Hick, in the second symposium, the concept of transcendence is far from obsolete. He argues that we are led to it, inductively, when we reflect on the equivalence found in the spiritual fruits of the world religions. We postulate a transcendent reality beyond all religions, which is above all but formal attributes. If it had substantive attributes it would be another particular manifestation of the transcendent, as are the other major religions. Critics of Hick's argument ask whether he is consistent in his views, since Hick claims that it is in this transcendent realm that human beings fulfil their potential, a process said to begin here on earth, and that appears to be a substantive claim.

Stephen Grover brings us back to the issue of intellectual distortions of religious belief. He argues that Hick's conception of transcendence is such a distortion, and that the hope connected with it has more to do with human desires than with the love of God. Hick's counter-claim is that without his conception of transcendence, we would have to accept a naturalistic view of life in which many lives end in wretchedness and hopelessness. Grover, on the other hand, is wary of Hick's categorical assumption that a minimum of social and economic justice is a precondition for any spiritual attainment.

If metaphysical conceptions of transcendence are abandoned, Richard Schacht asks, in the third symposium, whether it follows that we have no use for a concept of transcendence at all. Barry Allen had argued already that in the cultural artifacts we create we are enabled to transcend whatever historical state we are in. Schacht wants to argue, in a wider context, that there are many ways, moral and artistic, in which we seek to transcend the prosaic in our lives. We seek to create and sustain values which go beyond what is merely utilitarian.

In replying, Michael Weston asks us to step back, and to consider what we are doing when we make assertions such as Schacht's. What do we take ourselves to be doing, as intellectuals, and as philosophers in particular, when we attempt to reach conclusions concerning the place, if any, of transcendence in human life? If this question has to do with the meaning of our lives, is this something we can lecture on and about which we can come to an intellectual conclusion? Is the issue resolvable in that way? What if philosophical attempts to answer this question in the affirmative are themselves obstacles to raising the question in any real way? According to Weston, the intellectualization of the issue of transcendence and the meaning of life obscures the fact that the issue is a *personal* one; one which every individual must face for himself or herself. Here, truth is subjectivity, not a philosophical thesis.

In the fourth symposium, Ninian Smart challenges Weston's conclusions. Prior to any claims about transcendence arrived at by an individual, surely that individual has an obligation to try to understand what various religions have said about transcendence. Empathic understanding is prior to personal judgement. This is not an attempt to have 'a view from Nowhere'. We must be ready to learn from other religions. There is no such thing as the philosophy of religion, only philosophies of religions.

J. A. Di Noia certainly does not want to deny that we should make an effort to understand religions other than our own, but, as he and others point out, we are in danger of ignoring a feature of any serious religious belief: it makes a claim on one. We cannot take for granted that the claims of different religions amount to the same thing. Di Noia argues that dialogues between religions are at such an early stage that we cannot say what the outcome will be. The situation must not be oversimplified. Any philosophical or theological account of such dialogue must allow logical space for the possibility of coming to the conclusion that a religious claim is false.

In the fifth symposium, issues of truth and falsity loom large, since it concerns the possibility of a state of affairs which is said to transcend the limitations of this life, namely, survival after death. The discussion between William Rowe and Gareth Moore again reflects the fundamental divide between the papers in the collection. Is survival after death to be equated with eternal life, and is a transcendence we may be said to share with God after death, to be equated with an extension of our lives beyond the grave? Can we settle the issue of whether death is intrinsically bad or not independently of any context, or of any moral or religious perspective on the dead? If not, does this mean that death can be extrinsically but not intrinsically bad? In this symposium we are presented with the central issue of what the issue of 'transcending death' has become for us in our philosophizings.

This is precisely what Marina Barabas asks us to consider in the final symposium. Is 'transcendence' to be explored as though we are investigating a factual state of affairs? Is it a matter of asking what we want, wondering whether it exists, and, if it does, considering how we can attain it? Barabas asks us to consider the notion of transcendence in a radically different way, namely, via a notion of 'the beautiful'. She asks us to think of the way in which we can be drawn by the beautiful, how it can create an attention in us which is a response of gladness. Conceptions of transcendence may show us what we are not: a beauty and purity which does not exist among us. What exists among us, our hatreds and our other vices, should not be, while what should be, the pure and beautiful, does not exist, but draws us beyond ourselves. Such contexts show one way in which we can reappropriate the notion of transcendence from what it often becomes in our philosophical discussions.

Yet, as Michael Hodges points out, Barabas' emphasis can be misunderstood. It is not being claimed that the beautiful *must* draw us to itself. There is no necessity about our being drawn to what is transcendentally pure. People may be in the situation where some are so drawn, and yet walk away from it. They may talk of the situation in quite different terms.

This brings us back to the issue raised by Weston, namely whether 'the appropriation of transcendence', if it is to mean anything, is something which can be settled in a general way by philosophy. Weston insists that the issue is a personal one. But, then, is not *this* something that philosophy can recognize? We can arrive at the philosophical conclusion that it is confused to turn 'the meaning of life' into a philosophical theory about such meaning. This philosophical conclusion would not itself be a personal appropriation of the issue. Weston seems to suggest that even this philosophical engagement may be an evasion of the personal issue, and should be revoked. Such evasion may occur, but need it change the character of the philosophical task? No doubt interesting questions may be asked abut what one's conception of that task would be if it were accompanied by *blatant* evasion of the personal issues. But to recognize the limits of the philosophical task itself would not be a reason for revoking it.

The disagreements which are all too evident in this collection testify to the need for continuing philosophical engagement and discussion; a need which will persist as long as we are puzzled by what it can mean to speak of appropriating a concept of transcendence in our discourse. To repeat what we asked at the outset: Is the concept of transcendence in a perilous state because of what we, as philosophers, have made of it? My editorial hope is that this collection shows us, at least, that that question needs to be faced.

Part One
Transcendence – A World Well Lost?

2

The Ambition of Transcendence

Barry Allen

Thomas Nagel calls for philosophy to acknowledge an 'ambition of transcendence'. It is necessary, he says, 'to combine the recognition of our contingency, our finitude, and our containment in the world with an ambition of transcendence, however limited may be our success in attaining it. The right attitude in philosophy is to accept aims that we can achieve only fractionally and imperfectly, and cannot be sure of achieving even to that extent.' We are called to rise above the particular, historical, cultural, and physical, 'to reach a position as independent as possible of who we are and where we started'. The whole idea of philosophy, as Nagel understands it, is the pure desire for objectivity, the desire to transcend every 'particular point of view and to conceive of the world as a whole', bringing 'one's beliefs, one's actions, and one's values more under the influence of an impersonal standpoint'. Nagel evokes a Neoplatonic image of the soul ascending through celestial spheres toward the Absolute – toward a god's-eye view from nowhere. 'We may think of reality as a set of concentric spheres, progressively revealed as we detach gradually from the contingencies of the self.' 'What really happens', Nagel thinks, 'in the pursuit of objectivity is that a certain element of the self, the impersonal or objective self, which can escape from the specific contingencies of one's creaturely point of view, is allowed to predominate. Withdrawing into this element one detaches from the rest and develops an impersonal conception of the world.' Bernard Williams calls this the 'absolute conception of reality', which, he thinks, the very idea of knowledge 'seems to call for'. 'If knowledge is what it claims to be, then it is knowledge of a reality which exists independently of that knowledge, and indeed ... independently of any thought or experience. Knowledge is of what is there *anyway*.'[1]

Nagel admits that absolute objectivity, his view from nowhere, is an endless quest, and *might* even be impossible. 'The sceptic' may be right; perhaps we simply cannot know the truth about reality, the absolutely objective truth. I suppose Nagel takes this idea seriously because unless scepticism makes sense, Nagel's picture of transcendence and objectivity make no sense either. Anyway, for him the important thing is not attaining truth but striving for it, having the right intention. Cognitive success (absolute truth) would be nice, but it is not the heart of the matter. The most important thing is the effort. By straining for ever icier heights of detachment we advance 'our understanding of the world and of ourselves, increasing our freedom in thought and action, and becoming better'. Transcending one's own point of view toward the ontologically transcendent being of reality as it is in itself – the god's-eye view from nowhere – 'is the most important creative force in ethics'. 'If we did not have this capacity then there would be no alternative to relativism.'[2]

What is wrong with this picture? A good deal, I think. My discussion is organized around three ideas.

(1) An idea about subjectivity: The idea that there is an important difference between genuine knowledge and belief, opinion, doctrine, subjective conviction, and so on.

(2) An idea about truth: The idea that *it* is the appropriate concept in terms of which to interpret this difference – that the difference between knowledge and non-knowledge is essentially the difference truth makes.

(3) An idea about objectivity: The idea that the value or good of knowledge consists in its objectivity.

KNOWLEDGE AND TRUTH

Plato does not own the distinction between knowledge and opinion, which does not have to be drawn in absolute, metaphysical terms, and need not presuppose the ontological transcendence of beings-in-themselves with which true knowledge corresponds. That is not to say that there is no such difference to speak of, nor even that so ontological a thinker as Parmenides was entirely wrong in his understanding of it, disdaining 'the opinions of mortals, in which there is no true reliability'.[3] Parmenides contrasts the unreliable *doxa* with 'motionless truth', which suggests that truth makes the difference between knowledge and opinion. While I shall argue that that is a mistake, it remains sound, I think, to hold that the difference between knowledge and opinion is a matter of reliability. More precisely, the reason it is sensible to value knowledge, to prefer it to the variety of forms of non-knowledge, is that knowing implies an enhanced performative capacity which makes the knower more reliable in doing and making. Performative reliability is thus not the logical essence of knowledge, but its *raison d'être*, what gives knowledge a point and value, and gives practical, pragmatic significance to our distinguishing between knowledge and the varieties of non-knowledge, including errors and doctrines that *pass* for knowledge without really having that value.

I suggested that Parmenides takes the wrong path when he tries to understand the difference between *doxa* and philosophical knowledge in terms of truth or *aletheia*. Is it *truth* that makes the difference between knowledge and pretenders like subjective belief, conviction, or doctrine? Why *must* knowledge be true at all? According to A. J. Ayer, it is a 'linguistic fact' that 'what is not true cannot properly be said to be known.'[4] Abilities to use a sextant, harrow a field, or dye tissue for microscopy are 'not true'; they are, of course, also 'not false'. Yet they are excellent examples of knowledge. To say that such abilities are cases of 'knowing-how' and therefore somehow do not count or must take second place to propositional 'knowing-that' merely begs the question whether knowledge is essentially propositional knowledge of truth. No appeal to definitions can settle this question; knowledge is not true 'by definition'. If dictionaries say otherwise, it is because they have been corrupted by Platonizing philosophers mistaken for experts about knowledge.

'But', it may be said, 'if something we thought we knew is found to be wrong, to be an error or falsehood, we revoke our belief, and speak no more of it as knowledge.' That is right as far as it goes. What it shows is not that knowledge must be true, but that something we consider to be an error is not, of course, something we are going to count as knowledge. Certainly knowledge cannot be false. But 'true' and 'false' are contrary, not contradictory, terms. Knowledge does not have to be one or the other. From the mere fact that no knowledge *is false* nothing follows about truth as a logical ingredient of knowledge.

Consider this inference: (1) *Socrates knows that p*; so, (2) *p*. Many find the inference valid, and it might occur to a philosopher to adduce it as proof that knowledge has to be true.[5] On the face of it, though, the inference is contrived. Who would reason this way and to what purpose, especially since it is no easier to determine when somebody (really) knows that *p* than it is to determine whether *p* is true? Perhaps the inference depends on what Wittgenstein called logical grammar. To speak as we do, say not '*S* knows that *p*' unless you yourself believe that *p*. Perhaps. But that does not show that a logical property of *being true* partly constitutes knowledge, or that knowledge could not be what it is were it not *knowledge of the truth*.[6]

If knowledge must be true, then a claim to know must be a claim to know that something is true. Not that it is warranted, reasonable, or justified – those would be different claims – but that it is *knowledge* and as such is the very truth. But knowledge that has to be true cannot be fallible. The only claims that could reasonably be asserted as knowledge would be ones which (you suppose) could not possibly be incorrect. So the more implausible it is to hold that knowledge is an immutable body of infallible truth, the more dubious it should be that truth is a logical condition of knowledge. But why emphasize fallibility? What recommends this attitude toward knowledge? As Hume and Kant argued, to know is not to enjoy a specular representation or mimetic depiction of a thing-in-itself apart from its relation to anything else. Instead, as Nietzsche and Rorty say, it is to know the relations, to know some cross-section of relations among an entire ensemble of things (including sentences). I would add that as such relations are constantly changing, so must knowledge change to retain its empirical validity, the structure and content of knowledge being no more immutable than the environment in which it makes sense. This vital flexibility distinguishes knowledge from belief, doctrine, or genetic hard-wiring. But it also means that merely to retain empirical reliability knowledge requires what Peirce called the attitude of contrite fallibilism.

The difference between knowledge and mere subjective belief or opinion is the difference reliability makes. Why then speak of truth? Why insist that knowledge, to be what it is, has to be true? It may be answered that the reliability I make much of actually presupposes the truth of knowledge. Is it not the correspondence of knowledge with reality (its *truth*) that explains why some beliefs are reliable (knowledge) and others are not? Freud may have such an argument in mind when, in a rare descent into metaphysics, he defends a correspondence theory of knowledge and truth: 'If there were no such thing as knowledge distinguished among our opinions by corresponding to reality, we might build bridges just as well out of cardboard as out of stone, we might inject our patients with a decagram of morphine instead of a centigram, and might use tear-gas as a narcotic instead of ether.'[7]

The answer to this argument is that we have no idea which beliefs or conceptions correspond with reality (or are true) apart from their reliability. We cannot independently distinguish a property of correspondence and correlate it empirically with an independently established quality of reliability. Consequently, there can be no evidence for 'correspondence' except the very reliability it is invoked to explain. The so-called explanation is therefore vacuous. To say that a conception 'is true' is not to endow it with a quality that explains why it is useful or reliable. The reason we do not build bridges out of cardboard is not that *it is true* that they would disintegrate in the rain. It is that *they would disintegrate in the rain* (among other reasons). *Being true* or *corresponding to reality* are not, however, extra reasons in favour of building with stone rather than paper.[8]

Knowledge is not essentially true because what 'is true' in any case is a statement or proposition, and knowledge is not essentially linguistic or propositional. It is a presupposition, not a fact, that knowledge must admit of propositional representation, or that it presupposes true belief. Propositional 'knowing-that' is neither the central or most important sort of knowledge, nor is it really different from practical know-how, of which it is properly a species. Propositions, sentences, or statements are artifacts, things we must know how to make or use before we can know that they are true. So the knowledge it takes to know that a proposition is true is not propositional knowledge of truth. To know, say, that *Australia lies in the Southern Hemisphere* is true, you have to know how to discover and assess evidence, weigh plausibility, consult authorities, refute objections, and so on, including perhaps knowing how to get there from here.[9] All knowledge is like this, building on operational, effective know-how, and the artifacts that we know how to use (including the artifacts of conception and communication).

The conviction that knowledge requires truth, or that the best knowledge is propositional knowledge of truth, should fade in proportion to the clarity with which we grasp its practical, performative character. All our knowledge is built upon and ultimately goes back to operational, effective know-how – knowing how to perform tasks, render judgments, use tools, including the tools of conception, measurement, analysis, description, and communication. The *unit* of knowledge is not the true sentence or true belief, but the artifact (linguistic or otherwise). What makes knowledge good, what makes it desirable and worth cultivating, has nothing to do with the ontological truth of knowledge (its correspondence with a being-in-itself), depending instead on the difference knowledge makes to our performative reliability. The same practical quality, and not ontological, transcendent truth, makes the difference between genuine knowledge and belief, opinion, doctrine, myth, ideology, orthodoxy, and so on.

KNOWLEDGE AND OBJECTIVITY

For Nagel, beliefs and conceptions are objective to the extent that they are transparent, letting us see right through them to true being. Nothing about them is conditioned by circumstance. The more disinterested a perception, the more impartial a conception, the more transparent they are to beings in themselves. Nagel should find little to disagree with in Heidegger's idea of truth as disclosure. 'To say that an assertion "is true" signifies that it uncovers a being as it is in itself. Such an assertion states, points out, "lets" a being be seen … in its uncoveredness.' This 'predicative exhibition of a being', Heidegger says, has the character of unveiling letting-be-encountered. The 'being-true' of a true statement 'must be understood as *being-uncovering*'. The very being which was meant 'shows itself *just as* it is in itself; that is, *it* (in its selfsameness) is just as *it* (in the assertion) is shown, uncovered, as being'.[10]

Nagel holds up the 17th-century doctrine of primary and secondary qualities as the model to emulate the breakthrough to objectivity. As a result of taking this step we now know that an entire field of subjectively valuable qualities (colour, taste, texture, and so on) are not really *there* in things, not after you subtract their relation to us. A more disinterested view reveals a colourless world of corpuscles. This view of the world is not literally from nowhere. But it is on the road to nowhere, a step in the right direction, the sort of move we need a good deal more of. The rise and acceptance of the primary/secondary quality distinction proves that Nagel's vision of a possible view from nowhere is not the empty dream of a spirit-seer. When we are at our best as knowers, our best knowledge *does* disclose reality as it is in itself, from *its* perspective, *its* own 'self-identity'.

It is strange to regard the primary/secondary quality distinction as a blow for detachment. Galileo, Descartes, Boyle, and Newton – all advocates of the distinction – were clear about their interests. They wanted a quantitative measure, a natural philosophy of questions posed in quantitative terms, which they had learned (from an alchemical tradition some of them pretended to spurn) to associate with the mastery of reliable capacities for technical effects. It was not *disinterestedness* but rather a *different interest* (in contrast to prevailing scholasticism, where colours mattered and mechanics did not) which moved these philosophers to distinguish primary and secondary qualities. Their discovery (if we must) was not that colour is less 'objectively real' than spatial extension, but that there are reliable quantitative operations whose result is indifferent to the so-called secondary qualities of the material. *Mass* and *shape* are human conceptions as much as *red* and *stink*. It may be useful to ignore the difference between being coloured and being extended, especially when your interest is limited to questions whose answers are quantities: a measurement, a number. But the success of quantitative prediction does not prove that so-called secondary qualities are less real. What 'is there' depends on what you are looking for or are trying to do. Colour is not there if you are trying to weigh something. A wall or floor is not there for the neutrino that falls through them.[11]

Nagel expects a lot from the primary/secondary quality distinction. In reaffirming its importance he reasserts (in a 'scientific', 'modern' way) the old Greek dichotomy between appearance and reality. His ideal objectivity implies that the true objects of knowledge are 'identical to themselves', they have an identity which is somehow *their own*, precisely the quality Plato held to be the criterion of a substantial being.[12] With all Platonists, Nagel believes that when we transcend personal subjectivity we take a noble step toward something Absolute, toward a perspectiveless god's-eye view of beings-in-themselves. He calls this realism. Williams too thinks he is being seriously 'realistic' in his idea of an absolute conception of reality. But there is nothing particularly realistic about this so-called realism. A better description of Nagel's philosophy is Neo-neoplatonism. Instead of remaining locked in the interested partiality of our sensuous nature, philosophers and lovers of truth have a kind of moral obligation to raise their minds from the trough of subjectivity and ascend toward the light. Only then can they attain *knowledge* (a vision of true being).

Nagel's attachment to the rationalistic presuppositions of Greek metaphysics is obvious. Consider the distinction he makes between 'mere information', which any animal 'accumulates', and 'true knowledge', a thing apart, something completely different. 'We are', he says, 'encouraged these days to think of ourselves as contingent organisms arbitrarily thrown up by evolution.' – True (apart from the 'arbitrary' bit), and for sound reasons. – 'There is no reason in advance to expect a finite creature like that to be able to do more than accumulate information at the perceptual and conceptual level it occupies by nature.' There is no reason in advance to assume *anything* about the course of evolution. And no animal merely 'accumulates information'. What it perceives and what, if anything, it conceives, is a function of its neurology, and the result (insofar as it is not hard-wired) is *knowledge*, that is, a capacity for reliable performance in the environment which has co-evolved with that neurology. 'Not only [Nagel continues] can we form the pure idea of a world that contains us and of which our impressions are a part, but we can give this idea a content which takes us very far from our original impressions.' The question is whether such a 'pure' idea is possible. Can an idea be so pure, so disinterested, that it becomes *transparent*, letting us see the truth of beings in themselves? I think Nagel would have to do a lot more to show that this isn't merely a world-picture embraced by wishful thinking. To show that ideas can be so perfectly unconditioned by the environmental circumstances under which we conceive them as to become transparent it is not enough to trot out the primary/secondary quality distinction. Berkeley understood that colour and taste are *there* just as much as extension or matter is. In Heidegger's terms, there is no 'there' where beings can 'be' (presence) apart from *our* presence and their *relations* to us and to the environing world. Nietzsche is probably right to argue that 'the human intellect cannot avoid seeing itself in its own perspectives, and *only* in these. We cannot look around our own corner: it is hopeless curiosity that wants to know what other kinds of intellects and perspectives there *might* be.'[13]

The key question (as I see it) is whether 'objectivity' adds anything to the conception of knowledge that is not already entailed by the reliability which distinguishes knowledge from opposite forms of belief. You cannot explain the reliability by alluding to the objectivity, for the same reason you cannot explain reliability by referring to truth. Our knowledge is 'about objects', in the sense that when we practice that knowledge we are 'about' or intentionally involved with objects, and the 'objects of knowledge' are as various as the objects we are about when we use it in action. Such objects are not of one ontological sort (fact, state of affairs), nor is our involvement with them one kind of relation (representation). The point of knowledge is not to attain a unique, transparent *view* of a thing. The point is to get something (a conception, understanding, or theory) that works every time. To 'know' is to be able to work with things – objects, if you like; it is to be able to work with lots of them, with complicated, ontologically heterogeneous assemblies of tools, materials, conceptions, symbols, calculations, and so on. No one of these objects is *the* 'object of knowledge'.

Knowledge is different from belief, doctrine, ideology, and the like, even though the idea of objectivity is not useful for understanding the difference. Instead of the misleading opposition between an 'objective' knowledge and a subjective belief or perception, it is better to think in terms of how good the best knowledge of a time can be. It is only to be expected that the best knowledge should go beyond the original impressions of an untutored mind. Our *original* impressions are the product of past generations' conceptions and experiments, passed down by cultural inheritance to become 'the given' for later generations. To allow us to go beyond this inheritance, to transcend *this historical-artifactual given*, which human beings give to themselves as they reproduce their environment, is indeed a quality of the best knowledge.

To have 'the right attitude in philosophy' Nagel thinks you have to want to climb outside of your own mind, 'an effort that some would regard as insane and that I regard as philosophically fundamental'. I would say it is merely silly. It simply *isn't* possible to think our way out of our neurology, which is the effect of an evolutionary past that is contingent (I did not say arbitrary) yet inescapable. All that we have to think with – our unique neurology, our senses and the instruments we have contrived to enhance them, our cultural traditions and languages – are good for knowing only the environment in which all of these and ourselves have co-evolved. Everything about the human environment, including the instruments and practices of knowledge that reliably work in it, is artifactual, conditioned by the same evolutionary processes that are fundamentally responsible for our existence. The difference between

knowledge and non-knowledge (whether error, ignorance, or subjective conviction) has nothing to do with mirrors or mimetic fealty.
To 'get things right' is to get them right in our terms. It calls not for
Neoplatonic self-effacement or a fatuous god's-eye view from
nowhere. More important than objectivity, truth, or Platonic realism
is the fact that those who act from knowledge reliably get what they
aim for. Knowledge as we know it is the product of interacting artifacts, including our neurology, and only *works* in an environment
that is itself both artifactual and ceaselessly changing.[14]

KNOWLEDGE AND MECHANISM

At the conference for which my paper was first prepared, my com-
mentator was to be Hilary Putnam. He was, however, unfortunately obliged to miss our meetings, and Timothy Tessin took
over the task. In anticipation of an exchange with Putnam I wrote
this next section, discussing his idea of the transcendence of reason.
I let it stand here because Putnam's ideas are worth more discussion by philosophers of religion, and also because it allows me to
introduce a comparison between Putnam and Michael Oakeshott
and introduce a critical concept of *rationalism*.

Nagel's Neo-neoplatonism is an obvious example of the 'metaphysical realism' Putnam criticizes. Yet he too speaks up for transcendence, which is not well lost but poorly understood. His
argument supports a peculiar transcendence for reason or rationality. 'Reason can go beyond whatever reason can formalize'; 'reason
can transcend whatever it can survey.' 'There is a notion of
justification which is transcultural ... not simply a creature of the
local epistemology and the standards of the time.' To prove these
claims Putnam relies on a number of technical arguments. They
mostly come down to the thought that what is technically known as
'computability' – what can be written down as an algorithm, an in-
struction a machine (computer) can carry out – presupposes intelligence which *cannot* be so formalized, which 'transcends' algorithm,
which does not compute, does not follow a rule mechanically. The
'totality of possible human modes of reasoning and conceptualiz-
ation' is 'unsurveyable', irreducible to mechanical instructions
however complicated. There is no algorithm, no computable
method, no purely physical, extensionally definable property that
all cases of rationality, reasoning, intelligence, or knowledge have

in common. Intelligent human practice is therefore something wholly different from computation.[15]

It is instructive to translate Putnam's argument into the terms of Michael Oakeshott's distinction between technical and practical knowledge. Every human act involves knowledge, and all such knowledge has two moments which, however, never appear in isolation, the practice of knowledge necessarily involving both. One moment of knowledge is technical – how-to knowledge of technique. Whether or not it has been written down, such knowledge is formalizable – it can be described in a series of instructions 'whose application is, as nearly as possible, purely mechanical, and which does not assume a knowledge not itself provided in the technique'. In Putnam's terms, such knowledge is 'surveyable'. Oakeshott is careful not to reify this abstract moment of knowledge. There is no self-standing, purely technical (computable, mechanical) knowledge. Any knowledgeable, rational, intelligent action involves more than sheer technique. All knowledge, however formal, has also an inherently practical moment which cannot be formalized, but without which there is no formal knowledge. This Oakeshott calls practical knowledge, or knowledge of tradition. It can be communicated, but not by reducing it to written rules, being imparted and acquired through imitation and apprenticeship. 'It exists only in practice, and the only way to acquire it is by apprenticeship to a master – not because the master can teach it (he cannot), but because it can be acquired only by continuous contact with one who is perpetually practicing it.'[16]

The synergy Oakeshott describes between technical and practical knowledge seems close to that between what Putnam calls the normative (or intentional) and the computable (or mechanical). 'Rationalism' is Oakeshott's term for the habits of thought and action which wrongly assume that the *best* knowledge ('rational knowledge') is abstract technical knowledge. For the rationalist, it is a triumph for rationality when some new aspect or department of life is 'discovered' to be following a mechanical rule which can then be administered and managed 'for the greater good'. The 'sovereignty of reason' championed by the Enlightenment was this one-sided sovereignty of technique. What this movement fails to appreciate is that mastery of technique presupposes practical knowledge. To master a technique is to *translate*, to *reformulate* existing practical knowledge. Success in this movement across generations presupposes a human touch that constantly escapes reduction to a mechanical procedure. The informal, customary, habitual, tacit – everything rationalists dismiss as accidental, contingent, arbitrary, merely traditional or irrational – are really the indispensable prerequisites of acquiring, applying, teaching, and building technical knowledge.

Again Oakeshott's thought comes very close to Putnam's point that reason transcends whatever reason can survey. For Putnam, 'reason is both transcendent and immanent'. In Oakeshott's terms, rational action has both technical and practical moments. But Oakeshott would be unlikely to agree with Putnam's conclusion that 'we are ... committed ... to a property dualism ... the irreducibility of the intentional'.[17] It is not a question of dualism, of two self-subsistent realities. It is the folly of rationalism to think that technical knowledge is self-sufficient and that all knowledge, all practice, should be 'reconstructed' in strictly technical terms. *All* knowledge has technical and practical moments. No knowledge actually practiced could be *purely* technical, *purely* mechanical, nor should we wish it were otherwise. The rationalist ideal of knowledge requires that we abandon our best and most distinctively human qualities (our almost incredibly underdetermined and plastic neurology) and pretend that we are really something else, something simpler, stupider – a digital computer.

KNOWLEDGE AND TRANSCENDENCE

The foremost objection to Nagel's philosophy is the false choice it presents. We have to choose between 'objectivity' and 'relativism', between his unrealistic 'realism' and a mindless collapse into 'taste, sentiment, or an arbitrary ultimate choice'. We must resurrect the Greek idea of cognition as the revelation of being, or forsake the aspirations of the lover of knowledge. Yet when he says that it is necessary for us 'to combine the recognition of our contingency, our finitude, and our containment in the world with an ambition of transcendence, however limited may be our success in attaining it', I completely agree.[18] But what is transcendence? Is it a step outside circumstance, outside the human, a step toward a disembodied god's-eye view from nowhere? I don't think so. It is necessary to appreciate both the contingency and the transcendence of knowledge because there is more to knowledge than either alone. All knowledge has practical and technical aspects, computable or methodical and normative or intentional moments. We should think in terms not of either/or but of both/and. The reality of our experience and practice thoroughly mixes techniques and practical knowledge, computation and non-computational operations, the contingent given thrownness of existence and the necessity of transcending the given. Elevate any one of these at the expense of the others and you engender nothing but pseudo-problems, as you try to figure out how to get back what you have thrown away.

This language of 'the given' and 'transcendence' can be misunderstood. Nothing is *absolutely* given; there is no 'state of nature', the same for everyone everywhere, such as Nagel supposes when he speaks of 'original impressions'. I mean 'given' in Heidegger's sense of thrownness, which is very close to Rorty's conception of contingency. *What* is 'given' is everything of material and intellectual culture from the preceding generation, including the environment relative to which any of it makes sense. As for the transcendence of knowledge, the best knowledge (knowledge that can be tried and works) has to be practiced in order to survive, and such practice is much more than computation. Knowledge is transcendent inasmuch as its superior practice and therefore its cross-generational reproduction requires action which literally goes beyond everything that has been or could be written down or reduced to rule. Knowledge does not exist without opposite qualities, like creativity, innovation, improvisation, and an aesthetic sense of the appropriate. Such qualities transcend what is extant, customary, familiar, and obvious, and make the difference between ordinary and extraordinary, mechanical and vital, inept and ingenious. The transcendence of knowledge ascends in the direction not of True Being (Nagel's 'objectivity'), but of novelty and free invention. In a variation on a formula of Heidegger's, the essence of knowledge is freedom.[19] Freedom is the ontological *a priori* of knowledge – it is what *must be given* if there is to be knowledge at all. Knowledge requires superior practice to maintain itself, and such practice withers without freedom from rules. When everything mechanical, computable, purely technical, legible, and legislated about a task encounters the demands of circumstance, the quality of the outcome – whether innovative and appropriate or inelegant and inane – cannot be guaranteed by any formula.

Kant's idea of 'transcendental philosophy' makes the assumption that there can be reliable knowledge about the limits of knowledge. Transcending ordinary consciousness in a special philosophical act of reflection, such a philosophy deduces the 'transcendental conditions' that make empirical knowledge possible. The logical flaw in this conception was seen right away by the absolute idealists whom Kant unwittingly inspired. How did he know so much about knowledge? What kind of knowledge is philosophy itself? Kant seemed to have no answer to such questions. Hence, as Fichte concluded, 'there arises for philosophy itself – and within philosophy itself – an impetus to explain its own possibility. How can a human being who occupies the ordinary viewpoint raise himself to the transcendental one? ... This is a question concerning the very possibility of philosophy.'[20]

So it is, when philosophy is conceived after Kant's manner, as transcendental reflection. But there cannot be reliable knowledge about the limits of knowledge. Knowledge of what can be done is always retrospective, always knowledge of what has been done. 'In the beginning was the deed.' There is no prospect for the sort of 'transcendental philosophy' Kant envisioned, which would announce the limits of knowledge in advance. The only 'transcendental presuppositions' of knowledge are *practical freedom* plus the desire or ambition to transcend everything that is given, formal, mechanical, computable, or predictable.

It has been said that the clothes-button is only obvious once you see it.[21] The same can be said for most of our best inventions, which have the quality we find in the best art: they were entirely unpredictable, yet obvious and apparently inevitable in retrospect. It is important, however, not to be deceived by retrospective self-evidence. The best inventions, the best art, and the best knowledge are never the mechanical result of a method or technical rule. The idea we have about method, our extravagant estimation of its importance for the production of significant artifacts (including knowledge), is among our greatest self-imposed limitations, and a threat to the freedom without which knowledge cannot exist.

The simple fact is that no innovation has ever been the result of somebody's following a technical method that could be formalized and taught to computers – not in the experimental or formal sciences, not in the plastic or literary arts, not in politics or philosophy. That we should hanker after such methods, that we should think we are making progress when we reduce difficult choices in medicine or political administration to algorithm, policy, or formal decision procedure, are symptoms of the debilitating irrational rationalism of our time.

POSTSCRIPT

This paper has not been a direct contribution to the philosophy of religion, though I hope it has some indirect relevance to the issues discussed elsewhere in this volume. Much was said at the conference from which these papers arise about indirect communication. My paper concerns transcendence with respect to knowledge. The question here is much like one that arose often in our discussions. We asked whether religion presupposed the ontological transcendence of a salvific Being. John Hick thinks so. 'The Transcendent is thus the necessary postulate of the validity, not (as Kant proposed) of morality, but of religion' (this volume, p. 42). In a way, Richard Schacht agrees, although he draws opposite conclusions from this premise. Hick thinks that religious experiences provide good evidence for the existence of a transcendent Being. Schacht's assumption is that such a Being is a fairy tale, a metaphysical comfort we have to do without. God is dead. But, as Schacht well understands, Nietzsche is a religious thinker. Dionysus is the figure of a perfectly non-transcendent conception of deity, and Nietzsche the harbinger, for Schacht, of a post-transcendental religiousness. Ninian Smart shows that this much (if no more) would be a genuine agreement between Nietzsche's thought and some features of the religious traditions of Southeast Asia.

My question concerned whether knowledge posits something transcendent, as Hick thinks religion does. My answer was that it does not. I do not draw the conclusion, however, that the whole idea of transcendence – the adverbial idea rather than the adjective – should be dismissed in favour of the 'naturalism' which I suspect Hick wrongly associates with D. Z. Phillips. As an adverb, or a quality of personal action, I think there is a real, valid, ethically significant difference between transcendent actions and action which is not so much 'immanent' as inane, banal, extrapolative, routine, formulaic, mechanical, habitual, and so on. Such 'transcendence' may be called *ethical*, in contrast to the *ontological* transcendence that is the shared premise in the disagreement between Hick and Schacht. The argument about ontological transcendence concerns the existence of a Being whose qualities are transcendent. It makes transcendence into an issue about the existence of such a thing. When transcendence is viewed adverbially, as a quality of personal action, we see that 'transcendent beings' have nothing to do with it. There is a possible transcending for which we can aim in action, and which it is possible, though not easy, to hit. There is nothing spooky in this, nothing contrary to science to worry philosophers for whom 'naturalism' is a rallying cry.

I argued that knowledge requires, not the ontological transcendence of a being whose being (self-identity) makes our knowledge ontologically true. Knowledge does, however, require the ethical transcendence of superior technical practice. Knowledge is a function of *technē*, technical culture or ethos, our artifactual ecology. What knowledge requires for its continued existence and empirical validity is not the ontologically transcendent beings promised by a correspondence theory of truth, but rather the transcending action of those who know and do not merely apply a formula, follow a rule, make a calculation, or respond to a problem from habit.

I cast the question of the transcendence of knowledge in terms of the relation between knowledge and truth. As I see it, a conception of knowing that has no use for an ontologically transcendent object of knowledge is a conception of knowledge that drops the old assumption that knowledge has to be true, especially when truth is understood in the terms that it usually is by those philosophers who insist that knowledge *has* to be true. For such truth ('correspondence') presupposes the belief- (or consciousness-) transcending reality of beings (existents) whose being (presence, self-identity) makes our knowledge true. By arguing for the irrelevance of truth to knowledge, I meant to shift the question of the transcendence of knowledge from an ontological question about the objects of knowledge to an ethical question about the quality and context of personal action.

What this shift may mean for religion I do not know. At our meetings Ninian Smart took every opportunity to teach us to speak not of religion but of religion*s* – a plurality which goes beyond the great traditions almost to the level of personal world-views. A question I wish I could have asked Hick is whether the transcendent Being which he thinks religion as religion presupposes knows or has knowledge. Hick thinks it must have the power to ensure the ultimate fruition of human potential. What that implies for divine knowing is what I would have liked to ask him about. I suspect that an ontologically transcendent God with salvific power would be difficult to make sense of without granting it ontologically transcendent knowledge, full and perfect knowledge of the truth, the truth of beings. Or perhaps not? Getting clear about the *epistemic* assumption of this or that religion – what idea of knowing it operates with, whether as divine knowing or our knowing the divine – may be helpful to philosophers seeking clarity about the question of religion without transcendence.

NOTES

1. Thomas Nagel, *The View From Nowhere* (Oxford: Oxford University Press, 1986), pp. 3, 5, 6, 9, 74. Bernard Williams, *Descartes: The Project of Pure Enquiry* (Harmondsworth: Penguin, 1978), pp. 64, 66. See also Bernard Williams, *Ethics and the Limits of Philosophy* (Cambridge, Mass.: Harvard University Press, 1985), pp. 138–40; and Nagel's review, *Journal of Philosophy* 83 (1986), 351–60.

2. Nagel, *Nowhere*, pp. 6, 8, 186.

3. Parmenides, fragment 1, in K. Freeman, *Ancilla to the Pre-Socratic Philosophers* (Cambridge, Mass.: Harvard University Press, 1948), p. 42.

4. A. J. Ayer, *The Problem of Knowledge* (Harmondsworth: Penguin, 1956), p. 25.

5. For instance, Gilbert Harman, *Thought* (Princeton, N.J.: Princeton University Press, 1973), pp. 114–15.

6. Robert Brandom observes that 'attributions of knowledge ... are hybrid deontic attitudes in the sense that they involve both attributing and acknowledging commitments'. 'In taking someone to be a knower, one *attributes a commitment, attributes entitlement* to that commitment, and acknowledges commitment to the same content oneself' (*Making It Explicit: Reasoning, Representing, and Discursive Commitment* (Cambridge, Mass.: Harvard University Press, 1994), p. 202; see also p. 515).

7. Freud, *New Introductory Lectures on Psychoanalysis, Pelican Freud Library*, vol. 2 (Harmondsworth: Penguin, 1973), p. 213.

8. Richard Rorty may be right to suggest that when we say a statement is true we are not ascribing a property to it but only paying an automatic, empty compliment to reliable conceptions and useful knowledge. *Objectivity, Relativism, and Truth, Philosophical Papers*, vol. 1 (Cambridge: Cambridge University Press, 1991), pp. 6, 54–5, 140–1; and *Philosophy and the Mirror of Nature* (Princeton, N.J.: Princeton University Press, 1979), p. 10. Bruno Latour has a similar view, speaking of 'trials of strength' rather than of reliability. See 'Clothing the Naked Truth', in H. Lawson and L. Appignanesi (eds), *Dismantling Truth: Reality in the Post-Modern World* (London: Weidenfeld and Nicolson, 1989). My agreement with Rorty on this point does not, however, extend to wider agreement with his conception of knowledge; see my 'What was Epistemology?', in Robert Brandom (ed.), *Rorty and His Critics* (Oxford: Blackwell, forthcoming).

9. See Gilbert Ryle, 'Knowing How and Knowing That', *Collected Papers*, vol. 2 (London: Hutchinson, 1971), esp. pp. 224–5; Michael Oakeshott, *Rationalism in Politics and Other Essays* (London: Methuen, 1962), p. 9.

10. Martin Heidegger, *Being and Time*, trans. J. Macquarrie and E. Robinson (New York: Harper & Row, 1962), p. 261; and *The Basic*

Problems of Phenomenology, trans. A. Hofstadter (Bloomington, Ind.: Indiana University Press, 1982), p. 215. I discuss Heidegger's conception of truth in *Truth in Philosophy* (Cambridge, Mass.: Harvard University Press, 1993), Chapter 5.

11. On alchemy and the corpuscular philosophy of nature, see W. R. Neuman, 'Boyle's Debt to Corpuscular Alchemy', in M. Hunter (ed.), *Robert Boyle Reconsidered* (Cambridge: Cambridge University Press, 1994). On Newton's alchemy, see R. S. Westfall, 'Newton and Alchemy', in B. Vickers (ed.), *Occult and Scientific Mentalities in the Renaissance* (Cambridge: Cambridge University Press, 1984).

12. 'As he [Plato] never tires of repeating, really to be is to be "its own self according to itself: *auto kath auto*" ... there is no difference whatsoever between being and self-identity ... to be is "to be the same"' (E. Gilson, *Being and Some Philosophers* (Toronto: Pontifical Institute of Medieval Studies, 1952, 2nd ed.), pp. 10–15, 21). For examples, see *Phaedo* 78d, 100b; *Parmenides* 128e–129a; *Timaeus* 51d. I discuss this ontological conception of identity, especially as it bears on the classical Greek idea of truth, in *Truth in Philosophy*, Chapter 1.

13. Nagel, *Nowhere*, p. 70. Nietzsche, *The Gay Science*, trans. Walter Kaufmann (New York: Vintage, 1974), §374. I discuss Nietzsche's philosophy of knowledge in 'All the Daring of the Lover of Knowledge is Permitted Again', in B. E. Babich and R. S. Cohen (eds), *Nietzsche's Epistemological Writings and the Philosophy of Science*, Boston Studies in the Philosophy of Science (Dordrecht: Kluwer, forthcoming).

14. Nagel, *Nowhere*, p. 11. On the artifactual quality of environments, see R. C. Lewontin, *Biology as Ideology: The Doctrine of DNA* (Toronto: Anansi, 1991), pp. 83–92.

15. Hilary Putnam, *Realism with a Human Face* (Cambridge, Mass.: Harvard University Press, 1990), p. 125; and *Representation and Reality* (Cambridge, Mass.: MIT Press, 1988), pp. 2, 89, 93, 118–19. I discuss Putnam's philosophy at more length in 'Putnam und Rorty über Objektivität und Wahrheit', *Deutsche Zeitschrift für Philosophie* 42 (1994): 989–1005, and 'Critical Notice of Putnam', *Canadian Journal of Philosophy* 24 (1994): 665–88.

16. Oakeshott, 'Rationalism in Politics', pp. 10–11.

17. Putnam, *Realism and Reason, Philosophical Papers*, vol. 3 (Cambridge: Cambridge University Press, 1983), pp. 246–7, 302.

18. Nagel, *The Possibility of Altruism* (Oxford: Oxford University Press, 1970), p. 144; and *Nowhere*, p. 9.

19. 'The essence of truth is freedom' (Heidegger, 'On the Essence of Truth', in *Basic Writings*, ed. D. F. Krell (New York: Harper & Row, 1977), p. 125). I elaborate on this argument about the relation between knowledge and freedom in 'Forbidding Knowledge', *The Monist* (forthcoming).

20. Johann Fichte, *Foundations of Transcendental Philosophy*, ed. and trans. D. Breazeale (Ithaca, N.Y.: Cornell University Press, 1992), p. 472.

21. Lynn White, Jr, 'The Act of Invention', in *Machina Ex Deo: Essays in the Dynamism of Western Culture* (Cambridge, Mass.: MIT Press, 1968), p. 130.

3

Transcending Truth –
A Reply

Timothy Tessin

1. INTRODUCTION

Barry Allen argues for a divorce between the interest in knowledge and an interest in truth. According to Allen, 'What makes knowledge good, what makes it desirable and worth cultivating, has nothing to do with the ontological truth of knowledge (its correspondence with a being-in-itself), depending instead on the difference knowledge makes to our performative reliability. The same practical quality, and not ontological, transcendent truth, makes the difference between genuine knowledge and belief, opinion, doctrine, myth, ideology, orthodoxy, and so on' (p. 12).[1] He thus thinks that Richard Rorty 'may be right to suggest that when we say a statement is true we are not ascribing a property to it but only paying an automatic, empty compliment to reliable conceptions and useful knowledge' (p. 23). But whether or not Rorty's suggestion is correct, Allen is confident that truth is of little, if any, value for our dealings with the world about us. And since the pursuit of truth is fundamental to what Thomas Nagel calls 'the ambition of transcendence', Allen believes that we should give up as a confusion the desire for transcendence. At least, transcendence conceived as 'a noble step toward something Absolute, toward a perspective-less god's-eye view of beings-in-themselves' (p. 13). For Allen, 'Knowledge is transcendent inasmuch as its superior practice and therefore its cross-generational reproduction requires action which literally goes beyond everything that has been or could be written down or reduced to rule. Knowledge does not exist without opposite qualities, like creativity, innovation, improvisation, and an aesthetic sense of the appropriate. Such qualities transcend what is extant, customary, familiar, and obvious, and make the difference between ordinary and extraordinary, mechanical and vital, inept and ingenious. The transcendence of knowledge ascends in the direction not of True Being (Nagel's "objectivity"), but of novelty and free invention' (p. 19).

But Allen's confidence in his conclusion is misplaced. That truth, compared with reliability, is an outmoded category for evaluating what is said and thought, follows from the repudiation of truth conceived as a relation between thoughts or utterances and absolute reality, only if we assume that Rorty's reduction of truth to an 'empty compliment' is the sole alternative. The dilemma is a false one, however. Nagel and Rorty present us, not with jointly exhaustive alternatives, but with caricatures of what an interest in truth can be. Against the assumption of a dilemma, I wish to argue that we must change our bearings if we are to steer a safe course through the rough seas of the issue of this symposium. Asking 'What is the value of truth?' – or 'Does the concern for truth belong to a world well lost?' – in the abstract can only founder us in the shallows. We need to ask, rather, *when* and *for whom* does truth matter. Only by so situating the concern for truth can we begin to gain a clear understanding of what the expression of such a concern might mean.

Both Nagel and Rorty, and by implication Allen, fail to situate the interest in truth properly. I will return to Allen's critique of Nagel in Section 3. Let me first turn my attention to Rorty.

2.   OBJECTIVITY OR SOLIDARITY?

According to Rorty, that truth is worthy of our interest, 'not because it will be good for oneself, or for one's real or imagined community', but for its own sake, is the central theme of the Western philosophical tradition from the ancient Greeks through the Enlightenment.[2] Since the Enlightenment, however, we have witnessed the advent of an alternative tradition within which the pursuit of truth has become 'conscious of itself as a problem'.[3] For Rorty, this 'revaluation' has brought into question the old tradition's faith in the unconditional value of truth.

In allying himself with the Nietzschean project of 'revaluating the highest values', the value of truth in particular, Rorty does not mean to deny that someone might still say, or believe, that truth is worth pursuing for its own sake. More importantly, neither is his point to deny that truth is 'out there waiting to be discovered', as though to suggest that he has 'discovered that, out there, there is no truth'. Such a denial would just as much constitute a metaphysical commitment as the affirmation of a truth independent of human beings and the languages they create. Rather, Rorty claims only to *recommend* that 'our purposes would be served best by ceasing to see truth as a deep matter, as a topic of philosophical interest, or "true" as a term which repays "analysis"'. In short: he recommends that we stop talking about truth 'and see how we get on'.[4] What we should be 'getting on with' is the task of finding 'the best way of predicting, controlling, and generally coping with' our physical environment.[5] And the idea of truth as something worth pursuing for its own sake has nothing to contribute, indeed presents an impediment, to this undertaking.

The development of meteorology, for instance, may have proved 'better' than the rituals J. G. Frazer described in *The Golden Bough*, but only in the sense that it provides us with a more reliable means of, if not controlling, then at least predicting the coming of rain. To maintain, as Frazer did, that the development of a science such as meteorology marks a further stage in 'the slow, the never-ending approach to truth'[6] is expressive of what Rorty calls the desire 'to ground solidarity in objectivity'.[7] It is an attempt to justify agreement, and explain disagreement, about the best means for coping with our physical surroundings by appealing to a standard – objective truth – which transcends the boundaries of our culture and history. Thus, Rorty states,

> Those who wish to ground solidarity in objectivity ... have to construe truth as correspondence to reality. So they must construct a metaphysics which has room for a special relation between beliefs and objects which will differentiate true from false beliefs. They also must argue that there are procedures of justification of belief which are natural and not merely local. So they must construct an epistemology which has room for a kind of justification which is not merely social but natural, springing from human nature itself, and made possible by a link between that part of nature and the rest of nature. On their view, the various procedures which are thought of as providing rational justification by one or another culture may or may not really *be* rational. For to be truly rational, procedures of justification *must*

lead to the truth, to correspondence with reality, to the intrinsic nature of things.[8]

As an inheritor of the objectivist tradition, what Frazer failed to recognize is the point argued by philosophers and historians of science such as Thomas Kuhn: that his evaluation of the efficacy of so-called primitive rituals was made from *within* that historically and culturally conditioned practice called modern science.[9] Acknowledgement of the conditional character of his practice, and especially of the concepts which inform that practice, would have led Frazer to the further recognition that the best one can do in speaking about a way of life radically different from one's own is, following Quine's example, to declare one's allegiance to a conceptual scheme. 'For my part,' Quine says, 'I do, qua lay physicist, believe in physical objects and not in Homer's gods; and I consider it a scientific error to believe otherwise. But in point of epistemological footing the physical objects and the gods differ only in degree and not in kind. Both sorts of entities enter our conception only as cultural posits.'[10] Quine's judgement that 'The myth of physical objects is epistemologically superior to most in that it has proved more efficacious than other myths as a device for working a manageable structure into the flux of experience'[11] is thus justified only within the conceptual scheme of modern science, and in particular only in relation to the physical scientist's instrumental interest in the prediction and control of physical phenomena. No appeal to 'the intrinsic nature of things', or to 'the truth', can justify the scheme itself, because such notions derive from the confused belief that it is possible to step outside the conceptual scheme within which the physical scientist's practice has its sense.

For Rorty, however, the error at the heart of the objectivist tradition is not simply a confusion about the epistemological status of the physical sciences. He portrays it, rather, as a failure of *character*. To harbour an interest in truth for its own sake as the goal of inquiry is evidence of a desire to 'escape from time and chance'.[12] It is a desire to find a foundation for practical reason and discourse in something independent of – and transcending – the contingencies which all too often thwart the successful achievement of our ends. In a word, the pursuit of truth for its own sake is a form of *hubris*.

Against this *hubris*, Rorty recommends 'a willingness to face up to the *contingency*' of our lives.[13] This willingness involves, among other things, giving up the conception of thought and language as mirroring the world in its essence as well as of language as a medium for representing essences; giving up the idea that our utterances are 'made' true by their agreement with a reality common to all speakers; and embracing the historicist turn set in motion by Hegel, which according to Rorty 'has helped free us ... from theology and metaphysics – from the temptation to look for an escape from time and chance'.[14] 'A postmetaphysical culture', Rorty maintains, 'seems to me no more impossible than a postreligious one, and equally desirable.'[15]

The picture put forward as a substitute is of practical reason and speaking directed, not towards any Absolute, but towards novelty. For instance, 'To say that Freud's vocabulary gets at the truth about human nature, or Newton's at the truth about the heavens, is not an explanation of anything. It is just an empty compliment – one traditionally paid to writers whose novel jargon we have found useful'.[16] In general, the aim of inquiry is not to arrive at a true description of the world by means of 'an examination of the pros and cons of a thesis', but 'to redescribe lots and lots of things in new ways, until you have created a pattern of linguistic behaviour which will tempt the rising generation to adopt it, thereby causing them to look for appropriate new forms of nonlinguistic behaviour, for example, the adoption of new scientific equipment or new social institutions'. This kind of inquiry

> says things like 'try thinking of it this way' – or more specifically, 'try to ignore the apparently futile traditional questions by substituting the following new and possibly interesting questions'. It does not pretend to have a better candidate for doing the same old things which we did when we spoke in the old way. Rather, it suggests that we might want to stop doing those things and do something else. But it does not argue for this suggestion on the basis of antecedent criteria common to the old and the new language games. For just insofar as the new language really is new, there will be no such criteria.[17]

But how, then, on Rorty's view, are we to distinguish serious inquiry from shallow dilettantism? The sincere desire to persuade from sophistry? Or the struggle to find the solution to a problem from (what Nagel calls) 'cognitive wish-fulfillment'?[18] Marking

these distinctions does not require that we accept Nagel's conception of the growth of understanding as the movement from the subjective to the objective standpoint. But it does at least require that
we be prepared to give *reasons* for thinking a particular form of
inquiry to be futile, for wanting 'to stop doing those things and
do something else' – even if those reasons come from and are only
intelligible within the form of inquiry we wish to adopt.

3.   THE CORRESPONDENCE THEORY OF TRUTH

While Allen's discussion is imbued with Rorty's spirit, his discussion marks an advance in at least this respect: his is not merely the
recommendation, or expression of a preference, that we give up the
pursuit of truth, but a reasoned argument. We should give up
the idea that truth is worthy of our interest, and embrace historicism, because truth – as correspondence to, or agreement with,
reality – is not an intelligible object of human interest.

> [W]e have no idea which beliefs or conceptions correspond
> with reality (or are true) apart from their reliability. We cannot
> independently distinguish a property of correspondence and
> correlate it empirically with an independently established quality
> of reliability. Consequently, there can be no evidence for 'corres-
> pondence' except the very reliability it is invoked to explain. The
> so-called explanation is therefore vacuous. To say that a concept-
> ion 'is true' is not to endow it with a quality that explains why it
> is useful or reliable (p. 11).

It is in this context that Allen remarks that 'Rorty may be right to
suggest that when we say a statement is true we are not ascribing a
property to it but only paying an automatic, empty compliment to
reliable conceptions and useful knowledge.'
To see how Allen arrives at the judgement of the correspondence
theory's unintelligibility and of the possible correctness of Rorty's
suggestion, we might first consider a remark by William James,
which Allen quotes in *Truth in Philosophy*. 'Truth, as any dictionary
will tell you, is a property of certain of our ideas. It means their
"agreement", as falsity means their disagreement, with "reality".'
Both the pragmatist and the antipragmatist, according to James,
'accept this definition as a matter of course. They begin to quarrel

only after the question is raised as to what may precisely be meant by the term "agreement", and what by the term "reality", when reality is taken as something for our ideas to agree with.'[19] Substitute 'proposition' ('statement', 'utterance'), or 'belief', for James' 'idea', and we have the familiar formulation of the correspondence theory of truth: a proposition (belief) is true if, and only if, it agrees with (corresponds to) reality.

Many philosophers have held the correspondence theory to explain the meaning of 'true'. If they have questioned the adequacy of the explanation, then, like James, it has most often only been to the extent to which they have found a lack of clarity in terms such as 'agreement', 'correspondence' and 'reality'. Thus Tarski, to name just one example, can say of Aristotle's formulation – 'To say of what is that it is not, or of what is not that it is, is false, while to say of what is that it is, or of what is not that it is not, is true' – that its 'intuitive content … appears to be rather clear. Nevertheless, the formulation leaves much to be desired from the point of view of precision and formal correctness.'[20] But substituting expressions such as 'denotes' for 'corresponds to', and 'existing state of affairs', or 'fact', for 'reality', succeeds only in casting the illusion of clarity. For we have no clearer understanding of what is meant by 'denotes' and 'fact' than we have of 'corresponds to' and 'reality'.

But this difficulty notwithstanding, the relative 'precision and formal correctness' of the preferred terminological substitutions is a specious issue, since it fails to address the real difficulty. The correspondence theory could *explain* the meaning of our truth-predicates only were it possible to give a description of the correspondence relation – by whatever name we might call it – between our utterances and that to which our utterances are supposed to correspond which makes them true, which did not presuppose the understanding that the utterances in question *are true*. If ordinary usage is a reliable criterion, however, then 'is true' is *synonymous* with, not explained by, expressions such as 'corresponds to (agrees with) reality', 'denotes an existing state of affairs', 'fits the facts', 'accords with the way things are', and so on. To say that a statement corresponds to reality is just another way of saying that the statement is true. Imagine someone giving courtroom testimony. Asked whether he is able to confirm the testimony of a previous witness, he replies: 'What she said is true.' But we might just as easily suppose him to have said 'What she said fits the facts'; or simply 'That's the way it happened.' In neither of the alternatives has anything been added: as though the meaning of 'What she said is true' were unclear until we substituted an expression such as 'fits the facts' or 'accords with the way things happened' for 'is true'. But if the alternatives add nothing to the original statement, then neither can they explain the statement's meaning.

There are difficulties as well with speaking of 'reality' in the requisite sense. The primary difficulty lies in the supposition that we can *say* 'how things are in the world' independently of the various relations in which human beings stand to their environment and of the ways of speaking which are constitutive of these relations. Thus Allen, drawing upon Heidegger, states that 'there is no "there" where beings can "be" ... apart from *our* presence and their *relations* to us and to the environing world' (p. 14). 'What "is there" depends on what you are looking for or are trying to do' (p. 13). The point is not that our access to reality is limited by our particular interests and involvements – a limitation which might be overcome by taking a more objective standpoint – but that the *intelligibility* of speaking of 'what is there' is irreducibly bound up with our interests and involvements.

4.   THE DISINTERESTED SEARCH FOR TRUTH

I admit to sympathy with Allen's arguments against the correspondence theory of truth. I sympathize as well with his historicist orientation. But his conclusion of truth's valuelessness – that an interest in truth is, at best, *hubris*, at worst, unintelligible – follows neither from the arguments, nor from historicism. Indeed, I maintain that steering our way clear of the correspondence theory's pitfalls, combined with a (broadly) historicist orientation – conceived as encompassing what Wittgenstein called 'the anthropological method'[21] – opens the way to our seeing what can be meant by an interest in truth.

One reason for Allen's assumption that the conclusion follows from the argument is that he, like Rorty, confuses historicism with an instrumental naturalism. Thus we find in Allen's discussion remarks such as: 'What [an animal] perceives and what, if anything, it conceives, is a function of its neurology, and the result ... is *knowledge*, that is, a capacity for reliable performance in the environment which has co-evolved with that neurology' (p. 14); knowledge is 'realistic' in the sense that 'those who act from knowledge reliably get what they aim for' (p. 16) – where the preceding remarks make clear that 'reliable' means 'making successful adaptation to one's environment possible'. Only what serves the organism's struggles to adapt to a perpetually changing environment is worthy of that organism's interest. Since truth cannot be the object of human interest, naturalistically conceived, it seems to follow that talk of truth's value is an idle wheel.

But if historicism, as Rorty defines it, is the denial 'that there is such a thing as "human nature" or "the deepest level of the self"', and the affirmation 'that there is nothing "beneath" socialization or prior to history which is definatory of the human',[22] then neither Rorty nor Allen are historicist thinkers. Theirs is not a 'dedivinized' culture, shorn of absolutes, but a culture with new divinities: adaptation, reliability and novelty. They have toppled Lenin, if you will, only to make way for Adam Smith.

This confusion merits further consideration, if for no other reason than that it is central to Rorty's conception of liberalism as the belief 'that cruelty is the worst thing we do'.[23] But it rests on a further assumption; and it is to this second assumption that I wish to turn my attention.

Allen directs his arguments against the correspondence theory of truth. But the problem is not the theory *per se*. Rather, it is the correspondence theorist's own assumption that 'true', if meaningful, must name a property which human utterances have independently of the various practices and contexts in which we mark the difference between truth and falsity. The aim of inquiry, then, when understood as the pursuit of truth for its own sake, is held to be the discovery of this elusive, because 'transcendent', property. We find an analogue of this conception of transcendence in Nagel's definition of 'objectivity' in *The View From Nowhere*. 'To acquire a more objective understanding of some aspect of life or the world, we step back from our initial view of it and form a new conception which has that view and its relation to the world as its object ... A view or form of thought is more objective than another if it relies less on the specifics of the individual's makeup and position in the world, or on the character of the particular type of creature he is.' The definition leads Nagel to assert that 'The standpoint of morality is more objective than that of private life, but less objective than the standpoint of physics. We may think of reality as a set of concentric spheres, progressively revealed as we detach gradually from the contingencies of the self.'[24]

But we do not free ourselves from 'the contingencies of the self' *tout court* by studying and practising physics, though we may free ourselves of the contingencies which affect other types of human activity: personal relationships, for example, or the exercise of political power. This is, at least in part, the meaning of 'disinterested inquiry'. The disinterested inquirer is one who detaches the aims of his inquiry from interests in, for instance, acquiring wealth, self-aggrandizement or political accommodation. Throughout, however, disinterested inquiry remains motivated by *interests*. The issue in asking whether someone's inquiry is disinterested is the *kind* of interest that motivates the inquiry, not the absence of any particular interests.

One way we have of marking the distinction between disinterested inquiry and inquiry motivated, for example, by an interest in acquiring wealth, self-aggrandizement or political accommodation is to speak of the former as the search for truth. To pursue an inquiry disinterestedly is to be motivated by an interest in the truth 'for its own sake'. But misunderstanding of the interested character of inquiry has led some, such as Jane Heal, to dismiss the notion of the disinterested search for truth as vacuous. She says that 'The view that we value truth "in itself" (whether we give a correspondence or any other substantive account of it) has the implication that any instance of truth is, merely in virtue of being true, worth having.'[25] Thus the physicist who describes his research as a disinterested search for the truth should, according to Heal, be just as satisfied with learning the number of lecturers in the Swansea Philosophy Department as he would be with discovering the temperature at which a certain material acts as a superconductor.

I take Heal's remark to be an argument *reductio ad absurdum* against the conception of truth from which it derives rather than proof of the vacuousness of the idea of an interest in truth for its own sake. What she rightly criticizes is the idea that a theory of truth can determine the meaning of 'true' and 'false' *in vacuo* – as though what is meant by an interest in the truth could be severed from the particular context of inquiry in which the truth is being sought. Hegel saw the misunderstanding at the root of this idea when he stated that a concept, *qua* concept, is 'only something general and abstract'. It becomes the object of a genuine interest only through the activity of an individual situated in a particular context of action.[26] Grete Hermann states the point more explicitly when she says that 'The personal concern which differentiates genuine interest from the pure knowledge and judgement of value, is always directed towards concrete particular cases.'[27] Applied specifically to the concept of truth, Hegel's and Hermann's point provides us with a compelling objection to the project of a theory of truth. But rather than locate the interest in truth *in situ*, Heal assumes that the various theories of truth exhaust the possibilities for giving sense to expressions of an interest in truth; and she is thus forced into maintaining that the physicist's characterization makes discovery of something he calls 'the truth' the object of his interest rather than discovery of a superconductor.

I have no wish to suggest that no one might make this mistake – witness Nagel. I want only to make the point that it is in no way entailed by speaking of inquiry as 'disinterested' or as 'the disinterested search for truth'.

Following Hegel's and Hermann's lead, let me turn my attention to a particular case. Having been arrested for signing Charter 77, Václav Havel found himself in the following situation:

> I began to understand, toward the end of my stay in prison, that a trap was being laid for me: a relatively innocent turn of phrase – or so I thought at the time – in one of my requests for release was to be published in a falsified version in order to discredit me. I had no idea how to stop this from happening, or how to defend myself against it … I felt as though I were being, in a very physical way, tempted by the devil. I felt that I was in his clutches. I understood that I had somehow become involved with him. The experience of having something misappropriated in this way – something I had actually thought and written, *something that was true* – clarified for me with fresh urgency that the truth is not simply what you think it is; it is also the circumstances in which it is said, and to whom, why, and how it is said.[28]

What was clarified for Havel, we might say, was that an interest in truth, if a genuine interest, is not abstract and 'free-floating', but is situated within a particular context of action. It is thus subject to the same contingencies as any practical interest, intention or purpose, including the misappropriation by others. But the passage also presents us with a use of 'true' which resists the charge of vacuousness. It is not the misappropriation of *any* 'true proposition' which led Havel to the understanding that he 'had somehow become involved with' the devil, but the truth of *his own thoughts*

and words. And the context of his concern was a political arrange-
ment in which 'living in a lie' had been accepted as the norm in
exchange for material well-being.[29] Havel's remark thus presents us
with an application of Allen's own thought that 'Differences
between true and false do not exist apart from the practice in which
these values are produced and evaluated and statements made to
circulate as true, as known or probable, as information, news,
results, and so on.'[30]

5.   TRUTH OR RELIABILITY?

In spite of remarks such as this, and the acknowledgement they
imply of the place that talk of truth can have in a human life, Allen,
following Rorty, still maintains that 'true' can be nothing more than
an 'empty compliment' paid 'to reliable conceptions and useful
knowledge'. The reason is that Allen insists on posing the problem
of truth's value in the form: 'Truth or reliability?' – where 'or'
expresses an exclusive disjunction: one or the other, but not both.
Indeed, the relative value of truth and reliability only presents itself
as a problem because Allen assumes that we must opt for one or
the other. Once we take on board Hegel's and Hermann's point,
however, and cease to formulate the question in terms of the
merely abstract concepts of truth and reliability, we can see that
there is no *necessary* incompatibility. Both belong to the critical
vocabulary with which we evaluate actions, utterances and thinking. In some contexts, reliability is the appropriate standard
of evaluation; but in others, only truth will do. Replace 'true' with
'reliable' in Havel's remark and the result is a thought of a very different character. Or consider the difference in the character of courtroom testimony where the question of a witness's reliability was
severed from the question of whether his testimony was true.

Admittedly, none of these considerations provides conclusive
counter-arguments to Allen's criticisms. But then, my concern has
been to show that his (and Rorty's) approach to the question of
truth's value is misguided. Asking not 'What is the value of truth?'
but 'What value can truth have?' opens the way to an appreciation
of the expressions of a concern for truth that we find not only in
Havel's writings, but in Socrates, Kierkegaard, George Orwell and
Primo Levi.[31] And I will only suggest here that a similar reorienta-
tion towards the concept of transcendence is necessary if we are to

gain in understanding its significance in the lives of those for whom it is a matter of concern.

NOTES

1. References in the text are to Barry Allen, 'The Ambition of Transcendence', in this collection.
2. Richard Rorty, 'Solidarity or Objectivity?' in J. Rajchman and C. West (eds), *Post-Analytic Philosophy* (New York: Columbia University Press, 1985), pp. 3–4.
3. Nietzsche, quoted in Barry Allen, *Truth in Philosophy* (Cambridge, Mass.: Harvard University Press, 1993), p. 43.
4. Richard Rorty, *Contingency, Irony and Solidarity* (Cambridge: Cambridge University Press, 1989), p. 8.
5. See Richard Rorty, *The Consequences of Pragmatism* (London: Harvester Press, 1982), p. 11.
6. J. G. Frazer, *The Golden Bough* (London: Macmillan, 1987, abridged edition), p. 62.
7. Rorty, 'Solidarity or Objectivity?', p. 5.
8. Ibid.
9. Frazer, as I hope is obvious, is just one representative of a continuing allegiance to the objectivist tradition.
10. W. V. O. Quine, *From a Logical Point of View* (Cambridge, Mass.: Harvard University Press, 1980, 2nd ed.), p. 44.
11. Ibid.
12. Rorty, *Contingency, Irony and Solidarity*, p. xiii.
13. Ibid., p. 9.
14. Ibid., p. xiii.
15. Ibid., p. xvi
16. Ibid., p. 8.
17. Ibid., p. 9.
18. Thomas Nagel, *The View From Nowhere* (Oxford: Oxford University Press 1986), p. 10.
19. Allen, *Truth in Philosophy*, p. 61.
20. Alfred Tarski, 'Truth and Proof', in R. I. G. Hughes (ed.), *A Philosophical Companion to First-Order Logic* (Indianapolis: Hackett, 1993), p. 102.
21. See Rush Rhees, *Discussions of Wittgenstein* (London: Routledge & Kegan Paul, 1970), p. 101; also p. 50.
22. Rorty, *Contingency, Irony and Solidarity*, p. xiii.
23. Ibid., p. xv. See also Rorty's discussion of Orwell in Chapter 8 of the same work.
24. Nagel, *The View From Nowhere*, pp. 4–5.
25. Jane Heal, 'The Disinterested Search for Truth', *Proceedings of the Aristotelian Society* 88 (1987–8), p. 105.
26. See G. W. F. Hegel, *Vorlesungen über die Philosophie der Weltgeschichte, Band I: Die Vernunft in der Geschichte* (Hamburg: Felix Meiner Verlag,

1994), pp. 81–2. Wittgenstein's *Philosophical Investigations* §136 is also worthy of our attention in connection with Hegel's point; especially: '... it is as if we had a concept of true and false, which we could use to determine what is and what is not a proposition.'

27.   Grete Henry-Hermann, 'Die Überwindung des Zufalls' in Minna Specht and Willi Eichler (eds), *Leonard Nelson zum Gedächtnis* (Frankfurt a.M.-Göttingen: Verlag Öffentliches Leben, 1953), p. 43.

28.   Václav Havel, *Disturbing the Peace* (New York: Alfred A. Knopf, 1990), p. 67; emphasis added.

29.   See Václav Havel, *Open Letters* (London: Faber and Faber, 1991), especially 'Dear Dr. Husák' and 'The Power of the Powerless'.

30.   Allen, *Truth in Philosophy*, p. 4.

31.   The specific works I have in mind are: Kierkegaard's *Purity of Heart*; Orwell's 'Looking Back on the Spanish Civil War' and *1984*; and Levi's *The Periodic Table*.

Part Two
Transcendence and Truth

4

Transcendence and Truth

John Hick

'Transcendence', as indicating beyondness, is a very general idea
which waits to be given specific meanings in specific contexts. It is
perhaps most commonly used in contrast to immanence. However I
am not here focussing upon that polarity but am using the term to
refer to the characteristic in virtue of which the divine, the ultimate
reality is said to be other and 'greater' (in an Anselmic rather than a
spatial sense) than the physical universe. The area of discourse is
thus that occupied by the debate between naturalistic and what we
can, for want of a better term, call transcendental understandings of
the universe. The medievals used the term 'supernatural' here, but
that word has today shrivelled in meaning to indicate the occult,
ghosts, spirits, magic spells and the like. And so I shall speak of
transcendence, and of the Transcendent as that which, according to
the religions, transcends the multiple forms of discharging energy
constituting the natural or physical universe.

The natural or physical universe includes this earth and the
human and other forms of life on it, and thus includes the multi-
tude of human brains and their functioning, which in turn includes
the production of thought, language, feeling, emotion, and action.
Thought, feeling, emotion, and volition may or may not be identical
with physical brain processes – there is disagreement among naturalistic thinkers about this – but on a naturalistic view there can be
no mental life that does not continuously depend for its existence
upon brain activity, so that if there were no brains there would be
no sentient life, and in particular no human life – no thought,
feeling, emotion, language, personality, imagination, culture, social
interaction, artistic production, religion. And so if by 'nature' or
'the natural' we mean the physical universe, including human cerebral activity and the entire realm of mental life that depends upon
it, then by the Transcendent I mean the putative dimension or

range of reality that transcends this and that cannot be accomodated within a naturalistic understanding of the universe. We can say that the Transcendent is that which there must be if the various forms of religious experience are not purely projective but at the same time also responsive. The Transcendent is thus the necessary postulate of the validity, not (as Kant proposed) of morality, but of religion.

NATURALISTIC (= WITHOUT TRANSCENDENCE) CONCEPTIONS OF RELIGION

The most straightforward naturalistic view of religion is that it consists in individual and communal self-delusion. Ideas of the Transcendent – in the forms of God, or Brahman, or the Dharmakaya, or the Tao, and so on – are all products of the activity of human thinking, so that if there were no human brains there would be no God, Brahman, Tao, Dharmakaya, etc. If in imagination we compress the fifteen or so billion-year history of the universe into 24 hours, human life has only emerged during the last millisecond. Before that, on a naturalistic view, there was no God, Brahman, Tao, etc. And again, after either the heat or the cold extinction of life on this earth the Gods, the Brahman, the Tao, etc. that we create in our imaginations will have ceased to exist. According to naturalism, then, our planet is the locus of a momentary flash of conscious life within an otherwise unconscious universe; and we are in the extraordinary position of being part of this in some ways wonderful and in other ways appalling moment. As conscious individuals we may live for some seventy to eighty or so years and then simply cease to exist – like a word deleted from the computer screen! And one day, in its endless expansion or its 'big crunch', the universe will be as if the entire episode of human existence had never occurred.

The harsh implications of this view for our human self-understanding have probably never been so fully and honestly faced as by Bertrand Russell. In an early essay, 'A Free Man's Worship', written in 1902, he said:

That Man is the product of causes which had no prevision of the end they were achieving; that his origin, his growth, his hopes and fears, his loves and his beliefs, are but the outcome of accidental collocations of atoms; that no fire, no heroism, no intensity of thought and feeling, can preserve an individual life beyond the grave; that all the labours of the ages, all the devotion, all the inspiration, all the noonday brightness of human genius, are destined to extinction in the vast death of the solar system, and that the whole Temple of Man's achievement must inevitably be buried beneath the debris of a universe in ruins – all these things, if not quite beyond dispute, are yet so nearly certain, that no philosophy which rejects them can hope to stand. Only within the scaffolding of these truths, only on the firm foundation of unyielding despair, can our soul's habitation henceforth be squarely built.[1]

And in the third volume of his *Autobiography* Russell reprints a letter, written in 1962, in which he says, by way of self-criticism, that the language of this passage is 'florid and rhetorical', but adds 'However, my outlook on the cosmos and on human life is substantially unchanged'.[2]

Russell's picture constitutes an unflinchingly honest acceptance of the implications of a naturalistic understanding of the universe and our place in it. This world-view is, according to the Nobel-prize-winning physicist Steven Weinberg, who also espouses it, 'chilling and impersonal'.[3] Within such a naturalistic framework we can opt, with Russell, for a noble stoicism. We can accept our mortality and concentrate upon the immediate sources of happiness, including the attempt to reduce pain and misery in others, and can thus find meaning and satisfaction within our short existence. We can, with Russell, reject all notions of the Transcendent but nevertheless accept love, freedom, the search for truth, a commitment to reducing misery and promoting happiness, as intrinsically valuable (in the sense of being valued by us for no reason beyond themselves) despite their brief and insecure tenure of existence. We can recognize that human life has no ultimate purpose or meaning, that it is not a project aiming at any goal, and then proceed to make the best we can of it. Although I do not accept this outlook I nevertheless find that I can imaginatively identify with it and respect it.

In addition to this straightforward rejection of religion as illusion there is a school of thought which likewise presupposes a naturalistic understanding of the universe but nevertheless uses religious language to express certain important aspects of human experience. This is religion without transcendence. Ludwig Feuerbach was the first major thinker to formulate a version of it. He is often depicted as having a purely negative attitude to religion, whereas in fact he was advocating a positive appreciation of it, but only of religion without transcendence. This does not veto talk of God, Brahman, the Tao, the Dharmakaya, etc., but it denies that these concepts have any referent that transcends the natural. They refer to aspects of the natural world, and more specifically to ideas and ideals and speech acts produced by the human brain, and to consequent modes of individual and communal behaviour.

Religion without transcendence has room for the most exalted conceptions of divinity and for the highest moral and spiritual ideals and attitudes and forms of life. It can value the renunciation of the ego point of view, making no claim upon life but seeing it as (metaphorically) a gift and receiving its hardships and tragedies, as well as its delights, in a spirit of humble acceptance. Whilst still presupposing that human life is, in Russell's words, 'the product of causes which had no prevision of the end they were achieving' and that 'all the labours of the ages, all the devotion, all the inspiration, all the noonday brightness of human genius' are destined to be as though they had never occurred, religion without transcendence can nevertheless endorse the moral dispositions that have been so eloquently extolled in recent times by such writers as Tolstoy, Kierkegaard, Wittgenstein, Simone Weil and others. Putting it in terms close to those of Theravada Buddhism, one should live in the present moment, as the world being conscious of itself from one point of view within it, without being specially concerned about the particular point in the world process that is momentarily 'me', and so valuing equally oneself and others and delighting in all that is good in our human experience. Thus religion without transcendence can accept most of the moral teachings of the traditional religions, and can retain virtually the whole realm of religious language, although evacuating it of its metaphysical content. Among contemporary philosophers this strategy is advocated, for example, by our host Dewi Phillips, and among contemporary theologians by, for example, Don Cupitt.

THE UNCONSCIOUS ELITISM OF THIS FORM OF RELIGION

I now want to point to a feature of this position which is not usually recognized by its advocates. I have acknowledged that we can find positive meaning and fulfilment within a naturalistic interpretation of life. But who are the 'we' for whom this is true? We are the fortunate minority who have a reasonably secure sufficiency of food and shelter, of personal safety and freedom, of educational opportunities and cultural resources. We are the fortunate ones who are not chronically undernourished and living in fear of starvation, not oppressed or persecuted or enslaved, not refugees, not trapped in abject poverty and desperately anxious for our own and our family's and community's short-term future. We can, if we choose, recognize that we can do very little to end the injustices and sufferings of those who have been less lucky than ourselves in life's lottery, and proceed to enjoy our own lives as best we can, accepting the fleeting insignificance of the entire episode of human existence. But to think that *all* men and women are free to join in this positive response would be like saying that the desperately poor and starving in, say, the deprived and dangerous slums of Calcutta, or for that matter of Los Angeles, are free to rise into serenity and inner peace. This would be true only in a cruelly ironic sense. In principle they can do so, but not in reality. And so we must recognize that the 'we' for whom a religion without transcendence can be positively challenging, and even inspiring, consists in a minority who have been highly privileged by the accident of birth and other circumstances. In other words, to extol the value of religion without transcendence as other than the luxury of a fortunate minority is to ignore the immense fact of evil in the forms of physical pain and mental and emotional suffering caused by 'man's inhumanity to man' and by the structure of the physical environment.

I do not want to overstate this fact of evil, immense though it is, or to forget the many marvellous and enjoyable aspects of human existence. When we look back along the axis of history we must not be misled by the contrast between the comforts and cultural possibilities provided by modern wealth and technology, and the lack of these in previous centuries. There have been large tracts of history in which many people have lived in small tribal societies that were stable, largely egalitarian, generally internally peaceful, and with a sufficiency of food and fuel. In comparison with life in modern industrialized cities, life was then very simple and was lived at subsistence level, and with none of our modern medical remedies; but nevertheless there was quite possibly more contentment, a stronger communal feeling and sense of mutual support, and a readier acceptance of mortality, than in our affluent but fragmented and anxious Western world today.

But that having been said, the larger truth is still that the life of the majority of human beings has been, in the words of Barbara Ward and Rene Dubos, 'cramped with back-breaking labour, exposed to deadly or debilitating disease, prey to wars and famines, haunted by the loss of children, filled with fear and the ignorance that breeds fear'.[4] Restricting attention to our world today, the broad picture is that there are hundreds of millions of men, women and children who are suffering from one or more of the following calamities: being refugees with no fixed home, being physically or mentally ill and having no access to the kind of medical aid that is available to ourselves, being hungry, being chronically undernourished and lacking the protein necessary for full physical development, being desperately anxious for their own and their family's future, being caught in famines, earthquakes, floods, storms and other natural disasters, lacking even elementary education, being ruthlessly exploited by uncaring financial and political powers.

What I am suggesting, then, is that in the light of the massive reality of evil – that is, the pain, suffering, and deprivation caused both by fellow humans and by the environment – a naturalistic philosophy can only be accepted with equanimity by a privileged elite. For humanity as a whole, the naturalistic picture is very bad news. It means not only that evil has always been a massive reality, but that past evil is irreparable, in that those who have suffered from it have ceased to exist; and it must be expected that this will be true also of present and future evil. There can be no question of the universe being, as the religions teach, such that good is ultimately brought out of evil. I am not of course implying that naturalism is therefore false. It may be true. But I am arguing that forms of religion that presuppose naturalism – forms, in other words, of religion without transcendence – which present themselves as liberating and ennobling, are highly elitist. Further, this is something of which their proponents have hardly ever shown themselves to be aware.

THE PROJECT OF HUMAN EXISTENCE

Let me at this point introduce the idea of what I shall call the project of human existence. According to naturalism, human existence is not a project aiming at any fulfilment. It is just something that has been thrown up for a brief moment in the evolution of the universe. But for the religions, human existence as we know it is an unfinished project. All the great world religions teach that our present life is only a small part of our total existence, and that within that existence as a whole there is a realistic possibility for all human beings to attain, or receive, or realize what the religious traditions conceptualize as union with God, or with Brahman, or as nirvana, or as awakening to the universal Buddha-nature, and in yet other ways. The structure of reality, whereby this fulfilment is eventually possible for everyone, is very variously conceived. But the basic truth of the belief in a good outcome of the project of human existence does not depend upon the fulfilment of the specific expectations of any one of the religious traditions. We are talking about a mode of existence that is outside our range of experience and that may well take a form or forms that lie beyond our present conceptual and imaginative capacities.

Ludwig Feuerbach, the patron saint of religion without transcendence, perceptively noted that the idea of immortality is essentially involved in the idea of a benign God.[5] Let me spell out why this is so. Human nature includes wonderful potentialities which we see realized in the remarkable men and women whom we regard, in our customary Western term, as saints, or, in one of the Eastern terms, as *mahatmas*, great souls. I am not speaking here of those who have been officially canonized by the Catholic Church, although some of these are certainly among them. I am speaking of those whose lives show us, always of course in culturally specific ways, something of the heights of which human nature is capable. These include the great spiritual leaders whose impact has launched new religious movements – such as Moses, Gautama, Jesus, Muhammad; and great renewers or reformers of existing traditions, such as Shankara, Guru Nanak, Shinran, St Francis; and again innumerable individuals within every tradition who have been transformed by their response to Adonai, or the Heavenly Father, or Allah, or Vishnu, or Shiva, or to the Dharma or the Tao or the requirements of Heaven. In the modern period, with new possibilities opened up by the spread both of democracy and of a pervasive 'sociological consciousness', sainthood has increasingly taken political forms in such people as Mahatma Gandhi in India, Martin Luther King in the United States, Archbishop Romero in El Salvador, Dom Helda Camera in Brazil, Nelson Mandela in South Africa. As these examples show, the saints of the modern world are not perfect human beings – there can be no such thing – but people who, in response to a transcendent claim, have risen above self-concern to serve their fellows in very significant ways. In such people we are made aware of a human potentiality that is only very slightly developed in most people in each generation. It follows that if individual human existence ceases at death, the full human potentiality is only realized by those few who are able to realize it in this present life. But in the great majority of men and women the higher potentialities must remain for ever unfulfilled. Such a situation is clearly incompatible not only with a Christian belief in the limitless love of God but equally with Jewish or Muslim or Hindu theistic belief in the divine love and mercy, and with Advaitic Hindu or Buddhist belief in a universal destiny in union with Brahman or in the attainment of Buddhahood. There can be no loving God, and more generally no ultimate reality that is benign from our human point of view, if there is no continuation of human spiritual growth beyond the point reached at the time of bodily death. In a slogan: No theodicy without eschatology.

COSMIC OPTIMISM AND COSMIC PESSIMISM

Naturalism, then, including naturalistic religion – religion without transcendence – is a form of cosmic pessimism, whilst the great world religions are, in contrast, forms of cosmic optimism. Needless to say, I am not arguing that because the naturalistic possibility would be such bad news for the human race as a whole it must therefore be mistaken! I am concerned rather to try to see clearly what the two possibilities are, and wherein lies the difference between them. The difference is so great and all-encompassing that alternative versions of a given religion, one affirming and the other denying transcendence, amount to two radically different forms of religion; and this is so even though they use a common stock of religious language. Thus traditional Christianity is much closer to traditional Islam or Judaism or Hinduism or Sikhism or Jainism or most forms of Buddhism than it is to a form of Christianity without transcendence. For the traditional religions all affirm that the physical universe is the partial expression or manifestation or creation or emanation – all of these different concepts are used – of an ultimate reality which neither begins nor ends with the history of the physical universe and which transcends its ever-changing character as temporal process. The basic religious faith is that this reality, which I am calling the Transcendent, impinges upon distinctively human consciousness in the many forms of what we call religious experience. On the basis of this the religions declare – and this is their character as gospel, or good news – that the Transcendent is benign in relation to humanity in that the project of human spiritual growth continues to what in our various belief systems we refer to as the Vision of God, union with Brahman, moksha, Nirvana, awakening to the universal Buddha-nature, etc.

TRUTH FOR RELIGION WITHOUT TRANSCENDENCE

Now my remit is to consider the notion of truth in religion without transcendence, and this is best done in contrast to the notion of truth in transcendental religion.

Let us consider first a Christianity without transcendence. All the statements that are regarded as true in traditional Christianity can still be accepted as true, but the religiously central ones in a radically different sense. Historical beliefs, such as that Jesus of Nazareth lived in the first half of the first century CE, remain unaffected. But theological, or religious, statements – for example the statement that 'God loves us' – become true in a totally different sense.

However before looking at such beliefs as this we need to clear out of the way a complication which might seem to, but does not, affect the real issue. This is that a great deal of religious language is metaphorical. That God is great is not intended to mean that God occupies a large volume of space. That God is high above us is not intended to mean that God is further from the center of the earth than we are. That God is our Heavenly Father is not intended to mean that God is our biological father. And so on. And it is important, even though elementary, to see that the issue between religion with and religion without transcendence is not whether such statements should be understood literally or metaphorically. All sensible persons in both camps will agree that they are metaphors.

Turning, then, to the belief that God loves us, this means in the naive realism of traditional Christian belief that there is a personal Being who has created the universe, who is unlimited in knowledge and power, who intervenes from time to time in the course of history, and who loves his human creation in a manner analogous to that of an ideal human father. This belief entails that in addition to all the human consciousnesses that currently exist there is another consciousness which is the consciousness of God. But for Christianity without transcendence there is no such Being. There is the *idea* of such a Being, and there is the *language* in which the term 'God' plays a central role, and there are *forms of life* and *outlooks on life* which use the word 'God', and theistic language generally. But there is nevertheless no God in the sense that I spelled out above, involving (minimally) a divine consciousness in addition to the millions of human consciousnesses.

The same principle of interpretation applies to other central traditional Christian beliefs, such as the belief in a life after death. Here the non-realist (or 'without transcendence') understanding has been very clearly set forth by Dewi Phillips in his book *Death and Immortality*. It would, he says, 'be foolish to speak of eternal life as some kind of appendage to human existence, something which happens *after* human life on earth is over. Eternal life is the reality of goodness, that in terms of which human life is to be assessed ... Eternity is not *more* life, but this life seen under certain moral and religious modes of thought.'[6] Again, he says that from his point of view 'Questions about the immortality of the soul are seen not to be questions concerning the extent of a man's life, and in particular concerning whether that life can extend beyond the grave, but questions concerning the kind of life a man is living'.[7] Now it is a good Fourth Gospel metaphor to say that 'this is eternal life, that they know thee the only true God, and Jesus Christ whom thou hast sent' (John 17:3). But it is, surely, obvious that this is not intended to be inconsistent with the belief, present throughout the New Testament, in a continuation of this beyond the present life. Heaven is described in the New Testament, particularly in the Book of Revelation, in what some understand in a naively realistic way and others regard as imaginative imagery. Either way, it is surely clear that the reality of an 'eternal' quality of life now does not preclude its continuation, or its attainment, after death. But Phillips apparently assumes at this point an exclusive either/or. The contrast, then, between a realist and a non-realist interpretation of Christian eschatological language is stark. According to Phillips there is no continuation of consciousness after bodily death, although the traditional language about it can be used to refer instead to a quality of our present living. According to the traditional Christian understanding, on the other hand, it is true both that a present right relationship to God has 'eternal' value, and also that life embodying that value continues beyond death, and indeed that life continues after death *in order that* this value may be more fully and more widely realized.

A CRITICAL REALIST UNDERSTANDING OF
TRANSCENDENTAL RELIGION

I have referred to Phillips' unwarranted either/or. More generally, many advocates of religion without transcendence make the mistake of assuming that the only options are, on the one hand, a naive realist understanding of the Transcendent, and on the other hand a rejection of transcendence. The third option that they miss is a form of critical realism which holds that there is a transcendent reality that is limitlessly important to us, but that this reality is only known to us in limited human ways. We cannot know it as it is in itself, but only as it affects us. In Kantian terms, we do not experience the divine noumenon, but a range of divine phenomena to the formation of which our human religious concepts have contributed. But rather than risk getting distracted by Kantian exegesis I shall take as my text for critical realism in religion the extraordinarily fertile statement of St Thomas Aquinas that 'Things known are in the knower according to the mode of the knower.'[8]

I shall develop a critical realist understanding of religion, and of truth in religion, in terms of the concept of meaning: not semantic meaning, the meaning of words and sentences, but what I shall call pragmatic meaning. In order to get at this we can start from Wittgenstein's concept of 'seeing as' in the *Philosophical Investigations*, where he refers to ambiguous pictures such as Jastrow's duck-rabbit. We can see it *as* the picture of a duck's head facing left and *as* the picture of a rabbit's head facing right – though not of course as both at the same time. And we can see it in these two different ways because we possess the two different concepts of duck and rabbit, in terms of which we interpret the marks on paper. As Wittgenstein says, 'we see it as we interpret it'.[9] Now Wittgenstein thought that seeing-as is peculiar to puzzle pictures and other appearances, such as facial expressions, which are easily mistaken. So he said that '"seeing as ..." is not part of perception'.[10] He denied, in other words, that *all* seeing is seeing-as, pointing out that it would not be natural to say of the knife and fork on the table, 'Now I am seeing this as a knife and fork.' And indeed it would not. But I think he was mistaken in the conclusion that he drew. For the reason why this would not be for us a natural way of speaking is that we are so accustomed to knives and forks, as part of the familiar furniture of our culture, that we automatically identify them as such. There is for *us* no ambiguity. But it does not follow that what *we* know as a knife and fork could not be seen as something quite different by people of another culture in which knives and forks are completely unknown. Imagine Stone Age persons suddenly transported here in a time machine. They would see the items on the table, but might see them as small weapons, or as wonderful shining ornaments, or as sacred objects full of *mana*, too dangerous to be touched – and no doubt in various other ways. What the things are seen *as* depends on the concepts in terms of which the observer recognizes them. In other words, the activity of seeing-as, or recognizing, is relative to the perceiver's system of sortal concepts.

This is true not only of the recognition of objects but also of the more complex situations which objects jointly form. Let us at this point expand the concept of seeing-as to that of experiencing-as, of which seeing-as is the visual component. Thus I am experiencing our present situation as a meeting of a philosophy of religion conference – that is, as a gathering at which it is expected that this paper, having been circulated in advance, will be discussed. I am taking for granted certain aspects of the pragmatic meaning of the situation as I am experiencing it, such as the convention that critical remarks will be in order; that when you disagree with me or point out errors in my reasoning this is socially acceptable and I am not required to challenge you to a duel; that we shall not go on discussing indefinitely but will end at approximately the stated time, and so on. All this presupposes a vast cultural background, including a more or less civilized society in which people can meet at a specified time in a pre-arranged place and in a peaceful environment, and the existence of universities, the study of philosophy, the use of the English language, and so on and so on. But if Stone Age persons were dropped in among us at this meeting they would not experience the situation as we are experiencing it, because they would not have these concepts that are elements of our culture but not of theirs.

This suggests a way in which, taking a hint from Wittgenstein, we can formulate a critical realist epistemology. We live in a real environment, which we experience as having meaning for us, the kind of meaning (or the sense of 'meaning') in question being practical or pragmatic meaning. To experience the things on the table as a knife and fork is to be in a dispositional state in relation to them such that I shall use them in the ways in which in our culture we normally do use them. I shall not worship them or fight with them but shall use them as instruments with which to eat. To recognize them by means of our concepts of knife and fork is, in part, to be in this dispositional state. And for me to experience our present situation as a session of a philosophical conference is, again, to be in a dispositional state to behave within it in ways that are appropriate to that. The physical configurations of matter, simply as such, do not have meaning, but we endow them with meaning through what for other animals are recognitional capacities and for us are systems of concepts fixed and embodied in language. In general, then, to be conscious is to be discriminatingly aware of various selected features of our environment, recognized by means of our operative conceptual or recognitional system, so that we can act within it in ways that we take to be appropriate. So the meaning for us of our phenomenal world is its character as rendering appropriate some rather than other behavioural dispositions.

We can now apply to religion the complementary notions of experiencing-as and pragmatic meaning. Each religion trains its adherents to experience the universe as having a distinctive meaning which is reflected dispositionally in a distinctive form of life. This includes the experiencing of specific objects and places and events, and also of life as a whole. Thus in the context of the eucharist Christians experience the bread and wine, not simply as the natural objects that they know them to be, but as mediating the presence of Christ. Or a Hindu, bowing to an image of one of the gods who are manifestations of Brahman, and laying flowers or fruit before it, experiences the image not as just the piece of clay that she knows it to be, but as mediating and focussing a universal divine presence. And more generally, the Christian, for example, experiences the world – at any rate in consciously religious moments – as a divine creation, life as a gift of divine love, and its varied experiences, bad as well as good, as episodes in a pilgrimage through time towards the Kingdom of God, which in its fullness lies beyond this life. The difference between living and not living by a religious faith is a difference between living in the world experienced as having two different meanings, evoking different total dispositional states; and faith is the free interpretative activity in virtue of which we make (usually unconsciously) the cognitive choice between a naturalistic and a transcendental interpretation of the universe.

Let us now fantasize for a moment. If the different species all had their own conceptual systems and languages, these would be as different as the phenomenal worlds which they inhabit. And, to fantasize further, if the species had their own religions, these would also be built out of concepts peculiar to each species, which would accordingly think of the Transcendent in terms of concepts derived from their own forms of experience. As Rupert Brooke reminds us, the fish might believe that

> somewhere, beyond Space and Time,
> Is wetter water, slimier slime!
> And there (they trust) there swimmeth One
> Who swam ere rivers were begun,
> Immense, of fishy form and mind,
> Squamous, omnipotent, and kind;
> And under that Almighty Fin,
> The littlest fish may enter in.[11]

And returning to human life, a critical realist would expect us to conceive and therefore to experience the Transcendent in distinctively human ways – ways in the plural because there are different ways of being human, constituting the different cultures of the earth, which include different ways of thinking and experiencing the Transcendent. For critical realism in the epistemology of religion is the view that there is a transcendent Reality to which religious experience is a cognitive response, but that the forms that this takes within the different traditions depend upon their different sets of religious concepts together with their correspondingly different spiritual practices. The most predictable such concept is that of a limitlessly greater and higher Person – God. But there are also non-personal concepts, and hence non-personal modes of religious experience, of the Transcendent as Brahman, the Tao, Nirvana, the Dharmakaya, and so on. These different conceptualities, linked with appropriately different spiritual practices – for example, personalistic prayer and non-personalistic meditation – give rise to both the experienced God figures and the non-personal foci of religious contemplation.

I am thus appealing to the distinction between the Transcendent as it is in itself, beyond the scope of our conceptual systems, and the Transcendent as variously constructed within human religious experience. There is an analogy here with the physicists' language about the unobservable but inferred structure of the physical or natural universe. It is now a commonplace that advanced theories in physics have to be expressed either in mathematical or in metaphorical language. In contemporary works on physics we read of bundles of energy, of gluons and glueballs, of charm, of cosmic dust, of universes as bubbles within a mega-universe, of quantum tunnelling, of glitches and strings (which latter 'can be visualized as tiny one-dimensional rips in the smooth fabric of space'),[12] and so on in a riot of poetic metaphor. In religion, the analogous use of language is customarily described as mythological. In religious mythology we speak of the Transcendent in terms derived from the natural. And the truth of myth is a practical or pragmatic truthfulness consisting in its capacity to evoke (or tend to evoke) an appropriate dispositional response in the hearer. Thus the image of the Transcendent as a loving Heavenly Father tends to evoke a dispositional state which expresses itself in love for one's neighbours as fellow children of God. In so far, then, as the Heavenly Father is an authentic manifestation of the Transcendent to human consciousness, what is literally true of the heavenly Father – that he is good, loving, wise, etc. – is mythologically true of the Transcendent in itself. Again, insofar as the story of the Heavenly Father sending his Son to be born as a human being and to die for the sins of the world tends to evoke in us a trust and love that can illuminate and elevate our lives, to that extent the story is mythologically true. The same principle applies, of course, to the stories and mental pictures of the other great religious systems. Our language cannot be literally true of the Transcendent as it is in itself, but can be mythologically true of it in virtue of evoking an appropriate dispositional state in response to religious phenomena (the God figures, etc.) which are manifestations or 'appearances' to human consciousness of the Transcendent.

Such a view of the function of religious language is rather close to the Buddhist concept of *upaya*, 'skilful means'. This is the idea that religious teachings, including the Buddhist *dharma* itself, cannot be literally true because they refer to the Ultimate Reality which is empty (*sunya*) of our human conceptual projections. But the *dharma* can nevertheless be useful, indeed indispensable, as a skilful means to draw people towards the final experience of liberation, enlightenment, awakening, *satori*. Different teachings may be effective for different people, and for the same people at different periods of their life. But we should not cling to these teachings once they have served their purpose of helping us to move on to another stage of cognition. And so the Buddha told the parable of the man who crosses a river to safety by means of a raft and then, because the raft has been so useful, is tempted to lift it onto his shoulders and carry it with him. But he should go on, leaving the raft behind; and likewise, the Buddha said, the *dharma* 'is for carrying over, not for retaining ... You, monks, by understanding the parable of the raft, should get rid even of (right) mental objects, all the more of wrong ones'.[13] One is reminded of course of Wittgenstein's 'My propositions are elucidatory in this way: he who understands me finally recognizes them as senseless, when he has climbed out through them, on them, over them. (He must so to speak throw away the ladder, after he has climbed up on it).'[14]

The thought that our concepts apply to reality as humanly experienced, but not to reality as it is in itself, translates in religious terms into the idea of the ineffability, or in Eastern terms the formlessness, of the Transcendent. In the words of a fascinating saying in one of the Hindu holy books, 'Thou art formless: thy only form is our knowledge of thee.'[15] The Transcendent is not literally personal or impersonal, good or evil, purposive or non-purposive, active or passive, substance or process, even one or many; for these dualisms are aspects of our human conceptual systems. But in denying that the Transcendent is personal one is not affirming that it is impersonal, but rather that the personal–impersonal polarity does not apply to it. And the same with all the other dualisms. The Transcendent, as it is in itself independently of human awareness of it, is postulated as lying beyond the scope of human conceptuality. That is to say, it has no humanly conceivable intrinsic attributes, although its 'impact' upon us has of course to be described in terms of our human conceptualities.

There is however an obvious qualification to be made to this last statement. To say that X is ineffable is to say that X's nature cannot be described in terms of our human concepts. But of course to say that is already to describe it – namely, as being humanly indescribable. And so we have to distinguish between substantial attributes, such as goodness, power, personality, and purely formal and logically generated attributes, such as being such that our substantial attributes concepts do not apply to it. Ineffability must be defined in terms of the former, not the latter; and also in terms of the intrinsic nature of the Real, as distinguished from the effects of its presence upon ourselves.

The critical realist religious picture that I am proposing is, then, as follows. Using (perforce!) our human conceptuality, we can say that there is an ultimate source and ground of the universe in both its physical and its non-physical aspects – 'all things visible and invisible'. I have been referring to this as the Transcendent. The Transcendent is universally present, and affects human consciousness in many forms of what we call religious experience – within which I include the pervasive sense of living in the presence of God, and of being part of the samsaric process that leads towards unity with Brahman, and of oneness with the living universe that is an expression of the universal Buddha- nature, and as the sense of living in response to the Tao, or to the requirements of Heaven, as well as 'peak experiences' of enlightenment, awakening, visions and auditions and photisms and other such moments. These examples suffice to remind us that the impact of the Real comes to human consciousnesss in a variety of ways due to the different conceptual systems and spiritual practices of the religious traditions. The ultimate noumenal reality is thought, and therefore experienced, and therefore responded to in forms of human life in a range of ways, all formed by our different conceptual systems. The key concept of deity, or of the Transcendent as personal, presides over the theistic religions, whilst the key concept of the Absolute, or of the Transcendent as non-personal, presides over the non-theistic traditions. In each case the concept is made more concrete in terms of human history and culture. And so deity is thought and experienced, within Judaism specifically as Adonai, the God of Abraham, Isaac and Jacob; within Christianity as the Blessed Trinity of Father, Son, and Holy Spirit; within Islam as the strictly unitary Allah; within theistic Hinduism as Vishnu, who became incarnate as Krishna, or as Shiva, whose cosmic dance is the ongoing life of the universe; and so on. And likewise the ultimate as non-personal is thought and experienced within Advaitic Hinduism as the Atman which is identical with the eternal Brahman; within the different streams of Buddhism as *Nirvana*, or as the universal Buddha-nature of the universe; within Taoism as the eternal transcendent reality whose nature cannot be expressed in words; and so on.

What is the epistemological status of this suggestion? It is a theory, or hypothesis, offered as a 'best explanation' of the data provided by religious experience as reported in its plurality of forms by the history of religions. It is however offered as a (trans-cendental) *religious* interpretation of religion, i.e. one that accepts human religious experience not as purely projection and imagina-tion but as at the same time a response to the Transcendent. And insofar as it is correct it will be progressively confirmed in future experience beyond this life.

CONCLUSION

What I hope to have done in this paper is to draw out the contrast between religion with and without transcendence, showing in each case the sense in which religious beliefs can be true or false. The difference hinges upon different conceptions of the nature of reality as making or not making possible the ultimate fulfilment of the human project. And I have pointed out that we are not confined to a choice between a naive realist interpretation of religious language and the non-realist interpretation which issues in religion without transcendence. The third possibility is a critical realism which postulates an ultimate reality which is the ground of everything, including the possibility of the realization of the highest potential-ities of human nature; which is in itself beyond the network of human concepts, but which is humanly thought and experienced and responded to in the range of ways described in the history of religions.

NOTES

1.   Bertrand Russell, *Mysticism and Logic and Other Essays* (London: Edward Arnold, 1918), pp. 47–8.
2.   Bertrand Russell, *Autobiography*, vol. 3 (London: Allen & Unwin, 1969), pp. 172–3.
3.   Steven Weinberg, *Dreams of a Final Theory* (London: Hutchinson Radius, 1993), p. 41.
4.   Barbara Ward and Rene Dubos, *Only One Earth*, Report on the Stockholm Conference on the Human Environment (Harmondsworth and New York: Penguin Books, 1972), p. 35.
5.   Ludwig Feuerbach, *The Essence of Christianity*, trans. George Eliot (New York: Harper Torchbooks, 1957), p. 175.
6.   D. Z. Phillips, *Death and Immortality* (London: Macmillan, and New York: St Martin's Press, 1970), pp. 48–9. See also his *Religion Without Explanation* (Oxford: Blackwell, 1976), Chapters 8–9.

7. Ibid., p. 49.
8. St Thomas Aquinas, *Summa Theologica*, II/II, Q. 1, art. 2.
9. Ludwig Wittgenstein, *Philosophical Investigations*, trans. G. E. M. Anscombe (Oxford: Blackwell, 1953), p. 193.
10. Ibid., p. 197.
11. Rupert Brooke, 'Heaven', in *1914 and Other Poems* (Solihull: Helion Books, 1993), pp. 19–20.
12. Steven Weinberg, *Dreams of a Final Theory*, p. 170.
13. *The Middle Length Sayings*, vol. 1, trans. I. B. Horner (London: Pali Text Society, 1954–9), pp. 173–4.
14. Ludwig Wittgenstein, *Tractatus Logico-Philosophicus*, trans. C. K. Ogden (London: Routledge & Kegan Paul, 1922), 6.54.
15. *Yogava'sistha*, 1:28.

5

Transcendence and Truth – A Reply

Stephen Grover

I do not want to get sidetracked by the issue of elitism, but I think it is helpful to begin with Professor Hick's remarks on this topic.

Religion without transcendence, according to Hick, 'presupposes a naturalistic understanding of the universe but nevertheless uses religious language to express certain important aspects of human experience' (p. 43). This form of religion is elitist, Hick claims, because only those fortunate enough to escape starvation, slavery, persecution, oppression, grinding poverty, etc., 'can find positive meaning and fulfilment within a naturalistic interpretation of life' (pp. 44–5). The naturalistic picture is, for the vast majority of humanity, 'very bad news' (p. 46), so religion without transcendence can be liberating and ennobling only for that small minority for whom the naturalistic news is not so bad.

But what are the important aspects of human experience that religious language is used to express? Not, I think, complacent gratitude for the pleasures of a well-run pension-plan or a well-stocked grocery store, nor the humble acceptance of setbacks such as failing to make partner in a law firm or selling short in the stock-market. Comfortable lives are often those too smooth for religious belief to gain any grip, and those living such lives may be no more free to 'rise into serenity and inner peace' than are the slum-dwellers of Calcutta or south central Los Angeles, though for very different reasons. True religious feeling erupts into many people's lives when those lives are disrupted by tragedy, for then there are hardships to be overcome, or at moments of great joy that is known to be undeserved, bringing the recognition that we are creatures dependent upon grace. If lives are uniformly shallow there is no depth in them to be expressed, no matter how we understand the language that exists to express it.

Hick's description of religion without transcendence suggests that the aspects of human experience that gain expression in religious language are identifiable independently of the employment of religious concepts. The denial that talk of God, Brahman, the Tao, the Dharmakaya, etc. has any referent that transcends the natural is taken to mean that this talk refers instead to aspects of the natural world, and these aspects of the natural world can presumably be referred to in talk of other, non-religious kinds. This seems to me right as an interpretation of Feuerbach, or at least of Feuerbach's intentions (I suspect that his talk of infinite human consciousness is parasitic upon the theological language it supposedly replaces) but it is characteristic of many of those associated with the views that Hick is criticizing that they deny the possibility of translating religious language into language of another kind. If religious language is the only language in which these aspects of human experience gain expression, then these aspects will simply be absent from a description of the world that does not employ such language. I shall return to this issue later.

Hick's main concern over the elitism of religion without transcendence, however, is to do with theodicy. From the naturalistic viewpoint, evil is a massive reality that remains forever irreparable because those who suffer evil cease to exist and because the universe does not ultimately bring good out of evil. If, on the other hand, we somehow live on after our deaths, and if the universe somehow profits overall from the imperfections of its parts, then there is reparation for the many evils that most of humanity endures.

How does this tie in with the claim that only the fortunate are in a position to derive any comfort from religion without transcendence? If reparation has to be made for all evils, then it has to be made even for the lesser evils endured by the fortunate minority, and there is no reason to suppose that the members of this minority are ignorant and selfish enough to espouse a response to evil that works for them but not for the vast majority of humanity. If, on the other hand, the proper religious response to the reality of evil is to give up the demand for reparation, then the fact that there is no reparation is not bad news for anyone, or not in religious terms at any rate. Because the accusation of elitism is a serious one, Hick describes the elitism as 'unconscious' and generously supposes that its proponents are unaware of the implications of their own views. But those who reject reparation theodicies know perfectly well that some people are more fortunate than others. Their reasons for rejecting such theodicies gain their force precisely because of the massive reality of evil: the discomforts of the fortunate might, perhaps, be explained by some good that derives from them – 'no gain without pain' is surely a mantra of the bourgeoisie alone – but nothing can be brought out of horrifying evils that could be said to explain, let alone justify them. A God who inflicts suffering in order later to make reparation for it is a moral criminal.[1]

If we are on the lookout for elitism, Hick's own claim that 'in the great majority of men and women the higher potentialities ... remain for ever unfulfilled' (p. 48) might itself raise an eyebrow. Surely we are more often shown something of the heights of which human nature is capable by quite ordinary men and women, and the suggestion that a continuation of human existence after death is required for all but those few who realize their human potential in this present life is peculiar. We cannot all be Nelson Mandela or Archbishop Romero: 'If the whole body were an eye, where were the hearing? If the whole were hearing, where were the smelling?' (I Corinthians 12:17). Nor is it obvious that a failure to realize human potential before death can be compensated for by a continued existence under quite different conditions after it. If my life is scarred by some deep and unmendable regret, say for an injury that I have done to another, that is a burden that I bear as the individual that I am, and a future in which the notion of an individual's existing or not existing is inapplicable seems of no help. Perhaps the literal truth of a survival after death that afforded an opportunity to make reparation for the wrong that I have done would make a difference to me, but nothing so definite is offered up when literal truth is exchanged for mythological.

What is it then, that the proponents of religion without transcendence have missed, but have failed to see that they have missed? Presumably, it is something like the following: that religion without transcendence would be rejected by the vast majority of suffering humanity because their lives are such that it cannot provide meaning and fulfilment for them. Perhaps this is true. But by much the same token, Hick's critical realism would be rejected by the vast majority of ordinary religious believers. I think it is only an elite that can greet the claim that 'Our language cannot be literally true of the Transcendent as it is in itself' (p. 55) as good news, for only an elite ever talks or thinks in these terms. Someone for whom the 'story of the Heavenly Father sending his Son to be born as a human being and to die for the sins of the world' (p. 55) is true does not equate its truth with the tendency of the story 'to evoke in us a trust and love that can illuminate and elevate our lives', but thinks of it as true to the exclusion of the 'stories and mental pictures of the other great religious systems' (p. 55). Given a choice between naive realism, non-realism and Hick's critical realism, I think the vast majority of religious believers, and perhaps especially those whose lives are filled with deprivation and pain, would vote for the first.

But is this the choice that we face? These three possibilities – naive realism, critical realism and non-realism – are described by Hick as 'interpretations' of religious language (p. 58). The suggestion that religious language in general stands in need of interpretation is an odd one. Much in religion is obscure, especially when the religious tradition is one with which we are unfamiliar, but the kind of interpretation that we need when faced with such obscurity is internal to religion, and is itself given in religious language. So that is not what is going on here.

Instead we have a contrast between three theories or hypotheses (p. 57), one naive and two sophisticated. These theories offer rival explanations of 'the data provided by religious experience as reported in its plurality of forms by the history of religions'. The analogy with philosophical accounts of physical-object language is deliberate: the naive realist allegedly believes that physical objects are just as they appear to us to be; the non-realist denies that there are any physical objects as the naive realist understands that term; the critical realist distinguishes in Kantian fashion between objects as they are in themselves (and about which we can say nothing) and objects as they appear in human experience. Naive realism supposedly presents us with the metaphysics embedded in ordinary language, whilst the other two offer themselves as revisions of that metaphysics forced upon us by the difficulties inherent in naive realism and by other pressures deriving from scientific investigation into the natural world.

How does the dichotomy between realism and non-realism relate to the issues of truth and transcendence in religion? On Hick's view, the mapping is simple: naive and critical realism are both versions of religion with transcendence, non-realism of religion without. Hick describes religion without transcendence as evacuated of metaphysical content (p. 44), but what this means is that it is evacuated of the metaphysical content of realism, naive or critical, not that it is not a metaphysical theory. The metaphysics is just that of naturalism.[2]

If metaphysics is always nonsense, albeit sometimes deep non-sense, then none of these three theories is the right one, because the idea that we need a theory is itself a mistake. Our host, Dewi Phillips, has repeatedly repudiated the label of non-realist on just these grounds. Phillips regards the dichotomy – realism or non-realism? – as a false one. And he regards the dichotomy as false not merely in relation to religious beliefs, but when applied to beliefs of any sort. But perhaps it is better to examine this view at its source.

Wittgenstein describes the conflict between the realist and ideal-ist as an idle one: the convinced realist and the convinced idealist teach their children the word 'chair' in the same way, and so by all criteria relevant to the determination of the meaning of the word 'chair' the two sets of children will mean just the same by it.[3] Of course, when the realist challenges the idealist to accept as a definition of the meaning of the word 'chair' some such expression as 'physical object existing independently of all consciousness and providing a movable seat for one person', the idealist will reject the definition. But the disagreement is not over the meaning of the word 'chair' here, for the prefixed expression 'physical object exist-ing independently of all consciousness and ...' will provoke the same reaction whatever follows it. The meaning of a word is its use; meaning is what is explained in explanations of the meaning of a word. But the realist's prefix, and the equivalent expression from the idealist, are neither part of the explanation of the meaning of the word nor an aspect of its use.

If Wittgenstein is right, the realist and the idealist mean the same thing when they say, 'There is a chair in the unoccupied room next door,' and they mean the same thing when they say, 'I believe there is a chair in the unoccupied room next door' or 'It is true that there is a chair in the unoccupied room next door.' These are all just ways of asserting the same thing, though perhaps with varying levels of confidence. Evidence that they do not mean the same thing by the word 'chair' emerges only when one refuses to apply the word in a way that the other does, or when they behave differently in non-linguistic ways around chairs. Because such divergences do not correlate with the adoption of realism or idealism as a metaphysical stance, we can also say that realists and idealists share the same beliefs about chairs. There is agreement in language, and also in judgements; realists and idealists believe exactly the same things about chairs, and about all physical objects. The grounds on which we might attribute differing beliefs to them are lacking. They do, of course, come into conflict over sentences such as 'There are physical objects' but as all such sentences are misfired attempts to express what cannot be expressed in this way, we do not here have a case of a conflict of beliefs.[4]

Is there agreement in language between theists and atheists? Sometimes there is. Richard Swinburne and John Mackie are largely in agreement over the meaning of religious language, but disagree over the probability to be assigned to the hypothesis that there exists a god who is omnipotent, omniscient, etc. Bayes' theorem is useful in adjudicating their dispute precisely because theism is here treated as an explanatory theory, and it is easy to imagine someone assenting to Swinburne's assessment of the probabilities whilst remaining spiritually untouched. Feuerbach, if we read him as Hick suggests (p. 44), uses 'God' to refer to aspects of the natural world; someone agreeing about the meaning of the word but denying that there is a God would presumably be saying that these aspects of the world are themselves illusory.[5] Here religious language is treated as reducible to language of some other sort.

Wittgenstein's account of the conflict between the believer and the unbeliever rejects both these ways of construing the conflict. Religious language says what it says, and nothing else will substitute for it;[6] but it does not say what it says by offering empirical hypotheses that are subject to our ordinary methods of verification. Hick would certainly agree to the second point: the verification that assures us of the fact-asserting status of standard religious discourse is eschatological. If religion with transcendence is true, then religious believers will, finally, participate in an end-state of the universe that confirms beyond all possibility of doubt that their faith is justified. Without such experiential verification, the truth of religious myth is 'a practical or pragmatic truthfulness consisting in its capacity to evoke (or tend to evoke) an appropriate dispositional response in the hearer' (p. 55). Pragmatic meaning and pragmatic truth fit nicely together: to experience the environment as having pragmatic meaning is to be in a certain dispositional state in relation to that environment (p. 53): if the dispositional state is appropriate then the language is pragmatically meaningful and true. But this is all compatible with religion without transcendence: it is the step beyond pragmatic meaning and truth that gives content to the notion of a transcendental interpretation of religion, and whether such an interpretation is correct is something that 'will be progressively confirmed in future experience beyond this life' (p. 58).

The myths of the world's religions describe this future experience in numerous ways. Each myth is, for Hick, pragmatically true, and so although each religion says what it says and not something else, one can indeed substitute something else, namely, any other myth that has the same tendency to evoke the appropriate dispositions in the hearer. I am unsure how much Professor Hick thinks we can say about the future experience that will (if we enjoy it) progressively confirm the truth of the transcendental interpretation of religion: it seems to me to follow from what he says about theodicy that the experiences must be had by individuals, and under conditions that allow the application of the term 'human'. Otherwise, it does not seem possible for post-mortem spiritual growth to make up for the lack of growth displayed by so many lives before death. I find it hard to give any sense to the notion of my having experiences under conditions radically different from those that obtain now, and if as little can be said about post-mortem experience as can be said about the Transcendent, I do not see how the term 'experience' can be given any content here, or how these experiences could be said to be mine, or how it is appropriate to talk of any kind of verification.

The content of religion with transcendence that supposedly outstrips that of religion without it consists in a reality, the Transcendent, about which we can say nothing, for it is neither personal nor impersonal, neither good nor evil, neither active nor passive, neither purposive nor non-purposive, and so on (p. 56). It is what must exist if religion is to be responsive, and not merely projective (p. 42). Yet Hick's theodicy requires that the Transcendent be 'benign in relation to humanity' (p. 49). These two claims appear to be in tension, for anything that is benign must presumably be good rather than evil, and if that goodness shows in the continuation of the project of human spiritual growth then the Transcendent must also, I think, be purposive and active. Or is it just us who do the growing, and the best that can be said for the Transcendent is that it does not get in our way, or not as much as the natural does? Surely this is almost as dispiriting a picture as the one that Hick finds within naturalism: unless we can say something about our relation to the Transcendent, we have no reason for thinking that adding it on to the natural makes the news better or worse, or leaves it much the same. It is just another piece of furniture, which we are not able even to unpack from the crate that it came in.

A better place to start in thinking about transcendence is the way that it shows itself in people's lives. The believer who gives thanks to God for some happy event may, for all we know, be thanking God just as she would thank her boss if he were to give her a raise. But we know that something distinctively religious is going on when she thanks God for unhappy events as well. When Job prays: 'Naked came I out of my mother's womb, and naked shall I return thither: the Lord gave, and the Lord hath taken away; blessed be the name of the Lord' (Job 1:21) we see what it means to transcend the natural. Is what is expressed here an important aspect of human experience, but one that might gain expression in other, non-religious language? This is as powerful a repudiation of Russell's 'A free man's worship', and its 'firm foundation of unyielding despair' as one might want, and it would surely be wrong to describe it as a natural response to misfortune, if by 'natural' one means 'naturalistic'. Job, in refusing to curse God, refuses to allow anything contained within a naturalistic inventory of the contents of the world to determine the status of his relationship with God, and so transcends all items in that inventory. In Kierkegaardian terms, he relates himself relatively to all relative goods and so relates himself absolutely to the absolute good. This is surely religion with transcendence, and yet no movement is made towards the theodicy, and accompanying eschatology, that Hick insists is characteristic of responses to the Transcendent.

Understanding the meaning of Job's response does not involve attributing to him either a theodicy of reparation or a commitment to the confirmation of some hypothesis in post-mortem experience. Indeed, there would be something paradoxical if a faith that repudiates all consideration of how the world goes depends, for its truth, on how the world goes. Must we nevertheless insist that the reality of the Transcendent is the necessary postulate of the appropriateness of a response to misfortune such as Job's? The notion of the Transcendent cannot be built into the meaning of religious language if the Transcendent is itself utterly without character or content. A belief in something about which nothing can be said cannot show itself in the believer's behaviour, linguistic or otherwise. So the role of the Transcendent must here be explanatory: it is something postulated in order to account for the religious experiences of mankind, and without which those experiences are merely projective, and not responsive.

Hick appeals to an analogy with physicists' language about the unobservable but inferred structure of the physical universe, in which theories are expressed either mathematically or metaphorically (p. 55). Talk of bundles of energy, rips in the fabric of space, and so on, provides an analogy to the use of mythological language in religion. But what, in religion, corresponds to the mathematical expression of theories in physics? The Galilean book of the universe, written exclusively in the language of mathematics, gives content to the distinction between how things are in themselves and how they appear in our ordinary experience. But no such contrast is available in the case of the Transcendent as it is in itself, for there is no language in which the Transcendent can be described that is non-metaphorical.

The Transcendent cannot offer us the kind of advance over merely mythological descriptions of reality that many philosophers have seen as being made available by replacing, say, our ordinary talk of objects as coloured with an account in which those objects are said only to reflect light of certain wavelengths, while the colours reside in us as subjective dispositions. This picture is itself confused, for all that science can explain here is, on the one hand, the physiological basis of our capacity for colour-discrimination, and on the other, why the world is such as to allow us to possess and use the colour concepts that we have with success. Nothing in this could force us to accept the view that objects are not really coloured or that ascriptions of colour to objects are subjective or relative. Analogously, we might expect of an explanation of religion only an account of those reactions and responses characteristic of the religious life, and of the world in which those reactions and responses have their place.

Just as, if we or the world were different in certain specifiable ways, our colour concepts would be useless, so our religious concepts might become obsolete. Perhaps, if we lived for ever and lacked for nothing, this would happen. But the world is not such as to rob religious reactions of their point, nor can these reactions be reduced to or identified with non-religious reactions of delight or acceptance. Those reactions, and the life that they underpin, give religious language its sense. But nothing can give sense to belief in the Transcendent, just as nothing can give sense to the realist's belief that there *really is* a chair in the next room. Our ordinary procedures for assessing the truth of claims about chairs are what give those claims their sense; equivalently, it is the practices of religious believers that give sense to claims such as 'God exists' or 'There will be a Last Judgment'. Attributing to religious beliefs a sense that cannot be specified in the use of religious language produces an epistemological and metaphysical mystery parallel to that espoused by the realist in relation to the chair, for just as the realist will not be satisfied even when the chair is seen and sat upon, so the religious believer is condemned always to see through a glass darkly, and never face-to-face.

NOTES

1. See, for example, D. Z. Phillips, *From Fantasy to Faith* (London: Macmillan, 1991), pp. 119, 198–9. For those who reject theodicy as itself misguided. Hick's slogan 'No theodicy without eschatology' (p. 48) lacks any bite.
2. Religious non-realists such as Feuerbach are not non-realists about everything; they are realists about whatever it is that they think religion reduces to. Reductionists are therefore those who are non-realists about whatever is reduced, but realists about what does the reducing, as Putnam has pointed out (H. Putnam, *Reason, Truth and History* (Cambridge: Cambridge University Press, 1981), 56–7). Putnam remarks that '[a] truly non-realist view is non-realist all the way down', which in context suggests that non-realists are those who reduce *ad infinitum*. But this view, if it is coherent, is not what Hick has in mind, for the proponents of religion without transcendence adopt the naturalistic viewpoint and this presumably means that assertions about the physical universe are not reducible to assertions of some other kind.
3. Ludwig Wittgenstein, *Zettel*, §§. 413–14.
4. Wittgenstein, *On Certainty*, §§. 35–7.
5. Feuerbach often speaks of the infinity of human consciousness, and identifies consciousness of God as consciousness of the infinity of human consciousness. Denying that there is a God might therefore be understood as the denial of infinity to human consciousness, and if we can give a sense to the expression 'Human consciousness is infinite' then this is what the religious and non-religious Feuerbachians are in disagreement about.
6. Wittgenstein, *Lectures and Conversations on Aesthetics, Psychology and Religious Belief* (Oxford: Blackwell, 1966), p. 71.

Part Three
After Transcendence – Alternative Ways of the Spirit

6

After Transcendence: The Death of God and the Future of Religion

Richard Schacht

New struggles. – After Buddha was dead, his shadow was still shown for centuries in a cave – a tremendous, gruesome shadow. God is dead; but given the way of men, there may still be caves for thousands of years in which his shadow will be shown. – And we – we still have to vanquish his shadow, too.[1]

I am going to take it as my point of departure in this paper that, as Nietzsche so vividly put it, 'God is dead', and go on to reflect upon the question of what this might mean for the future of religion. Among the 'shadows of God' remaining to be vanquished, I suggest, is the shadow of the idea of God itself, which has fallen over the whole realm of religion in the Western world for so long that it takes some doing even to conceive of what religion might look like out from under it. If religion is to have a future, however, or at any rate a future other than simply a prolongation of its past, and a new lease on life after the 'death of God', having any interest and significance for those of us for whom (as Nietzsche put it in his gloss on this notion in *Gay Science*)[2] 'the belief in the Christian god has become unbelievable', this is an effort that must be made. And I further consider it to be an effort well worth making. For I believe the possibility of what I shall call 'post-transcendence religion' ('PT-religion' for short) to be of crucial importance in connection with the problem posed by the 'advent of nihilism' Nietzsche heralded, and with the task of overcoming it that was his greatest concern. And as I read him, I think he would agree. Indeed, I see him as one of the discoverers and explorers of this new religious continent, and – his anti-Christian rhetoric notwithstanding – as one of the most important religious thinkers in recent times.

Like so many who conceive of themselves as religious, as well as so many others who do not, I used to think that the future of religion more or less depended upon the future of beliefs in the existence of a transcendent deity of some sort. I now think that is a mistake. I also went through a period in which I bought into the idea that one can throw out baths without throwing out babies, applied this picture to religion and the idea of God, and thought that it might be both possible and desirable to get rid of the former (religion) while hanging on to the latter (God), appropriating God for philosophy in the spirit of Kant. I now think that would be unwise if not simply mistaken, and that this is a case in which there is more to be said for the bath – suitably filtered and recycled – than for the baby.

To be sure, the idea of God, along with those of the soul and immortality, may have become so entangled with the idea of religion that it would require something like Alexander's approach to the Gordian Knot to sunder them, with consequences that might prove no less fatal to the prospects of religion than their continuing entanglement itself may be. Some would take this to be the case with respect to God and the possibility of life-affirmation, morality and values as well. I do not agree, and indeed think Nietzsche was right to discern the genesis of nihilism in this very linkage. And I take Nietzsche's death-of-God rhetoric and anti-Christian polemics, as well as his running battle with Socrates, Plato and their metaphysical progeny, to be his version of Alexander's Gordian strategy, intended not to put an end to religion once and for all (any more than he meant to do away altogether with values and moralities), but rather to give it a new and more promising lease on life. I would like to see this happen – and to rehabilitate some of the richest pieces of religious language, as not only Spinoza and Hegel but also Nietzsche himself sought to do.

In company with all three of them, I am unwilling either to resign myself to the monopolization of religious language by the religious traditions that have long held sway, or to repudiate it entirely, or to abandon it without contest to those who would appropriate and trivialize it in the manner of the purveyors of the so-called 'new spirituality'. One day recently, while working on this paper, I received a bulk-rate mailing (along with the usual assortment of mail-order catalogs and credit card offers) from a book-and-CD club calling itself 'One Spirit'. It contained an 'exclusive charter invitation' to join up. (My first four selections would only cost a dollar!) On the envelope, with appropriate art and photos, were the following enticements: 'Re-explore your religious roots. Meditate. Encounter the world's wisdom. Deepen your personal relationships. Discover alternative paths to good health. Hear angelic voices.' And, last but not least, right up there by the bulk-rate mailing mark: 'Unleash your own creativity.'

Now, what are we to make of this? Someone obviously is out to make a buck; but the commercialization is too blatant to be interesting – as is the silliness which allows for the equal treatment of everything from *The Oxford Companion to the Bible* to *Women Who Run With the Wolves* and *Intuitive Eating*. Of somewhat greater interest is the fact that there is no mention of God either in the come-ons or in the breathless letter of invitation to join. The 'angelic voices' and the 'One Spirit' rubric are as close as one comes. One can of course select books about God; but they are given no pride of place in this phantasmagoria of spiritual uplift, evoking images in my mind of what the religious market-place in the later years of the Roman Empire must have been like. God clearly has fallen upon hard times when his competition is not only other gods and graven images but body oils and yoga workouts. 'One Spirit allows room for a diversity of beliefs,' the Membership Director writes, and 'is, moreover, as open to possibilities as you are'.

This is not merely a travesty of the sort we are used to when the term 'philosophy' is used to refer to anyone's ideas about anything. It also represents a serious impoverishment of language as well as of thought. With Hegel, I consider 'spirit' a term worth fighting for, even if there is nothing transcendent to which it refers. With Nietzsche, I take the same stand where the term 'soul' is concerned, even if (as he has Zarathustra say) 'soul is only a word for something about the body'. And with Spinoza, I would take the same position with respect to 'God', even if it is agreed that it refers only to something about the world – provided that we succeed in curing ourselves of our transcendence-reflex in our understanding of it.

Yet we do well to give some thought to the undeniable appeal of the sort of stuff represented by my mailing. It appeals to a great many people who are well beyond the point of ripeness for both benighted superstition and blind fanaticism. Strong appeals bespeak strong needs. Is the need reflected here a basic trait of our human psyche, from which (perhaps) religions ultimately spring, and the fertile soil in which they grow? Or is it instead to be diagnosed as the consequence of an addiction that can no longer be satisfied in the old way, but that craves something similar in its effect? And to come more directly to the point: why should anyone for whom the death of God is a point of departure be interested in the possibility of religion without transcendence? The answer to this question is of no little relevance to the further question of whether the New Spiritualism will do as well as anything. If the only answer is that we had better develop some sort of spiritual methadone to assist in humanity's recovery from its transcendence-addiction (lest it either relapse into its old ways with a fanatical vengeance or else lose the will to live), I might concede the necessity, but would find nothing in it either for me or for a humanity that has gotten its act together. Indeed, there is something Grand-Inquisitorial about this way of thinking that I find deeply repugnant. In any event, if that were all that remained of religion in the aftermath of the death of God, it would surely cease to be of any further interest to any such company as the present one.

If, on the other hand, there is or at least can be more to it than this, in relation to which the 'One Spirit' types are but kindergartners at best – something healthier, more vital, more honest, and more significantly connected with the flourishing and enhancement of human life beyond any such pathology – even in the absence of any appeal to transcendence, and indeed *especially* in that case, then it will behoove us to turn our attention to it. And it may well be that as we do so we will discover both good reasons to hang on to some pieces of religious language and promising ways of doing so. Chief among my candidates for preservation and rehabilitation in this respect, beyond those already mentioned, is the idea of the divine. And there may even turn out to be some good and important work to do for its old counterpart, the demonic.

In proclaiming the death of God, Nietzsche was giving expression to his conviction of the bankruptcy of all notions of some sort of transcendent reality beyond this life and this world, making sense of them, explaining them, and endowing them (and ourselves) with meaning and value. That, as I have said, is my point of departure here. But for Nietzsche, that marks the end only of a long and rather sorry chapter in the history of religion as well as of philosophy and of humanity, and not the end of the book for any of them. He may indeed have heralded the advent of nihilism, as an inevitable withdrawal symptom in the aftermath of transcendence-addiction; but he looked beyond it, to a new affirmation of life unmediated by dreams of transcendence – and yet associated with what for him was very definitely and quite explicitly a newly envisioned alternative religious sensibility. He called it *Dionysian*, to give it a pedigree to match those of its transcendence-oriented rivals; and the importance he attached both to *Thus Spake Zarathustra* and to his idea of the 'eternal recurrence' follows directly and clearly from it.

Nietzsche's vitriolic attack upon Christianity and Judaism as he understood them is well known; but it is often overlooked that he attacked them so violently in the name and on behalf of life and its affirmation, to which he took them to be profoundly and insidiously detrimental. Indeed, he conceived the counter-movement to Christianity in explicitly if unconventionally religious terms, as in his late note on 'The two types: *Dionysus* and the *Crucified*'. Thus, after beginning by remarking 'To bear in mind: the typical *religious* person – a decadence-type?' he goes on to reflect:

> . . . but aren't we then leaving out one type of religious person, the *pagan*? Isn't the pagan cult a form of thanksgiving and affirmation of life? Mustn't its highest representation be a justification and deification of life?
>
> Type of a well-turned-out and ecstatic-overflowing spirit. ... A type that takes into itself and *redeems* the contradictions and questionable aspects of existence?
>
> It is here that I locate the *Dionysus* of the Greeks: the religious affirmation of life, life as a whole, not denied or divided; typical that the sex-act awakens profundity, mystery, reverence.
>
> Dionysus versus the 'Crucified': there you have the antithesis. It is *not* a difference with respect to martyrdom – the same thing has a different meaning. Life itself, its eternal fruitfulness and recurrence, gave rise to torment, destruction, the will to annihilation [in the former case]. ... In the other case suffering, the 'Crucified as the innocent', was taken to be an objection against life, as a formula for its condemnation.[3]

This way of thinking, which Paul Tillich approvingly used to call Nietzsche's 'ecstatic naturalism', is no mere post-religious nihilism or bland secular humanism. Indeed, it stands – and was *intended* to stand – in marked contrast to both. And this likewise is no odd moment in Nietzsche's waning months of incipient insanity, as his imagery began to run wild; for it is one of the central strands of his thought from first to last, as evident in *The Birth of Tragedy* and *The Gay Science* and *Zarathustra* as it is in his late published and un-published writings. It supplied the passion so evident (to pick but one example) in the remarkable concluding section of the Second Essay of his *On the Genealogy of Morals*, which ends with his evoca-tion of a higher humanity that 'must yet come to us' – the type of what he calls 'the *redeeming* man of great love and contempt':

> ... the creative spirit whose compelling strength will not let him rest in any aloofness or any beyond ... This man of the future, who will redeem us not only from the hitherto reigning ideal but also from that which was bound to grow out of it, the great nausea, the will to nothingness, nihilism; this bell-stroke of noon and of the great decision that liberates the will again and restores its goal to the earth and his hope to man; this antichrist [or: antichristian] and antinihilist; this victor over God and nothing-ness – *he must come one day*.–[4]

I have quoted these passages at some length in an attempt to convey something of the spirit of what Nietzsche was reaching for, beyond both the tradition of transcendence and its collapse. In the perspective of that tradition and under the shadow of the idea of God, in the ancient world as in our own day, this way of thinking may appear to be not only areligious but threateningly anti-religious, and even diabolical. But that interpretation is highly suspect, and is far from disinterested; and once we recover from its spell and banish the 'shadow of God' that lingers on as a habit of thought even after the demise of the figure casting it, we may find that Nietzsche was on to something not only of interest but of great importance.

There obviously can be no serious question of turning back the clock and reviving Greek or Nordic or any other pre-Christian form of paganism – or at any rate, this surely is not what Nietzsche had in mind, his early infatuation with the Greeks and the Wagner of the *Ring* notwithstanding. But he certainly would seem to have thought that it would be both humanly possible and highly desir-able to go beyond traditional and contemporary ways of thinking – religious, metaphysical, and also their latter-day sequels and reactions – to something akin in important respects to this type of outlook and orientation, in connection with which terms like 'religious' and 'divine' and 'deify' and even 'redemption' may very appropriately be employed. The future he envisioned for them may not be their only possible and actual future, for better or for worse; but it is a possible future, and one that I believe deserves to be taken quite seriously.

Nietzsche is by no means the only notable figure in the modern Western philosophical tradition to opt for a reinterpretation of the divine rescuing it from its relegation to transcendence. And here I do not merely have in mind Feuerbach, who certainly repudiated the idea of a transcendent God, but conceived of the divine merely as a projection of our own human nature writ large. Feuerbach's secular humanism may be all very well and good as far as it goes; but it is too anemic and anthropocentric to have much promise as a contender for religious honors. I am thinking chiefly of the two others I have already mentioned, who are bedfellows of Nietzsche not as strange as one might think: Spinoza and Hegel.

I take both Spinoza and Hegel, despite all their talk of 'God', to be thinkers for whom the transcendent God of the Judeo-Christian tradition is as dead as for Nietzsche – and yet for whom this likewise by no means meant the demise of the divine, but rather opened the way for its relocation in something about the world of which we are a part. Both have been deemed theists, atheists and pantheists; but the debate about which of these labels best fits them is well wide of the mark. For them, as for Nietzsche, if it still makes sense to hang on to the idea of 'God' at all, the best thing to do with it is to recast it in terms of something fundamental or salient about life and the world. Spinoza (rather like Einstein) looked to what he called 'nature' to provide a gloss on what he meant by 'God'; while Hegel looked to what he called '*Geist*', particularly as it unfolds in history, society and culture. Both thought that the idea of a God existing out there somewhere apart from and beyond what goes on in this life and this world is naive and untenable; but both also thought that a true understanding of what goes on in this life and this world can and should be something of a religious rather than merely analytically rational and bloodlessly intellectual exercise.

To be sure, the 'God' of which Spinoza and Hegel speak is neither capable of nor interested in doing anything for us individually, or of entering into a personal relationship with believers or anyone else. That is one of the reasons why their versions of this notion, if understood, undoubtedly would not be found very satisfying for much of humankind; and as both of them were prepared to allow, it might be best for most people to remain attached in a naive way to forms of religion of a more traditional nature and appeal. But for those who have arrived at a point at which this is no longer possible, Spinoza and Hegel too both offer alternatives that are very far removed indeed from Schopenhauerian pessimism and its nihilistic kin, and that may be taken to anticipate possible varieties of PT-religion different from but comparable to Nietzsche's. So Nietzsche has some good and respectable company.

The kind of alternative religious possibility I have in mind might be thought of as the kind of thing we might have come to have if the ideas of a transcendently conceived God, soul and immortality had never occurred to anyone in the first place. Our lives and deaths, our creations and losses, our successes and failures, our joys and our sufferings, and our relations to each other and to our world all would remain to be dealt with; but the horizon within which they would be dealt with would be the horizon of this life and this world, as our understanding of them may develop and change, but always understood to be the limits of all existence and reality that may have any relevance to us. Taking this possibility seriously, and being able to think about it not as contrasting miserably with the transcendent alternative we would prefer but rather as simply a reflection of the way things are and an invitation to make the most of it, will certainly take some doing, and some getting used to. But I share the conviction of Nietzsche and company that we had better get on with it. And part of this project involves making the experiment of thinking of all appeals to transcendently conceived realities as fundamentally mistaken.

The mistake made by religions of transcendence and their metaphysical philosophical cousins, in the perspective of the alternative with which I am concerned, is the *reification of divinity* (and of human mentality and spirituality along with it). And the 'de-deification' deemed by Nietzsche to be needful with respect to the world[5] might with equal aptness and urgency be conceived as the task of the *de-reification* of divinity (and of the psyche as well). The fundamental intention here is not the eradication of the divine from our experience and understanding of life and the world, but rather their *re-divinization* – or rather (since it would be no mere turning back of the calendar), the new revelation of their divinity. It is the *recovery* of the sense of the divine as pertaining profoundly and fundamentally to the basic character of life and the world, either as they eternally are or as they have it in them to become, rather than their mere secularizing prosaification that leaves them not only disenchanted but desolate or even repugnant in their utter alienness and absurdity.

Ironically, that nihilistic outcome is, on Nietzsche's analysis, the direct consequence of the mistaken reification of divinity which might well have had for its motto 'Transcendence or Bust!' This obsession with transcendence, culminating in an unwillingness or inability to esteem and affirm anything that has no transcendent reality or pedigree, is for Nietzsche not the mark of true religiousness but a symptom of something having gone profoundly wrong, and a dangerously pathological form of religious mentality.

To be sure, reification is (as Nietzsche observed) a commonplace and often very handy way to simplify things for purposes of comprehension, communication and action, and so may well have come to be a deeply ingrained feature of human thought for good pragmatic reasons. But of course (as Nietzsche also observed, although this is often overlooked), reasons of this sort have nothing to do with truth, and indeed may even reasonably be taken to create something of a presumption against it. The disposition to reification opens the way to stories about transcendent realities and realms that may be very appealing to many, particularly in view of the various respects in which life (and death) in this world may leave much to be desired. But if first the appeal of these stories and then one's addiction to them render one unable to appreciate and affirm or even endure life and the world without them, they do their adherents no real good, and very real harm. Moreover, they may easily foster and promote attitudes and interpretations rendering their adherents oblivious or even hostile (as Nietzsche lamented) to the very features of life and the world that are most crucial to the possibility of their disillusioned affirmation.

The reification of the divine makes possible its personalization, in ways having important consequences for the character of religion. For example, this gives strong impetus to anthropomorphism as well as anthropocentrism, and may make worship seem appropriate and prayer seem cogent. The de-reification of the divine likewise would appear to require (or at least create a presumption favoring) its depersonalization, and so to render both worship and prayer otiose, except perhaps insofar as they may be psychologically or otherwise mundanely beneficial to those who engage in them. Religion shorn of transcendence likewise would seem to have no intelligible place in it for the notions of sin, damnation, grace and salvation, unless they too are interpreted in a manner pertaining entirely to human life mundanely conceived. But these losses may seem paltry indeed compared to the deprivation of the prospect of immortality, reunion beyond the grave with loved ones, and the expectation that justice will be meted out both to those who follow the rules and to those who do not.

The human (and perhaps all too human) stakes in the personalization of the divine suggested by these remarks may be summed up in a phrase borrowed from elsewhere but having clear application here: 'the cult of personality'. I would not dream of denying or even doubting the importance of personality, personal identity and personal relationships in human life; and there can be no doubt about the fact that it is as particular persons that those who matter most to us do so. But we tend to find it hard to accept the idea that personality is as ephemeral as it is contingent, coming into existence and passing away in little episodes in the career of our species to which the universe is utterly indifferent. And so we are impelled to devise and cling to ways of thinking that translate the importance we attach to it into an appropriate kind of reality. If this requires a personalized reified deity, so be it. And if giving up the latter would mean giving up the former, forget it. For some it is the prospect of the demise of their own selves that is intolerable; while for others it is the thought or experience of the death of those they love that drives them. In either case the cult of personality has powerful roots and nourishment. And it does not draw upon them alone; for it is also prompted and sustained by the longing to feel that one *matters* in the larger scheme of things, not just as a physical entity or living creature or member of a species or society or culture, but as the particular person one is; and that it is not only one's existence as that particular person that matters, but also everything one does and everything that happens to one. This self-centeredness and sense of (or craving for) self-importance, as childish as it may be, can hardly be overestimated as motivating features in the thinking of many. And they too both feed into and are fed by ways of thinking that reify in order to personalize the divine.

Giving up such ways of thinking is by no means tantamount to giving up caring about and highly valuing human personality and particular human persons; and it likewise does not put an end to the idea that there is anything that matters about them in the larger scheme of things – or at any rate, in larger schemes of things than our own thoughts and feelings. But it does mean that post-transcendence religion, no less than post-metaphysical philosophy, is faced with the task of revisiting these issues in a radically altered context, and with the challenge of seeking some new way of helping real human beings to come to some sort of livable terms with them.

It is far from obvious, for example, that PT-religion would necessarily be restricted to passive acquiescence in whatever may befall one. Indeed, it is arguable that, by leaving nothing to the intervention of a supremely benevolent, wise and powerful deity, a PT-religion might actually be more effective than its transcendently-oriented rivals in working out ways of dealing with the slings and arrows of outrageous fortune enabling people to make the best of difficult situations. More generally, there is no reason why it should only be transcendence-oriented religions that are able meaningfully to address the fundamental question of our relation to the powers that affect us and those we love, however heedful or heedless of us these powers may happen to be.

The basic issue here is a large and important one; and it is not the monopoly of any particular religion or type of religion – or even of religion at all, even though religions have long sought to perform a mediating function here. The issue is that of the relation of human beings to the forces at work in the world around them and in the beginnings and endings of their lives. How we understand this relation makes a great deal of difference. Religions have specialized in providing ways of interpreting it, enabling people to make sense of it and to carry on with their lives through thick and thin. Ideas of transcendence have had a great and understandable appeal in this connection. But they are not essential to the very possibility of 'rendering life possible and worth living' (as Nietzsche put it in his discussion of the Greeks and their arts in *The Birth of Tragedy*).[6] Or at any rate, I would say (with Nietzsche) that they had better not be; for otherwise disillusionment with respect to them will have dreadful consequences, and the only escape from the nihilistic rebound Nietzsche expected to follow upon the death of God will be through recourse once again to dreams of transcendence.

Religions are (among other things) in the consciousness-transforming business, providing human beings with ways of transforming their consciousness of themselves and their lives and world in such a way that they are able to endure and even affirm what befalls them, particularly when it is hard to bear. The trick here is to develop a mentality enabling one to rise above ordinary ways of thinking about such things. One strategy for doing this is to devise an interpretation altering the significance of the events in question, rendering them more endurable or even desirable. Another is to cultivate a sensibility in which the aspect of the situation is transformed experientially, as was exemplified for Nietzsche by the alchemy of Greek tragedy. And another is to achieve a kind of identification and identity transcending (or at any rate departing from) the way of thinking in which the troubling events matter (or matter greatly), and sustaining one in the face of these events and their acknowledged prima facie distressing import.

I see no reason why these strategies cannot be pursued successfully without recourse to transcendence. Indeed, they have long been pursued, under such diverse banners as art, literature, science and philosophy, in ways giving only lip service at most to such recourse, or at any rate experimenting with strategies that do not depend for their efficacy upon it. I would take Shakespeare and Goethe, Mahler and Stravinsky, van Gogh and Picasso, Darwin and Einstein, and Spinoza and Hegel (not to mention Nietzsche) all to be cases in point. These very examples, and the many others like them that could also be cited, prompt many questions relating to the nature and demarcation of religion in relation to other domains of human life and experience. I believe that the blurring of these distinctions is inevitable, and indeed that the demise of traditional forms of religious organization and activity will require the recognition that the venues of PT-religion are sure to shift from separate times and places to those in which the activities manifesting them are carried on – including those associated with these hitherto distinct domains.

A further step in the direction of a rethinking of religion from a PT-standpoint, I would suggest, involves taking seriously a point of Nietzsche's that long gave me no little difficulty: namely, that the important thing about a religion – Christianity, for example – is not the belief-system associated with it, but rather the value-scheme it reflects and promotes, and the impact of this value-scheme upon the character and quality of human life. Like so many of my fellow philosophers, I long found it difficult to pass over the former consideration in favor of the latter. I was failing to appreciate the merit of Nietzsche's idea that the value-schemes religions reflect and promote are the motivators of the belief-systems they may involve and engender; and that these value-schemes deserve to be taken more seriously than the associated belief-systems as such. Indeed, I take the drift of his point to be something like this: it is a mistake to construe religions as sets of propositions about the way things are that are either true or false; and it is a further mistake to suppose that they are significant precisely *if* they are true rather than false, and *insofar* as they may be supposed to be true rather than false. The mistake in question is rather like the mistake that would be involved if one were to take works of art as putative representations of the way things are that are either accurate or inaccurate, and that stand or fall with their representational accuracy or inaccuracy.

Neither for Nietzsche nor for me, however, is the upshot of this move to reduce religion to a merely sociological or psychological phenomenon, let alone to mere fairy tales, or primitive and deluded substitutes for science or morality. From the PT standpoint, what religion is most importantly and profoundly about – and this includes traditional religions like Christianity as well as possible religions of the future – is *value and values*. Religions, I am suggesting, are fundamentally a matter of the expression, affirmation, elaboration and promotion of certain sets of values, and more concretely of the worthiness of certain forms of life, experience and activity. This point becomes all the more interesting, in my view, if one holds (as I do along with Nietzsche) that these and all other such specific values are no more ingrained or prefigured in reality, independently of anything creatures like ourselves may experience or do, than sculpture is already there in stone – *but also no less*. Religions matter, and have mattered and will continue to matter greatly, not because they involve revelations of Truth (with a capital T), but rather because of the way in which they figure in the *generation* of value and values. They midwife the birth and parent the development and nurture the life of values that they also help to create – thereby transforming human life, and helping to endow and infuse it with values and value it would not otherwise have – somewhat in the manner that art does. They thus are in the same business as art and literature – as are also, in different but related ways having equally little to do with pure and simple truth, history and politics, and even (in certain important respects) philosophy and science.

Religions thus (as I now understand them) do not stand or fall with the truth of the moralities, ontologies, theologies, mythologies, psychologies or any other such accoutrements with which they may come to be associated, and to which they give rise and sustenance. To ask whether they are true or false is to make a kind of category mistake, akin to that which one would be making if one asked the same sort of question with respect to operas or symphonies. And once they cease to be seen as being in the truth business at all (their own self-consciousness notwithstanding), these various kinds of associated apparatus assume the significance of some of the ways in which they may express themselves and carry on their work of value-creation and value-promotion – and also of revaluation of and competition with other value-schemes. In short: they are value-schemes with bells on.

In this perspective, one of the unfortunate things the apostles of transcendence and other overzealous partisans of particular religions have done is to turn non-cognitive *expressions* serving to promote certain values into literalistically conceived *presuppositions and conditions* of the reality or acceptability of these values – and indeed of any values worth living and dying for. That misguided cognitivism – an analog to which may be found in the history and philosophy of art – is at the root of the linkage Nietzsche discerned between the paradigmatic religion of transcendence (Christianity) and nihilism, which is the inevitable outcome of becoming wedded to the idea that the only real value is a transcendently grounded value. And, on the other hand, Nietzsche's attempt to break us of this habit and to reorient our thinking about value, beyond both transcendence and nihilism, is also an attempt to revamp our sense of what religion is and might be, by way of de-deifying the idea of the divine.

Here again, the case of Nietzsche is highly instructive; and I ought to have learned from it better and much earlier than I did. His basic concern, from first to last, was with the possibility of an affirmation of life, in a Godless world that is far from being attuned either to our wishes or to our happiness. The early Nietzsche – still under the influence of a way of thinking that would grant the accolade of reality only to things in themselves, that of truth only to the correspondence of thought to them, and that of value only to truth so conceived and grounded – thought that the possibility of such an affirmation required *illusion*. But he came to see a series of mistakes here, resulting from buying into an interpretation that is itself among what he called the 'shadows of God'. And he further (on my reading) came to envision the possibility of dispensing with all such illusions, along with overcoming these mistakes with respect to the ideas of reality, truth and value, and of attaining to a height of life-affirmation capable of justifying and redeeming all. His emblem of this attainment was his conception of the possibility of embracing the idea of the eternal recurrence; and his figure of the *Übermensch* symbolized his notion of the sort of enhancement of life that would at once make possible and express itself in this embrace. And it was in this context that he sought to reintroduce the idea of the divinity of life and the world, purged of the shadows of God and released from the requirement of transcendence.

The key to the affirmation of life, for Nietzsche, both in *The Birth of Tragedy* and subsequently, is learning to experience it as valuable – not owing to its satisfaction of some independently specifiable value standard, but on its own terms, for what it is or is capable of becoming. The development of this sensibility is the great trick – or, more gracefully put, the great magic – of the various forms of art as he discusses them in that work, Apollonian, Dionysian, and tragic. And that, I believe Nietzsche also understood, is what religion likewise can be and properly is most fundamentally and importantly about. This is an *acquired* sensibility; and without it nothing can be experienced as being endowed with aesthetic, moral or any other such values. It is only for the properly cultivated and attuned consciousness that things not only exist but *matter*, and bear the aspects that we may cherish. To come to experience them in this way – as valuable, estimable, admirable – enables one to affirm them, and indeed to celebrate them; and such celebration in turn reinforces and promotes the experience of them as valuable. This is the germ and vital core of religiousness without transcendence, both pre- and post-Christian, at least as Nietzsche would have it.

Whether or not illusion is taken to be involved, Nietzsche further observes that a crucial piece of the puzzle of how this can happen has to do with the phenomenon of *identification*. As long as one experiences what is going on in life and the world as alien to one's own identity and existence, affirmation and celebration will be difficult if not impossible. A central task of both art and religion, therefore (and, for Spinoza and Hegel, of philosophy as well), is to mediate one's consciousness and self-consciousness in such a way that one is able to *identify* – in a sustaining, satisfying or even exhilarating manner – with the forces at work in life and the world, or with something about life and the world that is taken to trump those features of them that one finds distressing. A part of the trick has to do with learning to understand and experience both them and oneself under some persuasive description that facilitates this identification. It may or may not also involve the promotion of a sense of *participation*, either in the effecting of what is going on in the world or in a human community of others with whom one is in it together. This has long been an important part of religions as we have known them; but it remains to be seen whether de-institutionalized forms of PT-religiousness will be capable of generating and sustaining such relations.

Another important point noted by Nietzsche in this connection, which has given rise to a good deal of confusion, has to do with what he calls 'value creation'. The basic and general affirmation and celebration of what Nietzsche calls 'life', with which his PT-revisioning of the divine is intimately connected, not only are taken to require a 're-valuation of all values' as they traditionally and commonly are assigned, but also are held to open the way to what might be called a wealth of spin-off valorization. Once one gets the hang of experiencing things as valuable in a general sort of way, many particular things or kinds of things may be seen with new and more appreciative eyes, enriching and extending the domain of the significant. And to have one's world enriched in this way is to be strongly reinforced in one's basic affirmation, and to be given further cause for celebration. In this way such spin-off valorizations can fund back into the larger affirmation that makes them possible and prompts them, inspiring and engendering further 'new values'. This circle or (better) spiral of valuation is anything but a vicious one, and indeed is in my opinion (as in Nietzsche's) our last and best hope as we look to a future without transcendence. And if religion as well as humanity is to have a future, I do not see what else that future might better be.

Let us now take a closer look at the alternatives that remain open in such a future – or at least at some of them. (I shall pass over the possibility, for example, of a PT-religiousness such as I take Confucianism to exemplify, focusing chiefly on the affirmation and celebration and elaboration of certain sorts of moral qualities – not because I reject this possibility, or take a negative view of it, but rather because I am more interested in what I consider to be the most robust forms of PT-religiousness that are humanly possible.) So – if the idea of any sort of transcendence is set aside, and attention is focused upon this life and this world as the only reality of which it is meaningful to speak (and if we dismiss or ignore the possibility of pantheism, which I simply cannot take seriously), what are we left with to work with as the focus or locus of a religion of the future? It had better be something about life and/or about the world of a rather general nature, rather than some particular existing creature or thing or kind of entity; for the deification of any such thing or things, while no longer objectionable in the way that idolatry was taken to be in rivalry with belief in the One True (and transcendent) God, is still grievously misguided. That way, as Tillich used to say, lies the demonic. Indeed, one profoundly important reason to attempt to open up and realize the possibility of PT-religiousness is to provide an alternative not only to nihilism but also to what might be called the 'demonic turn' for those for whom the death of God leaves a void that demands to be filled in one way or another. The problem is to come up with suitable candidates for ultimacy among one's possible concerns – candidates lending themselves to unconditional affirmation, identification and celebration that are capable of sustaining such an embrace and generating further reinforcing attendant values without corruption and destruction ensuing on the part either of their subjects or of their object. What is true of power is also true of deification, where anything finite that comes within the compass of human consciousness is concerned: deification tends to corrupt its influence, and to do so in proportion to the unconditionality of the embrace.

There is yet another danger that is also to be avoided if possible, to which Kierkegaard was acutely sensitive. That is what might be called the trivialization (rather than the demonization) of the place holders of the divine in one's experience. For Kierkegaard as for Nietzsche, despite their profound differences, there were to be no shoddy substitutes for the divine in our experience. Religion properly conceived, as the deification of the appropriately deifiable, was to be distinguished from other modes of valuation precisely by virtue of its commitment to a kind of meaning that does not depend entirely upon one's own individual subjective willfulness, choices and decisions, and also does not make either sensuously or socially conditioned and determined values the central determinants of one's existence. Genuine religiousness for them instead is taken to involve the experience that what matters most is nothing of either sort, and transcends everything of either sort. Kierkegaard, of course, did not stop there, and took it to transcend this life and world altogether; while Nietzsche, like Spinoza and Hegel, looked to something *about* them instead. For all of them, however, there is no sadder and more pathetic spectacle than that of someone trying to find the meaning of life in the sorts of things around which all too many people's all-too-human desires, inclinations and choices revolve. To be religious is to look beyond them, and beyond what

depends upon oneself alone, if it means anything at all. And it does
– for Nietzsche no less than for Kierkegaard.

Religion happens when something is experienced as divine.
Religious pathologies – or at least some of them – occur when this
experience is misplaced, and takes as its object something incapable
of sustaining so high a valuation. Turning the matter around, value
schemes and valuations assume religious dimensions only if they
are elevated and intensified to what might be thought of as 'trump'
status in relation to other values and considerations. That is what
Tillich had in mind in speaking of 'ultimate concern' in this connection. But this can happen, I would suggest, only if some fundamental part of the human spirit is tapped in a way that prompts a
powerful response, strong enough to override ordinary and all-too-
human dispositions, inclinations and motivations, and rich enough
to serve as an organizing and sustaining force in a person's life
even in the face of otherwise daunting and even devastating trials
and tribulations. (This, I might observe in passing, is the phenomenon or human possibility I take Nietzsche to have been trying to
get at in a post-transcendent way in the Third Part of *Thus Spake
Zarathustra*, culminating in the 'Midnight Song' that is the religious
high point of the entire work.) It takes a very special mode of valuation to be capable of these effects. It must be neither merely intellectual nor merely emotional, but rather must involve both
dimensions of our spirituality. And it will not endure if it does not
reach into and satisfy our need to feel that we are fundamentally
attuned to what really matters, or matters most, not only in our
own little selves and lives but in life and the world more generally.

But what might this be, if it can be nothing on the order of the God
whom I am supposing no longer to be a live option? What might one
fix upon that admits of being experienced as divine in a healthy and
life-enhancing rather than pathological, debilitating and destructive
way? The two most obvious general alternatives would appear to be
either something *elemental* about life and the world or something *developmental* about them. Borrowing Nietzsche's labels in *The Birth of
Tragedy*, one may accordingly distinguish the possibility of *Dionysian*
and *Apollonian* modes of PT-religiousness here. The former may be
thought of as centering upon the affirmation and celebration of the
basic forces at work in our lives and in all life and nature; while the
latter may be conceived as focusing more upon that which they have
it in them to become, and upon the realization of that potentiality.

These of course are Nietzsche's two basic types of art as well –
but not of art alone. On the contrary: he explicitly takes them to

have a more fundamental and extensive application than this; and their extension to religion is a very natural one. The fact that he goes on to distinguish a third type of art, culture and way of experiencing life – the *tragic* – thereby raises the further question of a similarly corresponding mode of tragic PT-religiousness. And indeed I wish to suggest that that is precisely what Nietzsche in the end held out to us, as the most attractive and powerful and ultimately affirmative and life-enhancing of them all. One may deify not only the elemental and the developmental, but also their transfiguration in the manner pioneered by art, the contingency and ephemerality of all such transfigured existence notwithstanding. And tragic art prefigures what may indeed be the highest and most admirable of human possibilities in the context of a radically de-deified reinterpretation of life and the world, the celebration of which is what we most need to become capable of, in ample enough measure to sustain us in the absence of transcendence. Hence Nietzsche's call for a new Dionysian religiousness, and my invitation to contemplate the idea of a kind of born-again paganism.

The three figures I have invoked repeatedly throughout this paper – Spinoza, Hegel and Nietzsche – represent for me the three modes of PT-religiousness I take to be not only real human possibilities but powerfully attractive and appealing ones in the aftermath of the death of God. One may look either to nature, to history, or to art as the locus of that about life and the world that bears the aspect of divinity. So, with Spinoza, one may experience nature as divine, and regard the divinity of nature as the flip side of what might be called the naturalness of the only divinity there is. So also, with Hegel, one may come to have a like experience of history, assimilating nature to it in an anticipatory and preparatory capacity. And so further, with Nietzsche, one may divinize art and all that is akin to it, seeing both history and nature as proto-artistic in character. All three interpretations of life and the world and of what matters about them are also fundamental modes of valuation; and each affords the possibility of a kind of identification that can at least compete for our spiritual allegiance, affirmation and celebration. Together they mark out what I take to be the main points on the compass of PT-religiousness, by means of which I suspect humanity is eventually going to have to find its way. There may of course be others I have overlooked: the gospel of love, for example. If so, that will be fine with me. We need all the divinity we can get.

It may be objected that none of them even pretends to do for us what Christianity and other such religions purport to do, by way of the devices of transcendence. That is true enough; but if we must learn to do without any and all such attractions and consolations, we ought not to complain that they are lacking here. One may well wonder whether it is even conceivable that anything like the institutions, ceremonies, communities, practices and other forms of religious observance associated with many traditional religions could be established in these cases. The seeming ludicrousness of the idea makes it seem doubtful, and indeed prompts the question of whether these, too, might be things it would be wrong-headed to expect or even desire. But if so, and if this line of reflection is extended, the upshot would appear to be that the religion of the future will look much more like the arts, sciences, philosophy and literature of the present – at their best, to be sure – than it will look like religions of the past. Some may find this strange, and hard to accept. For my part, however, I would take it to be a good and welcome thing.

NOTES

1. F. Nietzsche, *The Gay Science*, trans. W. Kaufmann (New York: Vintage Books, 1974), § 108.
2. Ibid., § 343.
3. Nietzsche, *The Will to Power* (New York: Random House, 1967), § 252; *KGW* VIII 11:55; my translation.
4. Nietzsche, *On the Genealogy of Morals*, trans. W. Kaufmann and R. J. Hollingdale (New York: Vintage Books, 1969), II: 24.
5. *Gay Science*, § 109.
6. Trans. W. Kaufmann (New York: Vintage Books, 1967).

7
After Transcendence – A Reply

Michael Weston

Religion, according to Professor Schacht, has traditionally provided us with an interpretation of our lives which fitted them into a wider perspective through which we can see them as valuable and which enables us to endure and even affirm whatever happens to us. Traditional religion has done this by reference to a 'transcendent reality beyond this life and this world' through which our lives and world have been given sense (p. 76). But we can no longer believe in such a reality, and with such loss of belief we are threatened with a loss of meaning in our lives. Hence the importance of developing a post-transcendent form of religion which would carry out the religious function without the transcendent reference. Such a religious interpretation would require our identifying ourselves with something about life and the world which will 'trump those features of them that one finds distressing' (p. 87). Three possibilities are proposed. We might identify ourselves with: (a) the basic forces at work in our lives and nature generally; (b) the developmental forces at work in our lives as historical; (c) the fundamental underlying character of both nature and history as a 'proto-art'. These interpretations he identifies with Spinoza, Hegel, and Nietzsche respectively. But each interpretation nevertheless 'affords the possibility of a kind of identification that can at least compete for our spiritual allegiance, affirmation and celebration' (p. 91). I must thank Richard for his stimulating paper. The stimulation is clearly to an engagement with this 'competition' for our spiritual allegiance. Such a competition is presumably to take place under the protocols of philosophical argumentation: a dispassionate appraisal of reasons for and against, whether this is in relation to his diagnosis of the situation, or to his claim as to the unbelievability of transcendent religion, or to the interpretations of a post-transcendent religion which he offers. Indeed, the three authors of these interpretations would agree with this characterization of the nature of our engagement with these issues. In each case, they did not imagine they were putting forward a merely 'persuasive description' (p. 87) but that they were revealing, in some fundamental sense, the truth about reality (even if this was that 'reality' is an 'interpretation') and that certain values and ways of life were required by that truth. In this way, their projects were close to that attributed by Schacht to transcendent religion. He criticizes transcendent religion for turning expressions promoting certain values into 'literalistically conceived *presuppositions and conditions* of the reality or acceptability of these values – and indeed of any values worth living and dying for' (p. 86), calling this a 'misguided cognitivism'. Yet the same role is played, it might be argued, by Nature, Spirit and the Will to Power in his favoured authors: these are the nature of reality and because of this certain values and the lives lived in accordance with them are *non-illusory* or true. The difference lies not in a contrast between cognitivism and non-cognitivism, but in the cognitive attacks on the notion of transcendent reality and of its necessity for making sense of our world and our lives. The new interpretations have their force through that of philosophical argumentation, and indeed through the development of new conceptions of what this consists in. The revelation of *several* interpretations which could fulfil the religious function in a non-transcendent manner obviously poses us the problem of determining how this competition is to be settled. Our engagement with this problem is to be in line with whatever our conception of philosophical argumentation may be; and indeed it is difficult to see how this could be otherwise if one's objection to 'transcendent religion' lies in the demonstration of the unbelievability of the Christian God. But then one's spiritual allegiance to one of the interpretations is going to rest on philosophical argumentation.

This seems obvious enough with relation to Spinoza and Hegel. But it is equally true of Nietzsche whose complaint about previous philosophers is that they did not question *enough*. They sought, he said, the rational ground of morality but 'morality itself, however, was taken as given'.[1] Morality here refers to values which have the character of commandments or obligations and so require a reference to an authority over and beyond the *individual* concerned.

Such an authority is found not merely in the reference to the Christian God but equally to Nature or Spirit too. Indeed, Nietzsche sees the development of the secularization of Western thought, of which Spinoza and Hegel are a part, as fundamentally a continuation of the movement which produced the appeal to God. This is why the proclamation of 'the death of God' could be nihilistic and not simply the affirmation of secularist values. What secularist and traditional religious views share is, thinks Nietzsche, a belief in there being 'the truth' about human life from which values can be derived. They are part of the history of the dominance of the value of truth. When truth becomes the supreme value, life is directed towards a 'fulfilment of some highest ethical canon'[2] justified by an appeal to the truth about human life. And that this is the truth will itself need justification in terms of some final metaphysical revelation of the nature of reality. Knowledge of this, Nietzsche says in a brief summary of the career of the will to truth,[3] is, in ancient philosophy, assumed to be available to the human intellect. But where truth is the supreme value, assumptions are to be questioned, so that it comes to seem that this assumption requires for its justification the further one that the world has been made to fit the human intellect. We need then to postulate God as creator whose plan may be apprehended, at least in part, here below by our thought. It is this God whose existence is in turn questioned by modern thought. The real world and God retreat to the status of ideas of reason with Kant, binding us as objects of faith and not knowledge. But positivism, consistently with the value of truth, shows that unknown they cannot bind us. Nietzsche now steps forward and proposes, again in terms of the value of truth itself, that these ideas should be abolished since they are manifestly of no use. 'Plato blushes for shame; all free spirits run riot'.[4] To question in a fundamental manner is precisely to question the assumption of the primacy of the value of truth, which marks the turning of 'truthfulness' against morality.[5] This questioning involves seeing that the 'value of life cannot be estimated. Not by a living man, because he is party to the dispute, indeed its object, and not the judge of it.'[6] All valuations of life are by life on life itself. None can claim to occupy a position from which its valuation could assert a primacy which was anything other than its own self-assertion. But some valuations, indeed the dominant ones in Western culture since Socrates, have claimed this *and* the very nature of their values demanded it. If we see that all valuations are perspectives on life by life itself, then these perspectives are precisely those which cannot accept this and whose values are those of a life which needs to believe in there being 'the truth' and in their own access to it. From the position of Nietzsche's more fundamental questioning, the new question thus arises: what form of human life sees life in this way? And the answer is that this is the perspective 'of declining, debilitated, weary, condemned life'.[7] A life which finds itself problematic and so seeks for something outside itself, obedience to which can give it some significance: 'whoever is incapable of laying his will into things, lacking will and strength, at least lays some *meaning* into them, that is, the faith that there is a will in them already'.[8] This revelation of the character of the servile life and its values opens one's eyes to 'the opposite ideal of the most exuberant, most living and most world affirming man'.[9] Such a form of life appears as a possibility through the overcoming of the value of truth through which has been formed the notion of the individual who understands his value as an example of an abstract humanity. It appears, that is, in this particular historical juncture, manifesting itself to individuals in the proclamation of the absence of any standards to which they are subject. 'My idea: goals are lacking and these must be individuals!'[10] Individual life which is its own 'law': 'We ... want to *become those we are* – human beings who are new, unique, incomparable, who give themselves laws, who create themselves'.[11] It is here that the notion of 'art' becomes relevant: the individual's life becomes a process of creation, 'conscious distinction, self-shaping'[12] through which one imposes form on oneself only to overcome it when it threatens to subvert one's freedom from *all* imposed form (including that imposed by habit). But this perspective on life is one demanded by intellectual honesty. Intellectual examination has revealed that *all* perspectives on life are 'creative', are forms of art, are not revelations of a hidden truth. Perspectives which need to believe they embody the truth are thus dishonest and are illusions, even if people need on the whole to believe in them. The only honest life is self-creative, accepting and affirming the very absence of any truth to which the individual is subservient. And in that case Spinoza and Hegel are peddling further illusions.

But can we stop here to determine where our spiritual allegiance should lie? Unfortunately not. Thought, as we know, moves on. This is hardly the place for a resumé of post-Nietzschean thought, even were I capable of it. But one direction of such thought ought to be indicated. It might seem that Nietzsche's conception of a post-transcendent life is not radical enough. For it might appear that his thought merely inverts the previous order and so is still dependent on the idea of the transcendent. The ideal of the individual who is his own law, it might be said, is just the opposite of that of the individual subject to a law outside himself. As opposite, it depends for its sense on the other term of the opposition and so on the notion of transcendence. But this notion was to be abolished. Nietzsche sometimes recognizes this, remarking that if you get rid of the idea of the real world you equally dispense with appearance.[13] But this merely shows how difficult, and controversial, it may be to articulate a post-transcendent form of life which does not, secretly, depend for its sense on the notion of transcendence which is at the same time held to be discredited. Both the later Heidegger and Derrida may be regarded as addressing this issue. Heidegger thus requires us to engage in a rethinking of the tradition of Western thought, grounded as it is in metaphysics, in returning to the original questionability to which early Greek thinking, not metaphysical, was a response. We can perhaps in this way set about formulating a non-metaphysical conceptuality of human existence and the world which would indeed be free of dependence on the notion of transcendence. For Derrida, however, this very strategy of Heidegger smacks too much of the metaphysical desire for finality and truth. What is needed, rather, is to 'reveal' (what cannot be revealed, made present) the 'condition' of the possibility of metaphysics (or Heidegger's strategy). Metaphysics in its history is a series of grounded structures which emerge in a sequence as the previous ground is re-situated as something itself grounded. What makes this constant re-interpretation, and so the historicality, of metaphysics (which is, of course, denied by metaphysics itself) possible is the differential nature of language which means that any term can come to mean differently when placed in a different context. Determinateness of meaning is only an effect of stopping the play of meaning. The unbelievability of transcendence occurs where this becomes apparent, with the advent of language into the 'universal problematic'. There can be no 'transcendental signifieds' which lie beyond the play of language and yet which ground significance: God, concept, subject, Spirit, Nature, and so forth. What is required is the deconstruction of the metaphysical oppositions these terms legitimize, as when the signified is thought as just another signifier thus making both terms impossible, since the notion of 'signifier' requires that of 'signified'. Hence the introduction of the term 'trace', which is not a trace *of* something. The terms associated with 'immanence' here are rendered as untenable as the transcendental ones they depend on for their meaning. Such deconstruction is intended to open up our conceptuality to the uncontrollability of the generation of meaning. Well, I admit, all this is difficult enough, and certainly open to dispute. But do I hear someone mention Bataille, Deleuze . . . ? And so it goes on.

So what is to be done in pursuit of our spiritual allegiance? Isn't there just a suspicion that something has gone wrong here, that we are even perhaps prevaricating? Johannes Climacus would have thought so. 'Let a doubting youth, but an existing doubter ... venture to find in Hegelian positivity the truth, the truth for existence – he will write a dreadful epigram on Hegel ... for an existing person pure thinking is a chimera when the truth is supposed to be the truth in which to exist.'[14] Philosophy treats the issue of the significance of life as a cognitive issue, and so requires, as such cognitive inquiries do, a relation of disinterest on the part of the inquirer. Disinterest involves subordination to the subject matter at issue in pursuit of the truth, and this subordination requires a particular relation of the inquirer to their results. As Climacus remarks of Hegel: 'Although the world-historical is something past, as material for cognitive observation it is incomplete; it continually comes into existence through ever-new observation and research.'[15] Treated as a cognitive issue, one's determination of the nature of the problem regarding the significance of life, the possible responses to it, the reasons pro and con, all these are always open to revision. In genuine cognitive studies, the results are held hypothetically in terms of the nature of the inquiry itself. But now, the philosopher proposes to treat life itself as the object of such a project of thought. Climacus thought this the stuff of comedy. Modern philosophy 'has not a false presupposition but a comic presupposition, occasioned by its having forgotten in a kind of world-historical absentmindedness what it means to be a human being, not what it means to be a human being in general, for even speculators might be swayed to consider that sort of thing, but what it means that we, you and I and he, are human beings, each one on his own.'[16] Philosophy claims the priority of the general over the individual: only if one knows the nature of the human being in general (or the nature of our historical situation, etc.) can the individual determine her or his spiritual allegiance and so resolve the doubt of their existence which, unsatisfied, must result in nihilism, a loss of meaning in life. But if 'the nature of the human' or of 'our historical situation' is an object of cognitive inquiry whose results are always subject to revision and so can only be held hypothetically, *and* the individual can only determine the meaning of their life by reference to such results, then the individual must lead their life ... well, hypothetically? What could this mean? Such a relation to life in general is impossible: 'As an existing person, he can least of all hold absolutely fast the annulment of ... existence.'[17] The philosopher, when not philosophizing, exhibits continually a conviction of the value of his existence which, however, should, in terms of his project, be suspended. And more, when he is philosophizing, he exhibits a commitment to speculation which in terms of the problem he claims to be facing should itself be suspended. For that question was directed to life itself, and isn't doing philosophy part of his life? As soon as we try to think of there being a general problem here, that of 'the meaning of life', which we must resolve prior to the determination of the significance of our own individual life, the matter becomes, Climacus thought, comical. And this marks, he diagnosed, a misalignment between the nature of the 'problem' and the supposed forms of resolution. If the philosopher has the general problem he claims, then he clearly must have a problem with his own life, and one which embraces that life in its totality since the issue is the 'significance of life'. But such a problem would not only then include his own intellectual pursuits and so his involvement in philosophy, but would have the character, not of disinterest, but of total despair. For how else is an individual to raise the problem of the meaning of her own life?

What we have to recognize here, Climacus claims, is that there can be no general issue of the significance of life which must be resolved in order to give the guidelines for the individual's life. To raise the question of life's significance is always something done by an individual, and for an individual the raising of that issue cannot be a matter of disinterested inquiry since it must involve *herself*: it is raised in despair. And this shows us the nature of the problem. When we speak of the 'meaning' or 'significance' of life, this is not something to be known or understood, but refers rather to what we speak of when we ask what a relationship, activity, and so forth, *means* to someone, where we are asking, for example, how committed they are to it, the nature of their involvement. And in that sense we can ask what doing philosophy means to someone, a question that is not to be resolved by philosophy: 'Even if a man his whole life through occupies himself exclusively with logic, he still does not become logic; he himself therefore exists in other categories'.[18] Let us say that these are the categories in terms of which I can have 'problems' with my own life, can find my life 'meaningful', can come to certain 'resolutions' of the problems I experience here. None of these notions can be understood in terms of the disinterest and impersonality necessary for 'cognitive inquiry', which doesn't mean that there isn't an appropriate sense of 'reflection' and 'thought' which can take place here, nor indeed that there cannot be a 'reflection' about such notions themselves (although a problem with this, and so with what I am doing now, will appear shortly). All philosophical reflection is the reflection of individuals, and so there is something prior to the philosophy done by them, namely, their own involvement with it. Here lie the 'categories' in terms of which the individual lives their life and where the notion of the 'significance of life' belongs. It is this which philosophy forgets: 'The passionate question of truth does not even come up, because philosophy has first tricked the individuals into becoming object-ive.'[19] Philosophy is involved in what Wittgenstein would have called a 'grammatical confusion'. It tacitly assumes the problem is firstly a cognitive one of determining the nature of a generality, the nature of human life, of our historical situation, and so on. What Kierkegaard *through* Climacus (I shall return to the significance of this in a moment) tries to remind us is that the 'problem' in this context is one an individual has with *her own life*, and thus has the character of despair and not intellectual puzzlement, whose 'resolu-tion' lies, not in an 'answer' in the cognitive sense, but in a redirec-tion or intensification of passion. The 'spheres of existence' which Climacus identifies, the aesthetic, ethical, and religious, represent, one might say, different degrees of passion with which the indi-vidual may live their life and which determine the forms of passion with which they relate to the various contents their life may have and the sorts of 'problem' they can experience in their lives. The 'dialectic' of these stages is due to their inadequacy to the issue for the individual of the meaning of their life in its totality, that is, as responses to the possibility of total despair. The revelation of such inadequacy and the move between spheres remain matters of passion, of despair and redirection and intensification of passion, and involve the relevant form of personal reflection, about the causes of one's despair and about what one can do about it. This means that the issue of the 'truth' of life for the individual is what could 'resolve' the problem of total despair. And it is here that Climacus provides us with a 'subjective' sense of the transcendent, that is, one formulated in terms of the problem an individual can have with their own life. For the 'resolution', as removal, of total despair is not something which the individual can do of themselves, whereas the other forms of despair which the aesthetic and the ethical may involve admit of an exercise of human capacity for their removal.

Can we describe the process towards recognition of this possibility? Climacus (but not of course Kierkegaard) gives some such account as the following. Aesthetically, an individual regards the meaning of her life as determined by what happens to her: the categories of the aesthetic life are fortune, misfortune, fate. Such an aesthetic 'how' of life conceals an implicit assertion of the 'I', for although I already find myself disposed towards counting certain kinds of result as fortunate or unfortunate, in order for me to act I have to go along with this disposition, a passivity which may be broken if the results desired are not forthcoming. Despair aesthetically comes from what is outside. Such a break, having the character of a certain degree of despair, may, of course, simply result in a realigning of myself with other objectives. But more radically it provides the possibility for a despair over aesthetic life itself, since what is revealed in the possibility of changing my attachment to other objectives from those which now appear impossible is that it was my adhesion to the latter which gave them their significance for me and not, as it appears aesthetically, that they gave significance to my life. They had the significance they had for me because I had implicitly chosen them. Hence such despair over aesthetic life as a response to the individual's problem of the meaning of their life may be removed by, as Judge William puts it, 'choosing choice itself'. Here the meaning of my life seems to lie in my imposing choice upon it without reference to results, through the imposition of commitment. But this project itself cannot be carried out and so contains its own possibility of despair. The issue of which commitments have priority and the application of what is essentially general to the particularities of life both introduce an element of the arbitrary which can only be resolved by an appeal outside commitment and so to the 'myself' upon which commitment is imposed. The project, to impose commitment on myself, cannot be carried out, although here what precipitates despair comes from within. To despair both over what happens to me and over what I can do or will is to despair over the possibility of my being the source of the significance of my life and presents me with a despair I cannot remove of myself. Hence initially the recognition of this requires a negative movement against my proclivity to regard myself as the source of the value of my life, that proclivity which has progressively become explicit through the dialectic. But were I no longer to live in such a negative movement, which Climacus calls 'infinite resignation', but absolutely without reference, positive or negative, to myself as such a source, then this could occur only as a 'gift', by 'grace', of selflessness or love. As Simone Weil says: 'It is a question of being delivered from self, and this I cannot do by means of my own energy.'[20] Total despair is the limit of attachment to myself: as despair it still indicates a sense that I matter, that I am in some way the source of my own significance. To remove it totally would be to lose that sense, which I of course cannot do of myself. It is either given or not.

The transcendence which philosophy has found unbelievable is its own product, a move in its objectification of the issue of the meaning of life, its construction of it as a general intellectual problem. Thinking that in order to know how to live we should first have to establish the truth of the nature of the human being, it may seem that we must therefore establish that there *is the truth about ourselves and the world* and that we have access to it. Such a guarantee can only be provided by something beyond ourselves and our experience of the world to which we nevertheless in some sense can relate: the *logos* of the world which we can apprehend with the 'divine spark' in man, *nous*; Spirit which comes to know itself through us in the dialectic of history; and so on. But these transcendent entities (at least as far as the individual philosopher is concerned) are brought into play in relation to an 'objective' problem: the 'truth' of life has already to be construed as an object of intellect in order for the move to a transcendent object to appear necessary. When it appears in modern philosophy that we have no reason to believe in the existence of such a 'truth' or in our access to it, then the 'transcendent' is seen to be an illusion. But that, as far as philosophy is concerned, simply leaves us with a further intellectual problem: without transcendence, how is life to be given meaning? Which assumes, as Nietzsche, Heidegger and Derrida all do, that meaning has depended on a reference to transcendence in the sense this has in philosophy. This is why the revelation of its unbelievability is seen as threatening us with nihilism, creating the context within which discussion of alternatives can take place. Take away transcendence and you're left with what? With immanence and its values, or, if this has sense only in opposition to transcendence, then the task of liberating thought from this dependency through Heideggerian 'destruction' of metaphysics or a Derridean deconstruction. But for Johannes Climacus all of this is beside the point, a prevarication. Thinking the nature of human existence is something which is done by *you* or *me* and so must have the form of self-examination. It can only take place in the first person: only so can we really recognize that *we* are what we are examining. And in terms of this understanding of the 'problem' and possible 'resolutions' perhaps we may invoke a non-philosophical notion of transcendence, which would embrace the notions of 'grace' – and of 'God'. Perhaps. 'We': that is, you or me, singly, each one for ourselves.

Climacus says that God has no objective existence. That is, God cannot be made the topic of an objective inquiry into God's existence. The reason for this, Climacus tells himself (the importance of putting it in this way will appear later) commenting on Hegel, is that 'God does not play the role of the Lord in the world-historical process as it is seen by human beings ... one does not see God, because if he is not seen in the role of Lord, one does not see him'.[21] God cannot be 'Lord' or 'sovereign' (Lowrie's translation) if subordinated to the demands of the human intellect, since the relation to God requires the giving up of all human pretence to determine the significance of human life (and doing philosophy is, one supposes, part of that). Nietzsche declares that 'God is dead', but *this* God is the God who is the object of intellectual inquiry, the point of reference brought in to guarantee human access to the truth about the world and about ourselves. That that God is dead is no news since that God was never alive: it was always the product of human desire, whether intellectual or otherwise, and so could not give significance to human life in its totality. 'God is the God of the living':[22] that is, the God of the individual's, the person's, life in its totality (which is the only way the issue of the significance of human life in its totality can be raised by a human being). God does not exist objectively. But 'God is ... only for subjectivity in inwardness'.[23] If the individual can despair of life in its totality (which is the only way the problem of the meaning of life can occur for a human being); if then this despair (which still asserts the desire for a humanly determined significance and, in the meaning which despair gives to its denial, maintains a final claim to such significance) can be given up in the movement of 'infinite resignation' so that the attempt is made, against oneself, to live for nothing; and if then one can believe that this resignation will be transformed into positive love, then there is 'belief in God', 'God comes into existence for him'.[24] This, then, would be the 'subjective' analogue of the objective notion of 'transcendence'. But if one thinks one understands this, Climacus says, one doesn't, since what is at issue here is what could give significance to any aspect of human life, understanding included. 'In my relationship with God I must learn simply to give up my finite understanding, and with it the drawing of distinctions that is natural to me'.[25]

The question of the significance of life can only be raised in the first person by an existing human being (the 'living'). The 'truth' of this could only be the 'resolution' to the 'problem': if the problem is total despair (and the giving up of this itself), then the 'resolution' lies in the gift of 'the peace that passeth understanding'. Truth as love, as the transformation of subjectivity: this is what 'truth' would have to mean here. And, since the problem is first-person, so is the 'solution': this 'truth' can only be expressed in relation to *oneself*, but precisely by this it gets its universality. Yet, as I shall note shortly, it is just this which prevents one person saying this 'truth' to another – which suggests there is something wrong with *this* presentation. 'Only the truth that *builds up* is truth *for you*. This is an essential predicate in relation to truth as inwardness, whereby its decisive qualification as upbuilding *for you*, that is, for the subject, is its essential difference from all objective knowledge, in as much as the subjectivity itself becomes the sign of truth'.[26]

What motivates the individual in the 'existential dialectic' is despair, and the nature of this depends on whether the individual will, as Climacus puts it, venture further out, whether they really want what they claim to want, the truth. For there is a generality involved here, but one which emerges from the individual themself. The individual finds meaning in life in a particular way, but only on condition that they think it, under some description, as having more than individual significance. This may not be articulated, of course, but may be reflected in their regarding those who don't live like that as being foolish. As Socrates says, all humans desire the reality and not just the appearance of good, since the goodness, significance, of all else depends on it.[27] And it is this which provides the motivation for *communication* of the significance individuals find in their lives, its expression in such a way that others may be brought to share it. I want now briefly to consider how this may complicate the apparently 'disinterested' character of *this* communication.

For Kierkegaard doesn't write like *this*. There is no 'description' of the 'existential dialectic' such as I gave above in Kierkegaard's writings. Rather, it occurs in a pseudonymously written work, *CUP* (and in other pseudonymous works). In *CUP*, the author, Johannes Climacus, says that it is impossible to give reports or reviews of the pseudonymous writings 'because a report takes away precisely what is most important and falsely changes the work into a didactic discourse'.[28] What is taken away is the manner of the writing. In the *Journals* Kierkegaard, writing for himself, says 'if existence is the essential and truth is inwardness ... it is also good that it be said in the right way. But this right way is precisely the art that makes being such an author very difficult'.[29] Reports, reviews, commentaries: they speak in a way inconsistent with the truth as inwardness. Such forms of writing attempt a 'direct' communication where the persons involved in the communication are irrelevant to what is said and who withdraw in disinterest for a better apprehension of the object. But the pseudonymous writings are involved with a thinking that cannot be abstracted from the persons of the thinker and the possible recipient. Climacus calls this 'subjective thinking' and in relation to it 'direct communication' is impossible: the subjective thinker 'must not communicate himself directly'[30] because his thinking is involved in a 'double-reflection'.

The subjective thinker's thought is 'doubly-reflected' in being reflective, and so concerned with the nature of human life, thus claiming universality for itself, but at the same time being *personal* and therefore always having to show a recognition of this in the character of its expression: 'the subjective thinker as existing is essentially interested in his own thinking, is existing in it. Therefore, his thinking has another kind of reflection, specifically that of inwardness, of possession, whereby it belongs to the subject and no one else.'[31] The subjective thinker thinks about their *own* existence and through this thinks what applies generally. That universality is one which applies to each individual *in their own concern* with the meaning of *their own* lives. The subjective thinker indeed thinks about the nature of human existence. But whereas the philosopher claims to do this by ascending in disinterested inquiry to the universal and only after that descending to its application to the individual (and so himself), the subjective thinker thinks human existence *interestedly*, from *within* the existence he thinks about. His thinking is universal by being personal and not personal through firstly being universal, as philosophy claims it must be – a move which delays indefinitely its being personal at all.

But the thinking must *be* personal. It is in the context of personal concern with the meaningfulness of one's own life that the questions about the 'truth' of life, the significance of birth and death, immortality, God, and so forth are raised. And this means that these notions and questions contain essentially a personal reference: what is the truth of *my* life? am *I* immortal? what is the significance to *me* of *my* death?[32] These are questions and notions which anyone can appropriate, of course, but only *personally*. They cannot figure in a disinterested thinking. (E.g. 'But essentially the question of immortality is not a learned question; it is a question belonging to inwardness, which the subject by becoming subjective must ask himself.')[33] The subjective thinker thus 'thinks the universal but as existing in his thinking, acquiring it in his inwardness, becomes more and more subjectively isolated'.[34]

Thought about human existence by a human being can only be personal and thereby universal. But then the primacy of the personal (that the questions and responses always essentially contain a first-person pronoun or adjective) means that communication can only take place through the *appropriation* of these first-person expressions by another. They cannot therefore be 'directly' communicated since they cannot be formulated into the impersonal forms necessary for direct communication. Thus, for example, there is no question of 'the meaning of life' which can be raised in disinterested inquiry. There is only the question of the meaning of *my* life, which, of course, anyone can raise in relation to their own, but then only in the appropriate way and to which only certain responses are appropriate. Communication in these essentially subjective (first-person) matters cannot consist in one person telling something to another – as I have done above in the description of the existential dialectic and, indeed, here! Rather, the subjective thinker in engaging in self-examination frees herself in order to venture further out or realize she cannot bring herself to do so: frees herself for decisiveness. Just so, any communication can only have the role of precipitating such self-examination on the part of the other: 'Just as the subjective thinker has set himself free by the duplexity (i.e. of subjective thought, of what is thought and its essential personal form), so the secret of communication specifically hinges on setting the other free, and for that very reason he must not communicate himself directly'.[35]

This is why it is that Climacus appends to *CUP* a 'revocation' so that 'no-one bother to appeal to it, because one who appeals to it has eo ipso misunderstood it'.[36] What Climacus says cannot be appealed to as an authority since it is not uttered in a context where one person is in a position to tell another something. Rather, Climacus says, the book 'is about myself, simply and solely about myself'.[37] The book is a 'doubly-reflected' communication: it is Climacus engaged in self-examination and so speaking essentially in the first person. In reading the work one can, of course, take on this first person, but only if to do so consists in self-examination too.

Climacus's reflections, however, concern not only the nature of human existence but, as we have seen, the nature of reflecting about human existence. There is no abstract 'I': any individual is already existing, living and speaking in terms of some form of meaningfulness in their own lives. So what I have said above (parroting Climacus): that the question of the meaning of life is essentially subjective (first-person); that there is no disinterested position from which the question can be raised; that no individual stands here in a position of authority in relation to another; that there can only be 'indirect communication' here in which one says 'something to a passer-by in passing, without standing still oneself or delaying the other, without wanting to induce him to go the same way, but just urging him to go his own way'[38]; all this *is itself part of a view of life*. This is why Kierkegaard writes pseudonymously: 'I, by means of audible lines, have placed the life-view of the creating, poetically actual individuality in his mouth' he says in his own name in the appended 'A First and Last Explanation' to *CUP*.[39] Johannes Climacus is speaking from within his own sense of life's meaningfulness, which he says is that of a 'humorist' occupying the boundary that separates the ethical and the religious and from which the comedy of the human pretension to determine its own significance, whether in terms of what happens to them (in the aesthetic) or in terms of will (in the ethical) can be seen. What Climacus sees is not seen by the aesthete A or by Judge William in *Either/Or*. For example, from the point of view of the ethical, Judge William (appropriate name and title, of course) addresses A directly, commanding him to 'choose choice itself' and justifies this by appealing to his speaking from the universal standpoint: and so his mode of communication differs from that of Climacus. Kierkegaard, in other words (and disturbingly for us – I mean me), intends to show us that there is *no* disinterested position from which reflection about the nature of human existence can take place: and *that* is something which is seen *itself* only from within certain views of life. Hence Kierkegaard said that he had always been a religious author, for the *necessity* of writing pseudony- mously is one seen only from the religious or the religiously ques- tioned (as with Climacus's) position.

What, then, of this communication? Can I claim in the interests of a direct and impersonal presentation that this is neither a reflection about life's meaningfulness, nor one concerning the nature of such reflection, both of which would appear here to bear the subjective, personal imprint, but rather a reflection about the nature of the latter kind of reflection – that it is itself entangled in the former and so implicated in the personal? A 'trebly-reflected' communication, as it were. I suspect Kierkegaard would have regarded this as an evasion. For to engage in such a reflection means to have come to see that here 'truth is subjectivity' which implies a personal rela- tion to what this vision entails. This needn't, of course, be a relation of adherence – it may result in rebellion or rejection as inhuman or a recognition that in any case one isn't going to live in terms of such truth. If it is communicated by the nature of the pseudonymous writings that reflective confusions about the nature of the ethical and religious are themselves existential and so must be treated accordingly, indirectly, then that communication takes place itself indirectly.

There seems nothing else to do but to revoke the above and declare it concerns me alone – whoever that may be.

NOTES

1. F. Nietzsche, *Beyond Good and Evil*, trans. R. J. Hollingdale (Harmondsworth Penguin, 1979), p. 90.
2. F. Nietzsche, *The Will to Power*, trans. W. Kaufmann and R. J. Hollingdale (New York: Vintage Books, 1968), p. 12.
3. F. Nietzsche, *The Twilight of the Idols*, trans. R. J. Hollingdale (Harmondsworth: Penguin, 1978), p. 40.
4. Ibid., p. 41.
5. *WP*, p. 10.

6.   *TI*, p. 30.
7.   Ibid., pp. 45–6.
8.   *WP*, p. 318.
9.   F. Nietzsche, *Beyond Good and Evil* (New York: Vintage Books, 1966), p. 64.
10. *WP*, p. 154.
11. F. Nietzsche, *The Gay Science*, trans. W. Kaufmann (New York: Vintage Books, 1974), p. 255.
12. *WP*, p. 500.
13. *TI*, p. 41.
14. S. Kierkegaard, *Concluding Unscientific Postscript*, vol. 1, trans. H. V. Hong and E. H. Hong (Princeton, N.J.: Princeton University Press, 1992), p. 310. (Hereafter *CUP*.)
15. Ibid., p. 150.
16. Ibid., p. 120.
17. Ibid., p. 314.
18. Ibid., p. 93
19. Ibid., p. 33.
20. S. Weil, *Gravity and Grace*, trans. E. Craufurd (London: Routledge & Kegan Paul, 1963), p. 3.
21. *CUP*, p. 156.
22. Ibid., p. 156.
23. Ibid., p. 200.
24. Ibid., p. 138.
25. Ibid., p. 178.
26. Ibid., p. 253.
27. *Republic* 505d–e.
28. *CUP*, p. 283.
29. S. Kierkegaard, *Journals and Papers*, trans. H. V. Hong and E. H. Hong (Bloomington, Ind.: Indiana University Press, 1970), entry 633.
30. *CUP*, p. 74.
31. Ibid., p. 73.
32. See, for instance, ibid., pp. 165–82.
33. Ibid., p. 173.
34. Ibid., p. 73.
35. Ibid., p. 74.
36. Ibid., p. 618.
37. Ibid., p. 617.
38. Ibid., p. 277.
39. Ibid., p. 626.

Part Four
Transcendence and Pluralism

8

Transcendence in a Pluralistic Context

Ninian Smart

Mostly in this paper I shall deal with Buddhist and Hindu ideas and practice, so far as they bear upon notions of transcendence. Of course, that notion really splits into a number of varieties, since it is vital to say what something or other is supposed to be transcending. I consider, and have argued this in a paper originally presented in the 1960s,[1] that the concept of transcending space can be coherently stated, and, with suitable religious embellishments, is the key notion in Western theism. But there are other usages such as that something or other transcends thought or description and so forth. In this paper I wish to explore analogues from South Asian religions. But by way of contrast to the key idea of transcendence mentioned above, let me start by delineating a different model, as found in the Jain tradition.[2]

In Jainism the cosmos is pictured as being roughly in the shape of a huge human being. Corresponding to the waist of this being is a disc which contains various continents inhabited by humans and other living entities. Above are heavens, with gods in them of diverse rank. Below are purgatories. The size of the cosmos is immense. Its height is 14 *rajju*, each being the distance computed as that travelled in six months by a being going at two million miles per microsecond. At the summit of the universe is a region which is inhabited by liberated souls or life-monads (*jīvas*) who cannot go further since it is devoid of the medium of motion (which Jains distinguish from the geometrical system of locations). There can be no transactions between such life-monads and the rest of the cosmos, so there can be no communication with the great heroes of the religious tradition, such as Mahāvīra, the refounder of Jainism for the present world epoch. In short, temples may contain representations of divinity-like beings, but there can be no spiritual

113

exchange with them. Outside the cosmos are three layers of air, and then infinite space. This cosmology contains no 'room' for non-spatial transcendence.

The Jain cosmology is what may be dubbed material. Even the notion of karma is conceived as physical. It constitutes a substance of weight which keeps the life-monads down. With the annihilation of karma they float upwards like balloons until they reach the summit of the cosmos.

This archaic cosmology is interesting, but one would hardly think it to be credible in these latter days. Jains are not too worried, because they believe in any case that the religion is in decline during the present epoch and will die out completely until restored in a future age by a new 'Ford-maker' or spiritual teacher. Anyway, the Jain cosmology has this literal, non-transcendental aspect. It is by contrast with this that we can introduce Buddhist and Hindu notions.

Generally speaking, in the Indian context the serious contrast is between entities or states regarded as permanent, and those which are impermanent. For this reason, Indians often draw the line between soul and body in a way which frequently strikes Westerners as peculiar. Thus in general capacities and states known as *buddhi*, often translated 'intellect', and perceptions, etc., are treated as physical (though the matter is subtle). Consciousness lies behind the psychophysical organism, illuminating it, so to speak. In the Hindu tradition that consciousness is pure and permanent. So it transcends the bodily – the natural cosmos including psychophysical organisms. In Buddhism things are a bit different, because even states of consciousness are impermanent. However, nirvana is seen as permanent (though we shall need to investigate in what sense). But there is a manner in which it transcends the cosmos, in the Theravādin interpretation. In Mahāyāna things are more complex. It may be noted that by making the key contrast that between the permanent and the impermanent, Indian thinking tends to draw lines in unexpected places (from a Western angle). For instance, heaven is often pictured as lying beyond the cosmos: but in India it's often seen as part of the round of rebirth. Gods reside there over vast periods, but in the long run they have to come down to earth as humans before they can achieve ultimate liberation or nirvana.

The fact that consciousness in the Indian tradition is often identified with the permanent and so actually or potentially with a transcendent entity (the 'actually or potentially' I shall come to after a while) means that there can be many transcendents, whereas we tend to think in Western culture as if there is but one transcendent. Of course it can be the case that there is only a single transcendent: as for instance in Advaita Vedanta, since in Non-Dualism there is only one Ātman or Brahman. Sometimes the transcendent is conceived as being temporally other, but as all-pervasive in space. There is the possibility envisaged that there are many transcendents which are indistinguishable spatially, since they are all all-pervasive. Let me begin to explore the notion of transcendence in a relatively simple model, namely that in Rāmānuja's so-called Qualified Non-Dualism.

Here the line drawn between consciousness in the Hindu tradition and the psychophysical organism is well worth bearing in mind, since in Rāmānuja's system there is the explicit analogy drawn between the cosmos and the body of God. The cosmos, as being subservient to God's purposes, is like the body as serving the desires and purposes of the soul. For Rāmānuja (somewhat like Aquinas) there is something unnatural in a soul's being bodiless. The soul, then, of the cosmos is the Lord—the personal God and recreator of the universe. Occasionally this doctrine is labelled pantheism, but it is more properly panentheism: the soul exists independently of the cosmos, even though it naturally controls and 'inhabits' the world. In my view it is a fine vehicle of theism. Since it occurs in a Hindu context where mythologically there are many gods subordinate to and under the control of the Lord, one might label it transpolytheistic theism – a theism which transcends the many gods. Or, from another perspective, it can be seen as a *refractive* theism, in which the one God is refracted in the many images projected through the 'gods'. Anyway, it is certainly possible to use Rāmānuja's schema to expound Christian theism[3] or other forms of theism.

There are by the way some speculative thoughts at this juncture which take us away from the strictly South Asian context. It is possible to ask whether there may be more than one universe, in parallel, so to speak. Since modern cosmology has become so wild lately, we can permit ourselves a little imagination. If you use the model of God and her body, can she have many bodies? From an Indian point of view I do not see why not. If you can (by rebirth or reincarnation) have many bodies serially, why not simultaneously, if that is required? Naturally since time is in each case cosmos-bound, there would be trouble saying that the time in various cosmoi would be simultaneous: but in any case, let us settle for the notion of their being non-sequential. Anyway, I see no intrinsic objection to the Lord having a lot of diverse bodies (perhaps, if the notion makes sense, an infinite number or at least an indefinite number).

But though the main point of contrast between the transcendent and the cosmic is to do with time in the Indian tradition, there is also the notion that what is permanent exists, or can exist, outside the cosmos. Of course in one sense this idea is contradictory: for space like time is 'inside' the universe. To say that God is beyond the universe is a metaphor. It means for instance that She is non-spatial, and that She is 'behind' the universe as if our three-dimensional milieu were itself a kind of screen which shields us, so to speak, from the Power or Brahman behind. It usually implies that God or the Goddess is independent and the cosmos dependent. She is the causative force: our world is controlled by the Other beyond the cosmos.

It is worth mentioning at this point that Indian cosmoi do not begin. They pulsate, sometimes being dormant and sometimes active. In theistic systems the God sleeps between cosmoi, ready however to reactivate the creative powers which give rise to a new universe. The fact that God is always in the business of creation and re-creation does not mean that She is not totally in control. For one thing, in Rāmānuja's schema the cosmos, though God's body, is totally under Her or His control: unlike our bodies. We have bodies which of course we can move. It's the easiest thing to cross to the building opposite (assuming you do not suffer from a physical handicap). You can raise your right hand with ease. However, wiggling your ears is not so easy. Controlling the beats of your heart is more difficult still. And controlling your liver or your kidneys? Feeble is our control in such matters. In the Rāmānuja theory there is total control by God over her body. Anyway, there is no metaphysical feeling that you need to have a beginning to have *ex nihilo.* Because myth goes in time, the authors of *Genesis* seem to have thought that that was a necessary component of the absolute power of God. I do not see it so: why should not God have always been dancing the dance of creation?

This gets us on to another notion tied up with transcendence – namely the view that God has to be involved in transcendence in virtue of His or Her absolute power. How could She be controlling the cosmos from within? Surely She must in some sense be outside? Of course this cannot be literally outside, since if so She would be in some part of space. 'Outside' is after all a spatial concept. So it must be in some other sense that God is outside. One question

arising from this observation is: Can God be outside in some ana-
logical sense, and really so? That is, can analogy be ontologically
real? Well, one thinks 'Naturally so', since modern physics is full of
such strange uses of language. For instance, we have waves which
are not waves in anything, by some sort of analogy with the ocean,
even though there waves have a medium, namely water. If we can
throw away ether, we can throw away literal space in speaking of
God's being 'behind' or 'other than' the cosmos.

It is also worth commenting that since 'behind' is not a literal direction or location, neither is 'within' in talking of God's being
within all things. The difference between transcendence and immanence is therefore minimal, though transcendence does bring out
the thought perhaps that God would still be 'there' even if the
cosmos were not to exist: while 'within' stresses the point that the
cosmos has to be in existence if God is going to be within it.

Rāmānuja also conceived of the Divine Being as the soul of souls
as well as being the soul of the cosmos. He described the Lord as
the 'inner controller' or *antaryāmin* who guides individual souls and
administers karma (so to speak). In this way God is the soul within
living souls, which also function as the Lord's body.

Though the difference between transcendence and immanence
is from one point of view minimal, as I have observed, existentially the metaphor of God's being 'beyond' the world chimes in
with prophetic and devotional experience, namely experience
rooted in the numinous, since it conveys the perception of divine
Otherness. This is why it is possible to use the notion of transcendence as 'out there' and 'beyond' in the case of Hindu theism (similarly of course with all theisms). Since theism does not reign in
Buddhism, though virtual theism arises here and there, for instance in the Pure Land Schools, where Amitābha or Amida functions as a gracious God, the idea of transcendence is questionable
through much of that tradition. I shall come back to that point
anon. Anyway, God is seen in theisms, whether East or West (or
North or South), via the metaphor of 'beyond' which chimes in
with the religion of worship, born in part out of the numinous experience. But it is less appropriate in certain faiths or traditions
where the mystical or contemplative vision is emphasized and
where often the experience is felt as without the polarity of subject
and object.

This is most obvious in the case of Theravāda Buddhism.
Nirvana may be contrasted to the round of rebirth, but it is not

thought of as an Other lying 'behind' the cosmos. Actually its ontological status is very shadowy. There is of course nirvana conceived
as living liberation, achieved or realized by a saint in this life.
Beyond death however its status falls under the rubric of the unde-
termined questions. It is neither correct to say that the liberated
saint exists nor that he does not nor that he both does and does not
nor that he neither does nor does not. This is comprehensive negation indeed. In terms of the Buddha's metaphysics (as interpreted
in the Theravāda), the question as to whether a saint survives death
is radically inappropriate. But even if we were to simplify the subtlety of the teaching in this matter, nirvana would at best be a permanent condition, but not some unseen power or entity lying
'behind' the cosmos. Still, a limited form of transcendence could be
affirmed, in that without this nirvana would not constitute release
or liberation from the round of rebirth.

The situation in Mahāyāna Buddhism is different, and even more
complex. In the transition to Mahāyāna the teaching of emptiness or
the void (*sūnyatā*) emerges. According to this every event in the
cosmos is empty, that is it is without substance. It has no 'own-
being': partly because each event is dependent on others (some say,
as in Hua Yen, each depends on every other, like the jewels in the
magic net on Indra, each of which reflects all the others). Partly
every event is empty in the sense that all theories or ways to discourse about the universe are self-contradictory – for instance
because our worldly discourse is soaked thoroughly in the language of causation, and all theories of causation are contradictory,
as established by the dialectic deployed by Nāgārjuna. Before we
expand on this point further, let us turn aside to consider Advaita
Vedānta. This Hindu school was, it is supposed, deeply influenced
by Nāgārjuna: only entities in the cosmos are treated not as empty
but as illusory or part of the grand illusion or *māyā*. From the subjective side the world is the product of ignorance. However, there is
still a sense of transcendence in Advaita, because the higher truth
points to a single Reality, lying behind the illusion. This Reality on
its hither side can be seen from the lower level of truth as being the
personal Lord. He is actually illusory in the last result, being implicated in the very illusion which He creates. Still, there is a feel of
transcendence: so long as we remain within the illusion we can and
should worship God from a devotional perspective. On the other
hand, in so far as the One Reality is roughly equivalent, in the
Advaitin system, to the Emptiness in the thought of Nāgārjuna,
there is no theistic sense of transcendence attaching to it.

Let us return then to consider the status of nirvana in Nāgārjuna's philosophy, and more generally the Mahāyāna outlook. It is said that in higher truth nirvana and saṃsāra (the empirical world) are identical. We can understand this in the following way (though this account could be held by some to be over-substantializing in its formulation). First, the intrinsic nature of everything in the cosmos is its emptiness. From another perspective the contemplative experience itself reveals emptiness: for the higher experience of the Buddhist mystic is one of pure or empty consciousness. That higher experience is the realization of nirvana: so nirvana is emptiness, and samsara is emptiness. The two are identical.

Since by the way there is no subject-object structure to the contemplative experience, the saint in realizing nirvana becomes it, so to speak. Or to put matters a little differently: the saint attains the essence of Buddhahood, since *bodhi* or enlightenment consists in emptiness. And so nirvana does not only equal saṃsāra: it is also Buddhahood. Each one of us has the potential for enlightenment and therefore contains within herself the Buddha-nature. And so on.

A twist is that in saṃsāra we are really in nirvana. The only point is that liberation means realizing emptiness existentially. In short the difference between saṃsāra and nirvana is not an ontological one but an epistemological one: hence the importance in the Greater Vehicle of existential knowledge (or, as one may spell it, echoing gnosis, knowledge).

I think the exposition I have just given allows us to dispense with the idea of transcendence in Mahāyāna Buddhism. This is reinforced by the fact that the Buddha is supposed to have cast his teachings in the form of *upāya* or skilful means. That is, he adapted his teaching to the mentality of the people with whom he was consorting. He had a beautiful understanding of their attitudes. Such adaptation means that Mahāyāna is happy enough to treat aspects of the teaching as psychic engineering. This being so, then even the doctrine of rebirth could be a device adopted by the Buddha, rather than a real description of reality. So if you want a religion without transcendence a form of Mahāyāna is quite inviting. It should enable you to cultivate the holy virtues or *brahmavihāras*, namely love, compassion, sympathetic joy and equanimity, while under the spell of the imagery and teachings of the Buddha. The stories of the celestial Buddhas and Bodhisattvas would turn out to be inspiring, but whether they are true or not is not an issue. They would be part of the tradition's skill in means of leading the faithful onward and upward.

However, denial of the genuine reality of rebirth causes severe problems within the Theravādin framework. If there is no rebirth then there is no release from rebirth. Nirvana and saṃsāra exist by way of contrast, and in the absence of rebirth nirvana vanishes.

There is a further question arising from modern adaptations of the Advaita Vedanta. In particular I am thinking of the modern Hindu ideology as pioneered by Swami Vivekananda, Sarvepalli Radhakrishnan and more vaguely by Mahatma Gandhi. This ideology sees all religions as pointing to the same Reality. A version has been expressed by John Hick, and there are other variants by such as Frithjof Schuon. Does this philosophy also postulate a transcendent Being?

I think it has to. For one thing it concentrates on forms of theism. To the Theravādin it makes no sense to say there is one Reality which all religions point to. There is no such Ultimate in the Theravāda. There is of course an Ultimate Goal, but not a Being. The idea of a single Real manifests itself as so many diverse representations of the One. These manifestations are the objects of varying styles of devotion. Since the Theravāda does not have a single Real as its focus, it cannot fit the schema. Nor indeed could Jainism. By the way, the fact that the Theravāda cannot have a Copernican view of the religions helps to explain why its intellectuals have not worked out a theory of other faiths. Those theisms which rely on transcendental testimony or revelation do not fit the mold of Buddhist epistemology; and the Buddha is not a God like Christ or Allah. This lack of theory has been one factor in Sri Lanka's civil war, since no intelligible place could be found for Sri Lanka's Hindus and Muslims. Anyway, it is possible to hold a view of the Copernican Reality, provided you do not suppose that this view will easily account for the non-theistic religions. But in so far as it represents a way of reconciling theisms of differing traditions, the Reality of the universal Focus would imply a transcendent status. It fits in with religions of the numinous, that is religions of worship. It is therefore a consequence of unitive pluralism that it too does not make sense without the transcendent. Or at least it would issue in a shallow pragmatism, it being thought that the varied images of God would conduce both to peace and to various higher spiritual states which were good for the human community.

Oddly enough however the sense of the unity of all religions has tended to flourish more greatly among people who favor the mystical path, from Vivekananda to Aldous Huxley, and from Schuon to

Stace. This is in part because of the similarity of what mystics seem to say. It is in part because what they say often stresses the inexpressible. Also, because they appeal to experience they do not rely on śruti or revelation. Whether you are talking about the Veda or the Granth Sahib or the Qur'ān or the Bible (whichever version – Jewish or Christian), revelationists pin their faith to differing particulars, often in a rather literal way unrelieved by the esoteric interpretations of mystics. Often scriptures figure in ineluctably diverse rituals. Now these milieux of faith are nurturing and often very beautiful. The call of the muezzin sounds beautiful to one ear; the chant of Orthodox liturgy is heavenly to another ear; the sacred syllables of StJohn's Gospel are musical to another ear; the intoning of the Vedas are dauntingly tremendous to another ear; and so on. But they remain somewhat divisive. It raises the issue of how we can unite the diverse after all? Maybe by a theory of complementarity, differing faiths teaching diverse matters to each other: but unity? It does not seem really attainable. And these theisms all depend on a sense, a postulation indeed, of the transcendent.

In the foregoing I have explained to some degree and commented on the religions of South Asia, though in fact because Buddhism spread to Japan through every country in Asia but one, I have implicitly touched upon at least part of the East Asian experience. But there is much left out of religions both North and South. Nor have I said much about Judaism and Islam, nor of the many new and old religions of Africa and other continents. But at least I have tried to stretch debate into a broader sphere than it has often been conducted in.

NOTES

1. 'Myth and Transcendence', *The Monist* 50 (1966), 475–87, reprinted in Donald Wiebe (ed.), *Concept and Empathy* (1988).
2. On Jainism, see Padmanabh Jaini, *The Jaina Path of Purification* (1979), and Nathnal Taka, *That Which Is* (San Francisco: HarperCollins, 1994), See also my book *Reasons and Faiths* (London: Routledge & Kegan Paul, 1958) which started the postwar crosscultural philosophy of religion. Lately there has been published Thomas Dean (ed.), *Religious Pluralism and Truth: essays on crosscultural philosophy of religion* (1995).
3. As Steven Konstantine and I did in our book *A Christian Systematic Theology in a World Context* (1991).

9

Transcendence in a Pluralistic Context – A Reply

Joseph Augustine Di Noia O.P.

There are a variety of ways of approaching the question of whether there can be 'religion without transcendence'.

One might have it in mind to found a religious community, or, more modestly, develop a personal religious stance that allows no scope for the idea of transcendence. Perhaps personal integrity or ecological stewardship will come to occupy a place roughly analogous to some traditional form of religious commitment in one's own life, or in the lives of like-minded people.

But in this conference, and particularly under the rubric for this session, 'transcendence in a pluralistic context', what we seem to have in view are Hindu, Buddhist, Jewish, Christian, Muslim, and other actually existing religious communities which possess highly ramified doctrinal schemes. Certainly this is what Professor Smart has in view. He wants to examine something of the variety of ideas of transcendence as we find them in some religious traditions.

So we won't follow up on the interesting question of whether one could have a religion without transcendence if one were to set about constructing a religious stance for oneself or for others – except to say, in a preliminary way, that it certainly seems that this would be possible.

A related question brings us closer to home, but still seems somewhat far afield of the topic of our conference. Could one practice a religion that seemed, at least in the logic of its doctrinal scheme, to entail some concept of transcendence, and yet dispense with that concept? Again, this could simply be a personal matter. One could cultivate the religious affections, symbols, experiences and moral integrity fostered by one's religious tradition without actually embracing any beliefs that pointed to the existence of a transcendent being or to the attainment of a transcendent goal. Certainly, some people seem to have wanted to do this with their own traditions.

Closer to our topic would be the related possibility that this interest in cultivating aspects of a religious tradition without embracing its transcendent dimension would lead to the formation of a sub-community within the larger religious tradition, or a break-off community gathering together like-minded people who wanted to go off on their own. Such new communities would draw upon their parent religious traditions but omit or massively re-interpret references to and beliefs about a transcendent being or goal. Perhaps Nagarjuna's Mahayana Buddhism, as Professor Smart describes it, could be cited as an instance of this kind of transformation of a tradition. In this case we do in fact seem to have a living religious tradition that falls within our purview and that has dispensed with the idea of transcendence.

These reflections bring us close to what we seem to be doing at this point in our conference when we ask about transcendence in a pluralistic context. We seem to have existing religious traditions in view, and we are asking whether their doctrinal schemes entail some concept of transcendence, and, if they do have one, what it involves.

This inquiry supposes that we can fashion a concept of transcendence that is broad enough or inclusive enough to help us to understand the varieties of schemes we will want to discuss when considering the 'pluralistic context' of religions. Hindus, Buddhists, Jews, Christians, Muslims, Jains, and Confucians all believe different things and commend the pursuit of distinctive aims of life. Clearly, if we are interested in a variety of living religious traditions, it would not be helpful to develop and apply a concept of transcendence that is almost entirely dependent on a particular religious scheme, and then proceed to impose it on other religious schemes. This could lead us astray in a variety of ways, as Professor Smart suggests. If we come upon a religious scheme that is non-theistic – where, to employ the typology advanced by Smart's classic study *Reasons and Faiths*,[1] the mystical strand predominates – then we cannot impose a notion of transcendence that presumes the existence of a numinous transcendent like God. We will not get very far in our understanding of a doctrinal scheme that has no transcendent being for its central focus if we insist that the idea of transcendence entails an existing reality 'behind' or 'beyond' the world of sense-perception.

To be sure, we might undertake, on religious or philosophical grounds, to criticize a doctrinal scheme as inadequate if it did not possess an idea of a transcendent being or to suggest that such an idea is implicit in its doctrinal scheme. But in such cases, rather than trying to understand a particular religious tradition, we would be advancing another doctrinal scheme or at least another religious proposal as superior to the one under study.

So it follows that we need to approach the religious traditions we are interested in studying with conceptual tools that allow their differing notions of transcendence to emerge (if they have any) with their particularities more or less intact. Elsewhere Professor Smart has written: 'Religious doctrinal schemes are organic, and a particular notion of transcendence has to be taken in its context, if we are to attain a reasonably rich understanding of it.'[2] In the paper under discussion here, he remarks that the notion of transcendence 'splits into a number of varieties' depending on 'what something or other is supposed to be transcending' (p. 113). Even philosophers who believe that some notion of transcendence is essential to religion, as Professor Smart clearly does not, make a similar point. For example, Louis Dupré writes: 'The term transcendent, so essential for religion, develops dialectically and takes various meanings in different contexts. It is always transcendent in relation to what surrounds it.'[3]

Clearly, we will not want to take a stand beforehand on whether some concept of transcendence is essential to religion. Even less so will we need to have a definition of religion itself in order to proceed with our inquiry. As Peter Geach says somewhere, we don't need to have a definition of an elephant in order to distinguish one from a chipmunk. Something similar is true of religions. Although there certainly may be borderline cases, we do not need a definition of religion in order to identify and study what can reasonably pass for religions. Looking at these in all their wonderful diversity, we want to know how they deal with what we have been calling 'transcendence'.

But, although we can get along without a definition of religion, can the same be said about 'transcendence'? How will we know what it is we are looking for if we don't have some definition, even if only a rudimentary one, of 'transcendence'? We have seen that we need a concept of transcendence that will respect the particularities of the religious schemes we have in view. But what would this concept be like? What traits are we seeking to identify in a religious tradition when we ask about its notions of transcendence? Shall we look in standard dictionaries of the English language? Dictionaries of philosophy, including those specializing in the philosophy of religion, will prove to be of little help here: I have not found one that contains an entry for 'transcendence'.

So far, I have been using the term 'transcendence' as if we all knew what it meant. And, in general, I think we will have to admit that our understanding of the term has been shaped by the prominent role it has come to play in Western theism. Professor Smart is right to draw our attention to this factor, particularly as it bears on our study of non-Western religious traditions.

Discussing the topic elsewhere, Professor Smart has written that transcendence is a 'technical term', a 'sophisticated concept', one that 'belongs to the milieu of those religions which have well-developed doctrinal systems, such as Christianity (though not Christianity in its earliest days), Buddhism and Hinduism'.[4] While Smart is right to call 'transcendence' a technical term and to suggest that it helps us to identify certain scheme-specific features of well-developed religious traditions, it remains true nonetheless that the conceptual home of the notion as such lies in debates that are peculiarly Western. 'Transcendence' and, even more so, 'the transcendent' are expressions that have come to function as highly abstract ways of referring to God. It is beyond the scope of this response to enter into a lengthy discussion of the career of these terms in Western philosophy and theology. But it is worth noting, for our present purposes, that the way these terms are commonly used in Western thought predisposes us to approach the study of other religions with a hypergeneralized view of the object of religious devotion and quest already in place.

In their typically modern use in Western philosophy and theology, these terms lump together complex issues of God's existence and attributes in ways that would mystify a classical theologian like Aquinas. The distinctiveness and subtlety of classical discussions of the arguments for the existence of God and thus of diverse conceptions of the divine causality, not to mention their accounts of each of the divine attributes in turn – simpleness, perfection, goodness, limitlessness, omnipresence, unchangeableness, eternity, unity, omniscience and omnipotence – are often blurred by debates centered on an overly generalized concept of divine transcendence (along with its almost inseparable companion, the concept of divine immanence). Without commenting on the intrinsic merits of such debates, my point here is that neglect of the particularities and diversities of own's own religious tradition fosters habits of mind that are unprepared to take the particularities of other religious traditions sufficiently into account. It may be that this peculiarly Western predisposition to employ a hypergeneralized concept of transcendence lies behind the use of such terms as 'Reality', 'Ultimacy', and 'the Transcendent' by thinkers who advance implicitly theistic theories of religious diversity that Professor Smart terms, in the paper under discussion, 'unitive pluralism' (p. 120).

Rather than directly attacking this largely Western understanding of the concept of transcendence, Professor Smart employs a strategy of gently nudging us along in our inquiry. He proceeds directly to an examination of particular religious schemes without attempting to provide a prior account of transcendence, even one that is simply etymological or lexical. Although, as I have hinted, he has had a fair amount to say on the topic elsewhere, Smart's approach here is refreshingly minimalist. His rudimentary account – largely presupposed here but more fully developed with reference to Christianity in an essay to which he draws our attention[5] – relies on spatial metaphors.

While I welcome Smart's minimalism on this point, I want to try to expand the concept of transcendence just a bit in order to raise some questions that, far from overgeneralizing the concept, will in fact help us to see how irreducibly diverse are the features of religious schemes that entail what might be called a notion of transcendence.

When we ask whether the doctrinal scheme of an existing religious tradition in its present form entails some concept of transcendence, we seem to be asking roughly this: is there any sense in which the tradition in question points its adherents to an entity, a personal transformation, and/or a goal that are not fully or not at all encompassed by the ordinary limitations of earthly existence and/or experience?

Framed in this way, our inquiry remains open to the de facto variety we encounter on the world's religious landscape. To see what some of the possibilities might be, let us consider some types of religious schemes. When we have considered these hypothetical types, we will be in a better position to know what kinds of questions to address to existing religious traditions. We will be able to take account of the pluralistic context of our inquiry in determining the extent to which these traditions could be said to allow scope for transcendence in their conceptions of the objects upon which their schemes are focussed.

It might be that religious traditions that focussed primarily upon the cultivation of some human quality (like wisdom, detachment or love) or of some relation (like harmony or justice), or upon the worship either of a particular natural entity (like the sun or the earth), or of a particular individual or group (like the emperor or the state) could not be said to point their adherents to entities not encompassed by the limitations of earthly existence and experience. These entities are neither ontologically nor epistemically transcendent: that is to say, they share earthly existence with all other entities and are directly accessible to experience, knowledge and description.

But we have to tread carefully here. As William Christian noted in *Meaning and Truth in Religion*, since 'one function of a basic [religious] proposal of any type is to mark off its logical subject from all else in a special way ... any entity proposed as a religious object is in this sense transcendent'.[6] It would depend in part on how such religious schemes came to be developed – especially if the earthly entities in question were deemed to be 'symbolic' of unspecified hidden realities – to determine whether to identify some notion of transcendence there. But allowing for borderline cases, we would seem to be on fairly safe ground if we concluded that religious schemes of these types had conceptions of their religious objects that were largely non-transcendent.

The same would for the most part be true of quasi-religious schemes that explicitly rejected a transcendent focus and centered their attention on nature or humankind. But while neither nature nor humankind is ontologically transcendent, there is a real sense in which they are epistemically so. As Christian notes, 'neither are given in experience'. It requires a certain level of abstraction and generalization to conceive of nature and humankind as objects of religious interest.

We are on firmer ground with such religious objects as pure forms (e.g., the Good, Beauty, Humanity, Truth), pure being, or transcendent agents (e.g., Zeus, God, Allah, Shiva). These are objects that are generally thought not to be encompassed by the limitations of earthly existence. But the degree to which they are seen to be ontologically transcendent would depend on the scheme-specific references and predications that would figure in their descriptions in particular religious traditions.[7] Ontological transcendence might be secured with reference to an account of the divine sheer existence (the *ipsum esse per se subsistens* of Aquinas) or of permanence in contrast with impermanence (as Smart suggests is the case in Indian religions). Varying levels of epistemic transcendence would likewise be associated with these objects. While some religious traditions stress the radical unknowability and ineffability of God (for example, Christian apophatic theology), others seem to allow for a kind of perception or direct experience of the divine (for example, some forms of mysticism).

Most of the types of religious schemes discussed thus far have in common a practical bent. They not only direct their adherents to believe in, worship, or value some object of religious devotion. They often also strive to cultivate in their adherents certain attitudes and dispositions that may amount to something like a complete personal transformation. Depending on whether the experience or enjoyment of this new state of being is understood as encompassed by earthly existence (for example, inner harmony) or surpassing it partly or completely (for example, an other-worldly paradise), a further question about the presence of notions of transcendence (and, in particular, self-transcendence) would naturally arise with respect to the religious schemes in question.

In contrast to the types discussed thus far, some religious schemes might not direct their adherents to believe in, worship, or otherwise value any presently existing entity. The object of their doctrines and practices would be to direct believers exclusively to the attainment of some goal, involving either some form of personal transformation or some other new condition of existence or consciousness. If such a transformation or new state of being is by definition not yet achieved or attained by the seeker in question, then it cannot be said to be a presently existing entity of any kind; until it is achieved, it always remains a goal to be sought (for example, nirvana). If the new condition involves literally an arrival at some new location, then it could be said to be a presently existing entity which nonetheless remains the object of a quest on the part of the believer (for example, heaven). Again, the degree to which religious goals can be thought of as transcendent is a matter which can only be settled by careful study of the religious traditions in question (as Professor Smart has tried to show in his subtle discussion of this issue in his paper).

The result of this discussion of some types of religious objects and schemes surely would be that, in a pluralistic context, there can be no such thing as a univocally applicable concept of transcendence. This consideration of some types of religious schemes – by no means an exhaustive one – demonstrates the remarkable range of possibilities here. And while there seems to be no reason to rule out the possibility of religions without transcendence, there are good reasons to suppose that many existing religious traditions will allow ample scope for transcendence in their descriptions of that upon which their schemes of belief and practice are centered. It is the merit of Professor Smart's paper to have alerted us to the significance of this important fact about the Hindu, Buddhist, Jewish, Christian, Muslim, Jain, and other religious traditions we encounter in our inquiry about transcendence in a pluralistic context.

NOTES

1. Ninian Smart, *Reasons and Faiths* (London: Routledge & Kegan Paul, 1958), especially Chapters 1 and 2.
2. Ninian Smart, 'Myth and Transcendence', *The Monist* 50 (1966), p. 477.
3. Louis Dupré, *The Ultimate Dimension* (Garden City, N.J.: Doubleday, 1972), p. 16.
4. Ninian Smart, *The Philosophy of Religion* (New York: Oxford University Press, 1979), p. 29.
5. 'Myth and Transcendence'.
6. William A. Christian, Sr, *Meaning and Truth in Religion* (Princeton, N.J.: Princeton University Press, 1964), p. 178. My remarks in this and the following paragraphs are dependent in part on Christian's discussion of types of basic religious proposals.
7. See William Christian's illuminating analysis of the role of references and predications in religious discourse in Chapters 10 and 11 of *Meaning and Truth in Religion*.

Part Five
Transcending Death?

10

Death and Transcendence

William L. Rowe

To transcend death is to overcome it. The best way I know of overcoming death is to live through it. Failing that, the next best way is at some time after death to be reconstituted as the person you were while you were alive. According to the traditional teachings of the Catholic Church each of us transcends death in both of these ways. At the very moment of bodily death our immortal souls are transported to heaven or hell, or to purgatory if our final destination is heaven but we require some fine-tuning before we can move there. And at the end of the world we will all, the damned as well as the saved, be rejoined or reconstituted with our resurrected bodies and then continue in our state of heavenly bliss or eternal torment.

In this paper I will suppose that these beliefs are false, along with any other beliefs that imply personal survival of death. Specifically, what I will suppose to be false is that a human person survives death either in the sense of continuing to exist and having memories, thoughts, beliefs, and feelings or in the sense of coming back into existence at some later time and then having memories, thoughts, beliefs, and feelings (with or without a body). What I propose to explore is what sense, if any, can be made of transcending death on the assumption that we do not survive it by continuing to exist (or coming back into existence) and having experiences. Perhaps I should add that this exploration is not simply an intellectual pursuit someone might engage in who nevertheless is convinced that we do transcend death in the sense of continuing to exist (or coming back into existence) and having experiences. I believe there is no personal survival of death and also think there are good reasons to support this belief. This does not mean that I think that those who do believe in personal survival are irrational in holding this belief. It means only that I think that they are mistaken in holding this belief.

I

What is there about death that raises for us the question of whether we can transcend it? I believe it is the fact that death is seen as something that is bad. If we did not view death as a bad thing, the question of transcending it would not arise for us. It is because death is perceived by us as something bad that we feel a need to transcend it, to rise above it. If death were not a bad thing and we came to see that it is really not a bad thing, the problem of transcending death would simply go away. And one way in which philosophers have sought to dissolve the problem of transcending death is by trying to convince us that death is really not a bad thing, that it is not something that we have any need to transcend. But what if death really is a bad thing? What then can we possibly do about transcending it? If it really is a bad thing, transcending death would seem to be impossible. We can make efforts to prolong life. But this isn't transcending death; it is just postponing the moment of death. Death itself remains inevitable. We can perhaps engage in some kind of self-deception whereby we gloss over the fact that it is bad, or get ourselves to think of it as not bad, or get ourselves not to think of it at all. But this won't get rid of the badness of death; at best it will only decrease the occasions on which we are consciously aware of its badness. Moreover, we might feel that there is something inauthentic about this approach to transcending the badness of death. But, in any case, this head-in-the-sand approach, as comforting as it may be, contributes nothing to the philosophical problem of transcending the badness of death.

Our reflections thus far seem to leave us little hope in doing anything that will contribute to a philosophical solution to the problem posed by death. Either death is a bad thing or it is not. If it is not a bad thing then there is no problem to be solved, there is no real question about whether we can transcend the badness of death. At most, the work of the philosopher is confined to getting us to see that death is not something bad. On the other hand, if death is a bad thing, then, since we are powerless to alter its badness and powerless to escape it, death cannot be transcended at all. Thus, finding a way of transcending death seems to be impossible. Either there is nothing to transcend or the badness of death is ineluctable and cannot be transcended. Nevertheless, let us forge ahead and at least try to settle the question of whether death is a bad thing.

II

We need to distinguish death from dying. Dying is a process we live through until its very end. Death is a state or condition that commences when the process of dying is completed. Sometimes we use 'death' to refer to the process of dying. We say, for example, that someone had a good death. What we mean is that the process of dying was fairly peaceful, not filled with pain. But we do need to distinguish the two. Clearly, dying is sometimes dreadful in that it is sometimes protracted, painful, unpleasant for all concerned. But our question has to do with death itself, not the process initiating it. Is death itself a bad thing?

In discussions of whether something is good or bad, or perhaps neither, philosophers often distinguish between whether that thing is good or bad in and of itself (intrinsically good or bad) and whether it is good or bad as a means (extrinsically good or bad). When we ask whether a person's death – i.e., his being dead – is bad, are we asking whether it is intrinsically bad or extrinsically bad? Is a person's death something that is bad in and of itself, or is it perhaps only bad because of what it brings about or prevents from happening? I suspect that it is the latter, extrinsic badness, that we often associate with death. But what value, if any, belongs to death by virtue of its intrinsic nature? Is death intrinsically good, intrinsically bad, or neither intrinsically good nor intrinsically bad? My own judgement is that death is intrinsically neutral, neither intrinsically good nor intrinsically bad. Someone's being happy is intrinsically good, someone's being unhappy is intrinsically bad, but someone's being dead is neither intrinsically good nor intrinsically bad. It might be argued that life is something that is intrinsically good. And, if this is so, it might be thought that death must be intrinsically bad. But a state of affairs that is not itself intrinsically good and that logically precludes an intrinsically good state of affairs from obtaining need not itself be an intrinsically bad state of affairs. Someone's not being happy logically precludes everyone's being happy, an intrinsically good state of affairs. But someone's not being happy, as opposed to someone's being unhappy, is not an intrinsically bad state of affairs. We must distinguish between the mere absence of something intrinsically good and the actual presence of something intrinsically bad or evil. Thus, even if life is something that is intrinsically good, it hardly follows that death is intrinsically bad or evil. In the absence of a convincing argument to the contrary, I conclude that death is intrinsically neutral, neither intrinsically good nor intrinsically bad.[1]

III

Let's turn then to the question of whether death is extrinsically bad. Whether something is extrinsically bad is commonly thought to be a matter of its value taken together with the value of its causal effects. If it, together with its causal effects, increases the balance of intrinsic good over evil or prevents a decrease in the balance of intrinsic good over evil, then it is something that is extrinsically good. If it, together with its causal effects, decreases the balance of intrinsic good over evil or prevents an increase in the balance of intrinsic good over evil, then it is something that is extrinsically bad. What, then, of death? Is death always an extrinsically bad thing? It is clear, I believe, that the answer to this question is no. Someone's being dead at a certain time may be an extrinsically good thing because it increases the amount of intrinsic good in the world.[2] Of course, whether someone's being dead at a certain time has such an effect depends on what the circumstances are. One and the same thing may be extrinsically good in one set of circumstances and extrinsically neutral or bad in some other set of circumstances. In the appropriate circumstances, a person's being dead (a wicked tyrant, let us suppose) may be extrinsically good; whereas in other circumstances that person's being dead may be extrinsically bad. For the second set of circumstances may be such that his being dead results in a far more wicked tyrant taking his place. So it seems that there is no clear sense in which it is true that death is always a bad thing. For it does not seem to be intrinsically bad; and depending on the circumstances, a person's death may be extrinsically good or extrinsically bad or neither.

IV

Thus far we have been considering whether death is intrinsically bad and whether it is extrinsically bad. To the first question we have answered that death is intrinsically neutral, neither intrinsically good nor intrinsically bad. To the second question we have answered that death is sometimes extrinsically bad, sometimes extrinsically good, and, I would suppose, sometimes extrinsically neutral. But in asking and answering these questions we have appealed to the notion of intrinsic value and have claimed that some states of affairs are intrinsically good, others intrinsically bad, and still others intrinsically neutral. In addition, in considering whether death is extrinsically bad we have proceeded in a somewhat utilitarian manner to answer that question in terms of the total balance of intrinsic good over bad that results from someone's being dead at a certain time *t*. Some will undoubtedly object that we have not given much content to the idea of intrinsic value, and have stated no criteria for determining what things are intrinsically good, intrinsically bad, or intrinsically neutral.[3] And they will feel that until more has been said about this we really cannot judge whether death is or is not intrinsically bad. Nor, they may object, can we determine whether death is extrinsically bad. But even if we were to make some headway in responding to these quite reasonable objections, a more serious complaint awaits us. For we have discussed the extrinsic badness of death in terms of death's causal impact on the balance of intrinsic good over intrinsic bad. And many will surely feel that we have simply missed the central point underlying the common conviction that death is something bad. For, they will argue, this conviction is not concerned with what someone's death means for the balance of good over evil in the world. The conviction that someone's death is bad is centered on the idea that it is bad *for that person*. It's whether your death is something bad *for you* that is at issue. And no amount of speculation concerning whether one's death serves some cosmic good may be at all relevant to whether your death is something bad *for you*. Clearly, to make progress with the philosophical problem of death we must consider the value of death for the person whose death it is.

V

I will assume that nothing can be intrinsically valuable for a person at a time if the person is not alive and conscious at that time.[4] Thus, once you are dead nothing can be intrinsically bad for you. I believe this is the fundamental point Epicurus relied on when he argued that it is irrational for anyone to fear death. Epicurus says:

> So death, the most terrifying of ills, is nothing to us, since so long as we exist, death is not with us; but when death comes, then we

do not exist. It does not then concern either the living or the dead, since for the former it is not, and the latter are no more.[5]

When I am dead, death cannot be intrinsically bad for me, since I won't then be in existence to experience its supposed badness. And, of course, while I am alive, my death cannot be intrinsically bad for me, since it does not exist. The good news about my death, then, is that when it finally comes I won't be around to experience it. And if I'm not around to experience it, it really cannot then be intrinsically bad for me. Dreading your own death should not be compared to dreading the death of those you love. You may live through their deaths and go through the long days of having to get along without them. But you won't have to go through any long days once you are dead. Your death, once it comes, will mean nothing to you at all. And until it comes it cannot be intrinsically bad for you either. So why all the fuss about death?

VI

Perhaps we can begin to see what goes wrong in Epicurus's reasoning if we take a case where we want to say that someone's death at a certain time was a good thing for that person. Someone who has a terminal disease that brings with it an incredible degree of pain may take her own life rather than linger on for a few more months in constant agony. It was good for her, we might say, to have died when she did, as opposed to the alternative of a few more months of relentless pain and suffering. But how can her death at that moment in time have been good for her? For if Epicurus is right it wasn't good for her before it occurred because it had not yet occurred. And it wasn't good for her after it occurred because she no longer existed. So it simply couldn't have been good for her at all. But this argument is, I believe, unsound. For all that Epicurus has really established is that her death cannot have *intrinsic value (good or bad) for her*. There is still the matter of whether her death a few months earlier than she would have died had *extrinsic value for her*. When we say that something X is extrinsically good *for a person* we generally have in mind some intrinsically good experiences that person has because of the occurrence of X. Where X is someone's death, it is clear that X cannot be extrinsically good in this way. For a dead person cannot have intrinsically good experiences. But there may be another way in which X can be extrinsically good for a person. For X may prevent the occurrence of intrinsically bad experiences for that person, while preventing few, if any, intrinsically good experiences for that person. And my suggestion is that it is in this way that this person's death at that time is extrinsically good for her.[6] For if we compare her whole life given her death at that time with what her whole life would have been had she lingered on in pain and agony for the next few months, we can see how one might judge that her life with the earlier death is intrinsically better for her than her life would have been with the later death. And it is some such thought as this that leads us to say that her death at that earlier time was extrinsically good for her. It was not extrinsically good by causing her to have any intrinsically good experiences. But it was extrinsically good by preventing what otherwise would have been a final, brief segment of life that is overwhelmingly intrinsically bad for her. So, although Epicurus is right in holding that someone's death cannot be *intrinsically good or bad* for that person, we should not conclude from this that someone's death cannot be good or bad for that person. For, as we've just seen, someone's death at a certain time may be *extrinsically good* for that person.[7]

Just as there are circumstances in which someone's death a few months early is extrinsically good for that person, so too there are circumstances in which someone's premature death may be extrinsically bad for that person. A young boy with his life before him is killed in an accident. His death is a tragedy in the lives of those who loved him and looked forward to his having a good life. But is it something bad for him? His death at that time cannot be intrinsically bad for him. But it may well be extrinsically bad for him. Had his accidental death not occurred, we can suppose that he would have lived a good life, a life intrinsically far better than its early segment up to his accidental death. Certainly, some who die at an early age would have had such lives had their early deaths not occurred. Their deaths at those times are extrinsically bad for them, they prevent them from having many intrinsically good expediences. Of course, one advantage of their deaths is that they will not know what they have missed. Once dead, they will have no regrets that they didn't live longer. It is those who loved them and live on who will have those regrets. Their early deaths are not extrinsically bad for them by way of causing them to have intrinsically bad experiences. But they are extrinsically bad by virtue of preventing them from having many intrinsically good experiences. The early death of the young man may well have been his greatest misfortune.

VII

In the first section of this paper we noted that it appears to be impossible to transcend death. For if death is not a bad thing, there is no need to transcend it. And if death is a bad thing, then, since we are powerless to avoid it, the badness of death is ineluctable and cannot be transcended. We then sought to determine whether death is a bad thing. Refining the issue to whether death is a bad thing *for the person whose death it is*, we agreed with Epicurus that neither a person's death nor her death at a particular time is intrinsically bad for that person. In addition, we argued that, depending on the circumstances, a person's death *at a particular time* may be extrinsically bad, extrinsically good, or extrinsically neutral for that person. For the many people who live until their bodies naturally wear out, death, at the time it occurs, is not extrinsically bad for them. It is only those who, as it were, die before their time for whom death is bad. Moreover, when one's death is extrinsically bad, it may be that one could have transcended death's badness. For it is not death itself that is here at issue; it is death at a *particular time*, specifically, a death too early, that is extrinsically bad. And some of these deaths are not inevitable, but could have been prevented by careful thought or the cultivation of better habits. Thus, our preliminary conclusion is that for many of us there is no need to transcend death. For our deaths will not be bad for us at all, and may even be good for us.

If this preliminary conclusion should be true, why then do we persist in feeling that death is humankind's great enemy? Why is it that death is universally feared, or, if not feared, contemplated with sadness and regret? Why is it, as Thomas Aquinas remarks, that 'man naturally shrinks from death, and is sorrowful at its prospect'?[8]

Several answers suggest themselves. First, since dying before one's time is not all that infrequent a phenomenon, our persistent fear of death may just be the fear that our actual death will come before our time, before our continued life ceases to be on balance intrinsically good for us. Second, although we have distinguished death from dying, the two are closely connected. Since we do experience the process of dying, and since that process sometimes involves considerable suffering, it is possible that in fearing death we have simply transferred to death our quite natural fear of the process of dying. Third, it may well be that we have not sufficiently reflected on death to come to see the truth that Epicurus saw: that death is not intrinsically bad for us. Or perhaps we fail to see that death may come at a time when it is our friend rather than our enemy, when it is extrinsically good for us to die rather than linger on in senseless pain and suffering. Finally, it could be that we do understand all this and are simply irrational on the subject of death. It may be that even when we know at the conscious level that our death will probably not be bad for us we are, nevertheless, driven by unconscious needs to fear death. If any of these answers is correct then there is little the philosopher can do to help us transcend the fear of death. At best, the philosopher can try to help us see that (1) our actual death will not be intrinsically bad for us, and may well be extrinsically good for us, and (2) that death before one's time may be avoidable by taking normal precautions and cultivating good habits. But the philosopher can give no assurance that the process of dying will not be unpleasant, and she cannot assure us that we will not die before our time. Nor can the philosopher, qua philosopher, do much to alleviate our irrational fears of death. If the fear of death is driven by irrational forces buried in the unconscious, it is therapy, not sound philosophy, to which we must turn.

Let us suppose, however, that we have been enlightened by philosophy and have come to see that our own death may not be bad for us at all. That is, let us suppose that we see very clearly that our own death cannot be intrinsically bad for us and that it very well may be either extrinsically good for us or extrinsically neutral. Moreover, let us suppose that we have not confused the question of death itself with the question of premature death, that we realize that while we may reasonably fear premature death, it is not reasonable to transfer this fear to death itself, particularly when it is not premature. Let us also suppose that although we may reasonably be fearful about the process of dying, we see that such fear should not be extended to death itself. And finally, let us suppose that the fear of death is not driven by irrational, unconscious forces. Or that if it is, this problem can be resolved by a bit of therapy or the wonders of chemistry. What then remains of the problem of death? What remains to be transcended?

VIII

What remains to be transcended is not the *badness of death*. What remains to be transcended is the *fear of death*, our attitude of regret, sadness, and even dread on contemplating the fact that our life is a fleeting thing and that someday all too soon we shall simply cease to be. The ineluctable problem about death is not death itself, but the sadness, regret, and fear that may grip us as we contemplate the inevitable approach of death and our eternal annihilation. And the remarkable fact is that this attitude about death persists even when life itself becomes a trial, often filled with misery and unhappiness. Woody Allen notes this point in his own inimitable way in a few lines in *Annie Hall*:

> There's an old joke. Uh, two elderly women are at a Catskills mountain resort, and one of 'em says: 'Boy, the food at this place is really terrible.' The other one says, 'Yeah, I know, and such ... small portions.' Well, that's essentially how I feel about life. Full of loneliness and misery and suffering and unhappiness, and it's all over much too quickly.[9]

How are we to account for fear of death in the sense of a fear of ceasing to be? It cannot be viewed simply as a fear of death before our time, for it afflicts even those who have lived to the fullness of their years. As Thomas Huxley notes: 'It is a curious thing that I find my dislike of the thought of extinction increasing as I get older and nearer the goal! It flashes across me at all sorts of times.'[10] This fear of death is centered in the fact that death is the total extinction of the conscious person. Corliss Lamont expresses it well:

> To try to realize that when once we close our eyes in death, we shall never, never open them again on any happy or absorbing scene, that this pleasant earth will roll on and on for ages with ourselves no more sensible of what transpires than a dull clod, that this brief and flickering and bitter-sweet life is our only glimpse, our only taste, of existence throughout the billion infinities of unending time – to try to realize this, even to phrase such thoughts, can occasion a black, sinking spell along the pathways of sensation.[11]

Before we explore the question of what accounts for the fear of our permanent annihilation, it is worth noting that the experience of such fear does not appear to be a universal phenomenon among humankind. David Hume, for example, professed no such fear of death, but appeared serene in facing his extinction, content in knowing that he had largely accomplished his life's aims. However, so pervasive is the belief in the fear of death that Samuel Johnson simply refused to believe that Hume was really at ease about his own death. 'It is more probable that he lied than that so very improbable a thing should be as a Man not afraid of death; of going into an unknown state and not being uneasy at leaving all that he knew.'[12] And Boswell could account for Hume's serenity only by supposing that he was secretly a Christian.

The account of the fear of death that seems most plausible to me is that suggested by William Sherlock in the 17th century: 'The love of life, and the natural principle of self-preservation, begets in all men a natural aversion to death, and this is the natural fear of dying.'[13] Fear of death is parasitic on lust for life. It is life that we are driven toward and, therefore, death that we rebel against. If we did not long to live we would not live in fear of death. The only solution to the problem of death is to cease to care so much about life. But it seems that we can no more control our longing for life than we can control the movement of the tides. And so long as we are driven to live, so long will we continue to view our death with sadness, regret, and fear. And this will be so even when we come to see that in the economy of nature our death is as inevitable and as natural as the movement of the tides. Moreover, it will be so even when we come to see that death itself may not be bad for us at all. So long as we lust for life we will feel an aversion to death. For it is our lust for life that begets and fuels our fear of death.

IX

We began with what we called the philosophical problem of death. But in the end what we have seen is that the problem of *death* has been displaced by the problem of the *fear of death*. Philosophy's contribution to the 'solution' to the problem of death consists in helping us to see two important points: (1) that death itself cannot be intrinsically bad for us, and (2) that death is sometimes extrinsically bad for us, sometimes extrinsically good for us, and perhaps sometimes extrinsically neutral for us. The fact that neither of these points suffices to diminish the natural fear of death suggests that the ultimate source of this fear is not, as Epicurus may have thought, an intellectual confusion. The poet Philip Larkin saw this clearly. In his poem 'Aubade' he writes:

> This is a special way of being afraid
> No trick dispels. Religion used to try,
> That vast moth-eaten musical brocade
> Created to pretend we never die,
> And specious stuff that says *No rational being*
> *Can fear a thing it will not feel*, not seeing
> That this is what we fear – no sight, no sound,
> No touch or taste or smell, nothing to think with,
> Nothing to love or link with,
> The anaesthetic from which none come round.[14]

Our fear of death is rooted in our nature as animals and in our nature as rational beings. Because we can conceive of an endless expanse of time looming before us, an expanse throughout which we will not be at all, and because we lust for life and consciousness, we are subject to the fear of death. But it is not death itself that is bad for us, it is the fear of death. For to be in the grip of such fear is to have experiences that one can only wish to be without. Something of the flavor of these experiences is expressed by Carl Jung.

> When one is alone and it is night and so dark and quiet that one does not see or hear anything but the thoughts that add and subtract the years of one's life, and the long sequence of those unpleasant facts, which prove cruelly how far the hand of the clock has advanced, and the slow and uncheckable approach of that dark wall, which threatens to swallow up irretrievably all I love, desire, possess, hope, and strive for, then all the wise dicta go into hiding and fear descends upon the sleepless like a choking blanket.[15]

I say that these are experiences that one can only wish to be without because they are intrinsically bad and, so far as I can see, bereft of extrinsic value. Fear about the process of dying and fear about premature death may have extrinsic value. Both may prompt one to take precautions that may prevent an excessively painful dying or a premature death. But fear of what cannot be prevented or diminished is fear that is wasted.

Against what I have just said it can be argued that it is precisely this fear, or its begetter, the lust for life, that has led to the growth of gerontology and the development of precisely those factors that add to the quality of our later years and postpone the coming of the endless dark night. But I think the rational fear of premature death is all humankind needs to pursue developments in human longevity. At some point the quest for longevity reaches its natural limit. We can then only give in to the inevitable workings of nature. Unless we conjure up the supernatural magic of the gods, we must simply submit to the fact that our ultimate destiny lies in death and not life. And at that point the human goal should be to acquiesce to the inevitable, to cherish the lives we have been able to have, and to go gently and serenely into that dark night.

What keeps us from this quite reasonable goal, however, is not some mistake in logic, some flaw in reasoning. It is in fact the blind watchmaker, the forces of nature and natural selection that have so 'shaped' us that we lust for life, struggle to reproduce our kind, and fight for the last gasp of breath, rather than welcoming death as a fitting end to life.

X

Several years ago I had my vet put down my 14-year-old golden retriever. For a number of years he accompanied me on canoeing trips into the Canadian wilderness above Minnesota. These were exciting times for him. When the tents and canoeing gear were assembled he became excited, stayed constantly by my side, fearful that I would leave without him. When the morning of departure came, he was very excited and leaped gladly into the back of the station wagon, content with whatever small space had been left for him. As he aged and the trips became more difficult for him, I worried about the day I would have to leave him behind. I pictured to myself his helpless efforts at trying to get into the car before I left, his whimpering as I forced him back into the house before driving off. It never happened. When the arthritis set in and he was no longer able to get into the car without assistance, his desires changed. He sniffed but showed little interest in the tents and canoeing gear as they were assembled. On the morning of departure he arose and waited patiently until I left. But it was apparent to me that he was really waiting for this early disturbance of his slumber to end. As I left he cheerfully walked back to his bed, ready for a few more hours of well-earned rest. Nature dealt kindly with him. When he was no longer able to do what he loved, she removed that desire so that he did not feel deprived of something he deeply wanted. Or so we would like to think.

It would be grand if nature were so fine-tuned that when the lust for life had satisfied its biological purpose of reproduction, that lust slowly abated until the time when death due to the natural decline of the body would occur. At that point, having no compulsion to keep on living we could reflect with serenity over the course of our lives, regret our failings, take pride in our accomplishments, wish well those who will continue on, and go peacefully and without fear into that deep, dark night. But nature is neither benign nor unkind. Some of our desires disappear along with our ability to satisfy them. Others do not. I expect my desire to go wilderness canoeing will slowly abate with my capacity to perform the tasks necessary for the activity. But the lust for life is more primitive, not something we have acquired by experience and learning. Nature is not fine-tuned to our needs or feelings, and it is certainly not benign. It is simply sentimental on our part, or perhaps a need to humanize nature into a god, to think otherwise. Nature is utterly indifferent to the fact that the lust for life continues on beyond any useful need to the individual or the species. Many of us are destined to approach the dark night in the fullness of our years, frustrated by a longing for continued life that reason tells us cannot be satisfied. Moreover, we may well discover that reason is quite ineffective in eradicating our persistent longing for life. Some benefit, however, may come to us from understanding in advance that our longing for continued life will likely keep us company up to the moment of death. To understand why the fear of death persists at a time when we would be better off without it may make death somewhat less frightening to us. To attain any greater degree of transcendence over the fear of death may be beyond our grasp.[16]

NOTES

1.   Since we are taking a person's being dead to preclude that person's existing and having conscious experiences, a person's being dead precludes that person experiencing pain, remorse, regret, or having any other experience that would be something intrinsically bad.

2.   I have here shifted from the inevitable fact of *someone's death* (at some time or other) to the perhaps preventable fact of *someone's death at a certain time*. A person's death (at some time or other) is inevitable, built into the fabric of the universe by the process of aging and the laws of nature. A person's death at a certain time may not be inevitable. (I am indebted to David Widerker for making me aware that at crucial points in an earlier draft of this paper I used 'death' to refer both to someone's death at some time or other and to someone's death at a certain time.) When I discuss the extrinsic value of someone's death, I mean to be discussing the extrinsic value of *someone's death at a particular time*.

3.   At best, we've given only an example or two. Someone's being in pain is intrinsically bad; whereas someone's being happy is intrinsically good.

4.   A person's being conscious is only a necessary condition for a state of affairs being intrinsically valuable for that person. It is very difficult to provide a complete account of what it is for a state of affairs to be intrinsically valuable for a person. Perhaps the following may do as a provisional account of what it is for a state of affairs to be *intrinsically bad for person S*. A state of affairs is intrinsically bad for S just in the event that it consists in S's being in some conscious state that is intrinsically bad. For example, *S's being in pain* is intrinsically bad for S since it consists in S's being in a conscious state that is intrinsically bad. It should be noted that *S's being pleased upon contemplating the suffering of innocent children*, even though it includes the good state of affairs of *S's being pleased*, will be an intrinsically bad state of affairs for S insofar as the whole state of affairs consisting in *S's being pleased upon contemplating the suffering of innocent children* is itself an intrinsically bad state of affairs.

5.   Epicurus, *Letter to Menoeceus*, trans. C. Bailey, in Whitney J. Oates (ed.), *The Stoic and Epicurean Philosophers* (New York, 1940), pp. 30–1.

6.   A person's death at a certain time would prevent only a few intrinsically good experiences for that person provided it is true that had that person continued to live she would have had only a few intrinsically good experiences.

7.   I am indebted to Fred Feldman's illuminating paper 'Some Puzzles About the Evil of Death' for developing the idea of extrinsic value that I have used. His paper originally appeared in *The Philosophical Review* 100, no. 2 (April 1991): 205–27.

8.   *Summa Contra Gentiles*, Book III, Chapter 48, paragraph 6.

9.   Quoted in John Martin Fischer (ed.), *The Metaphysics of Death* (Stanford, Calif.: Stanford University Press, 1993).

10.   Quoted in Jacques Choron, *Death and Modern Man* (New York: Collier Books, 1964), p. 81.

11.   Ibid., pp. 82–3.

12.   Ibid., p. 99.

13.   Ibid., p. 80.

14.   Quoted in D. Z. Phillips, *From Fantasy to Faith* (New York: St. Martin's Press, 1991), p. 55. I thank Phillips for bringing this poem by Larkin to my attention.
15.   Quoted in *Death and Modern Man*, p. 81.
16.   I am grateful to Rod Bertolet, Jan Cover, Martin Curd, Jeff Jordan, William Wainwright, and David Widerker for helpful comments on an earlier draft of this paper.

11

Death, Value and Transcendence

Gareth Moore O.P.

The sting of death is sin. (1 Corinthians 15:56)

I

In the course of his paper *Death and Transcendence* Professor Rowe presents us with a dilemma:

> Either death is a bad thing or it is not. If it is not a bad thing then there is no problem to be solved, there is no real question about whether we can transcend the badness of death ... On the other hand, if death is a bad thing, then, since we are powerless to alter its badness and powerless to escape it, death cannot be transcended at all. Thus, finding a way of transcending death seems to be impossible. Either there is nothing to transcend or the badness of death is ineluctable and cannot be transcended. (p. 134)

I shall argue in the present paper that this apparent dilemma is a false one, that it can make sense to speak of transcending death, and that traditional religions, as well as ethical systems, have something to offer toward the realization of this possibility.

First it is necessary to draw out an important assumption underlying the supposed dilemma as Professor Rowe presents it. He understands the transcendence of death as the surmounting of an obstacle or the defeat of an enemy or an escape from an aggressor:

> To transcend death is to overcome it. The best way I know of overcoming death is to live through it. Failing that, the next best

way is at some time after death to be reconstituted as the person you were while you were alive. (p. 133)

In what follows Rowe treats these two best ways of transcending death as the only ways of transcending death, and they are assumed without argument to be unavailable. The traditional religious beliefs in the immortality of the soul (understood as the belief that one lives through one's death) and in the resurrection of the body (taken as the belief that one is reconstituted at some time after one's death) are assumed to be false. It is presumed that it is at least roughly clear what these beliefs amount to and that they are to be dismissed. Some such assumption seems all but universal in modern philosophical discussions of death. In making it himself Rowe ensures that his own treatment will not be far from the mainstream. But it seems to me at least a questionable assumption, particularly in the context of a discussion of religion and transcendence. A preoccupation with death and a history of meditation upon it is one of the major features of several important religions, including Christianity. It is not clear that the ways in which Christians talk about death are reducible to the two neat formulas that Rowe presents us with. Neither is it immediately apparent what Christian talk of the dead amounts to. It is actually quite difficult to get to grips with. For example, a Christian may happily say that her dead Uncle Sol is in heaven, with God, and also that he lies buried in the local cemetery. (She will not normally say that *part* of him is in heaven, and another part six feet under.) This makes it look as if it is possible, in the Christian view, to be in heaven and on (or in) earth at the same time. But if that is so there is a further question why it is only of the dead that it is said that they are in heaven. Why not of the living also? Again, some Christians think that they will rejoin their dead loved ones when they themselves die. Why do they not think they will join their dead enemies? What is the relation between the ante-mortem relationships of people and the way post-mortem relationships are envisaged? What is the relation (or what are the relations) between belief in a future life and belief in judgement on this present life? Questions like this are obvious ones, and any plausible answer to them must go far beyond a supposed belief in the survival or reconstitution of the dead. What Christians (not to mention adherents of other religions) say about death and what follows it is complicated and needs serious attention if it is to be understood at

a philosophical level. The general assumption of modern discussions of death, that it is final and that talk of life after death is to be
put to one side, may reflect a view of death and a religious poverty
widespread in some parts of the modern world, but it short-circuits
discussion of what religious people actually say about death and of
the ways they act in the face of death, a discussion essential to any
serious understanding of religion. Attempts have been made to
come to grips with religious language and practice surrounding
death by, among others, Wittgenstein[1] and Phillips.[2] It is a pity
their lead has not been more widely followed.

It is by no means evident, then, that the common assumption underlying Rowe's discussion is a wise one. Yet it would be a pity to
part company with him so early, since, I believe, much can be learnt
by following his reasoning. So I shall for the purposes of this reply
to his paper accept the limitations imposed by his assumption. I
will accept his rejection of the supposition that 'a human person
survives death either in the sense of continuing to exist and having
memories, thoughts, beliefs, and feelings or in the sense of coming
back into existence at some later time and then having memories,
thoughts, beliefs, and feelings' (p. 133). I shall also accept, for the
sake of argument, that the proposition here rejected is a reasonable
summary of what Christians believe about life after death.

Rowe characterizes living through death and being reconstituted
after death as the two best ways of transcending death. A consequence of ruling out both of these at the beginning is that we know
already, without argument, that any possible way of transcending
death that might emerge from the argument is going to be an also-
ran, a limping, third-rate affair. Indeed, it becomes clear very soon
after that Rowe believes no further way of transcending death is
going to emerge. If death is bad at all, 'we are powerless to alter its
badness and powerless to escape it', so 'death cannot be transcended at all'. We have already arrived at Rowe's dilemma. The
only thing left to argue about is whether death really is a bad thing,
one that we cannot transcend, or is not bad at all and does not need
to be transcended.

Already at this early stage, then, what we might have thought
would be the main problem addressed in the paper has been resolved, or perhaps sidestepped. Much of what follows is concerned
instead with the question of whether death is indeed a bad thing,
and questions of transcendence are apparently left behind. I think,
however, that this appearance is deceptive. Much of what Rowe

says on the question of the badness of death is in fact relevant to the original question, whether there is any way in which death can be transcended. In what follows I shall present a general criticism of Rowe's argument and then relate the points that emerge to the question of the possibility of transcending death.

II

There are four important elements in Rowe's argument. First, the philosophical problem of death is presented as the problem, not simply of whether a person's death is good or bad, but whether it is good or bad for the person who dies. Rowe presents the matter thus:

> The conviction that someone's death is bad is centered on the idea that it is bad *for that person*. It's whether your death is something bad *for you* that is at issue. And no amount of speculation of whether one's death serves some cosmic good may be at all relevant to the question of whether your death is something bad *for you*. Clearly, to make progress with the philosophical problem of death we must consider the value of death for the person whose death it is. (p. 137: Rowe's italics, here as throughout)

If you are contemplating your death, it is not what is good or bad for the universe in general that is important in your assessment of whether your death is or will be a bad thing, but what is good or bad for yourself. (Neither, therefore, is it a question of what is good or bad for some other person.) Note that this is presented not as a psychological generalization, not as stating what as a matter of fact people find important when considering their own death, but as a matter of philosophical principle. Hence a person rationally fears his death if and only if his death is really bad for him. To discover that your death is not really a bad thing for you is, if you are rational, to cease to fear death.

Second, the evil of death (if it is evil at all) can be, like other evils, of two kinds: intrinsic and extrinsic. If a person's death is bad it must be either bad in itself or because of its causal consequences for that person. Third, death can be neither intrinsically good nor intrinsically bad for a person; this is so because when we are dead we experience nothing. Fourth, death can, however, sometimes be extrinsically good and sometimes extrinsically bad.

I think there are weaknesses at all four stages. Here I wish to argue chiefly that the first and third of these steps are importantly wrong: I may fear my own death not because I think it bad for me, but because I think it bad, *tout court*; and it is implausible to locate value only, or even chiefly, in experience. I will begin with the latter point.

It is clear that fundamental to this stage, as to much of Rowe's argument, is the distinction between intrinsic and extrinsic good and evil.[3] Something has intrinsic value if it is good or bad in itself, regardless of causal effects. A thing's extrinsic value is determined by its relation to what has intrinsic value:

> If it, together with its causal effects, increases the balance of intrinsic good over evil or prevents a decrease in the balance of intrinsic good over evil, then it is something that is extrinsically good. If it, together with its causal effects, decreases the balance of intrinsic good over evil or prevents an increase in the balance of intrinsic good over evil, then it is something that is extrinsically bad. (p. 136)

The question concerning death is then: 'Is a person's death something that is bad in and of itself, or is it perhaps only bad because of what it brings about or prevents from happening?' (p. 135). Death is then judged to be neither intrinsically good nor intrinsically bad (p. 136), and this is given theoretical justification by a brief review of Epicurus's argument concerning death. This argument is to the effect that death is to be considered as nothing, since while we are alive we are not affected by our death, and when our death comes we are no longer around to be affected by it.[4] Hence death cannot harm us; it does not touch the living, and the dead are no longer there to be touched.

Since our death cannot be intrinsically bad for us, it can be an object of rational fear for us only if extrinsically bad for us, so Rowe then proceeds to a discussion of whether death might be extrinsically bad. But the argument moves too quickly at this point. It is difficult either to agree or to disagree with Rowe's judgement that death is not intrinsically bad until we are offered some criteria for something's being intrinsically bad, and Rowe does not attempt to do this.[5]

However, it is possible to deduce broadly what has intrinsic value in Rowe's eyes. At the beginning of his discussion of Epicurus, he says:

I will assume that nothing can be intrinsically valuable for a person at a time if the person is not alive and conscious at that time. Thus once you are dead nothing can be intrinsically bad for you. (p. 137)

This suggests a link between intrinsic value and experience of some kind or other, a link confirmed by the remark that

When I am dead, death cannot be intrinsically bad for me, since I won't then be in existence to experience its supposed badness. The good news about my death, then, is that when it finally comes I won't be around to experience it. And if I'm not around to experience it, it really cannot then be intrinsically bad for me. (p. 138)

Rowe assumes that an experience x can be intrinsically good or bad for me at time t only if I am alive and conscious at time t. He never offers any justification for this assumption, though it is not uncontroversial; it short-circuits, for example, the discussion surrounding the possibility of posthumous harm initiated by Nagel.[6] Why does this requirement seem so natural to Rowe? The answer seems to be that he locates intrinsic value in experience (even if what counts as experience remains somewhat vague). It is only experience or what I experience that has intrinsic value for me; a good experience is intrinsically good for me and a bad experience intrinsically bad for me (and an indifferent experience intrinsically indifferent). Thus he writes:

When we say that something X is extrinsically good *for a person* we generally have in mind some intrinsically good experiences that person has because of the occurrence of X. (p. 138)[7]

The requirement that I be alive at time t has the function of guaranteeing that in some fundamental sense I am able to experience x, among other things. It seems to follow that for x to be intrinsically bad for me I must experience it as bad; the experience of x must be a bad experience.[8] What is intrinsically bad for me is a bad experience, and what is intrinsically good for me is a good experience. It is because I cannot have any experience after death, and *a fortiori* cannot have any bad experience, that death cannot be intrinsically bad for me. From Rowe's assumption that for something to be intrinsically bad for me at time t I have to be alive and conscious at time t it seems to follow, then, that death cannot be intrinsically bad for me.[9]

There are at least two difficulties with this view locating intrinsic value in experience: first, it will not do the job that Rowe wants it to do, it cannot show that death is not intrinsically bad for me; and second, it is false. The first difficulty is connected with the vagueness of the notion of experience that underlies Rowe's presentation of it. If my death is the end of all experience for me, then of course at no time after my death do I experience my death as bad. What follows from this, given all Rowe's assumptions, is that my death is not bad for me at any time after I have died. But what Rowe needs to prove is that I cannot experience death, and experience it as bad, *before* I die. If I can experience my own death at some time before it happens, then it can be an intrinsic evil for me at that time, and it will then also be rational for me to fear my coming death.

At first sight this suggestion appears preposterous, for how can I experience my death before it is there to experience? This might seem a cogent objection on one normal view of experience, namely that to experience something implies being aware of its presence (for an object) or present occurrence (for an event). And presence apparently implies contemporaneity. But whether it in fact does so in the present context depends on how wide the concept of experience is that Rowe is using. The question arises, then: what counts, for Rowe, as experiencing something? Is it necessary to have some sensory awareness of it? Or will the memory of an event, or its anticipation, count as experiencing it? Suppose my wife is gunned down before my eyes by bandits. This would count as experiencing the murder of my wife on almost any account of experience. But now suppose my wife is murdered in a distant land and I learn of the event only through the post. Would we count this as experiencing her murder? I guess that most of us would, for most purposes, say not; we normally contrast learning of something at second hand with experiencing it directly. But if Rowe agrees with this, then he has to say that, since I do not experience the murder of my wife, I do not experience it as bad, either. But that in turn means that my wife's murder cannot be in itself bad for me. It can only be extrinsically bad for me, by causing bad experiences. This in turn implies that while my wife is still alive and travelling in a distant bandit-ridden land I cannot rationally fear her death unless I fear it because I think it will cause me to have bad experiences. But this is wildly implausible.

But it can be replied to thus: of course I do not necessarily fear my wife's death because I think it will be bad *for me*; I fear it because I think it will be bad *tout court*, bad in itself. I can surely have values which I do not relate to my own well-being.

This reply seems to me correct. The distinction on which it relies, between something's being bad for me and simply bad, is an important one, and one which I wish to develop later. The trouble is that Rowe does not appear able to avail himself of this response. At the only point at which he discusses contemplating another's death he writes:

> Dreading your own death should not be compared to dreading the death of those you love. You may live through their deaths and go through the long days of having to get along without them. (p. 138)

Thus he really does seem to think that fearing the death of my wife amounts to fearing the bad experiences I will have as a result of it. On the basis of Rowe's remarks, the badness, from my point of view, of my wife's death really does seem to be badness *for me*, and not badness *tout court*.

But, even granting this, the strategy employed here, of representing fear of an event as fear of what may follow that event, is misguided. It may of course be true that if my wife dies I will have bad experiences; I may spend months or years in inconsolable grief. But if I fear my wife may die I do not *ipso facto* fear that I will spend a long time grieving. I may *also* fear that this is what will happen to me; but I may not. And I may not fear it, even though I am pretty certain that is what is going to happen if my wife dies; in contemplating my wife's possible death I may simply not care about what may happen to me. The fear that she will die is not the fear that I will grieve after her death; the one is the fear of what may happen to her, and the other the fear of what may happen to me. Neither can the latter be the cause of the former. I cannot fear the death of my wife because I fear that I will grieve for her loss if she dies. I fear her death because I love her, because she is precious to me. And I will only grieve for her after her death if she is precious to me. If I do not value her I will be indifferent to her death or even greet it with rejoicing. My fear before the event of her death and my grief after it have the same explanation, my love for her. If I fear that I may grieve after her death, and fear it because I think it will be a bad experience, this fear has its source rather in my love for myself.

Rowe is in trouble, then, if he does not allow that learning of an event at a temporal and spatial distance is a way of experiencing that event; he has to deny the evident rationality of fearing an event which is not experienced. On the other hand, if he is willing to count learning of an event at a temporal and spatial distance as experiencing that event, then it seems I can after all experience my death before it happens.[10] As I can learn that my wife *has died*, so I can learn that I *will die*. There is a difference between the two, in that learning about my own death, unlike learning about my wife's death, must always be learning about the future. But the futurity of my death cannot be a relevant consideration at this point, since most things we fear we fear as future.[11] Anybody who held that it is irrational for me to fear my own death because it lies in the future would also have to hold that it is irrational for me to fear any future event at all. Rowe shows no sign of being ready to adopt such a radical position.

Rowe seems, therefore, to be caught in a dilemma of his own: he must maintain either that indirect learning of an event does not count as experiencing it, with consequent unacceptable restrictions on what can count as bad for somebody; or that indirect learning does count as experience, in which case the assumption that I must be alive and conscious at a time for anything to be bad (or good) for me at that time does not rule out the possibility of my now experiencing my own future death, so that my death can be intrinsically good or bad for me now even if, according to Rowe's assumption, it will not be after I die.

III

But there is a deeper and more fundamental problem with the whole of Rowe's argument. His thesis linking intrinsic value to experience is false. I wish to approach this aspect of the matter indirectly, by way of a look at another of Rowe's fundamental assumptions: his insistence that when we talk about the fear of death, what we have in mind is somebody's death's being bad *for that person*. There is a possible ambiguity about the idea of death (or anything else) being bad *for* a person. If we speak of a surfeit of lampreys being bad for a person we normally mean that it harms that person in the sense of being injurious to his well-being, particularly his physical health.[12] If his physical health is injured enough, death may result, and in that case we may say that the surfeit of lampreys has been *very* bad for that person (even if, having read our

Epicurus, we want to say that his death itself is not bad for him). If I am concerned that something may be bad for me in this sense my concern is for myself; it is self-regarding. In general, in this sense x is said to be bad for the person who has or does x, or to whom x occurs, or who is affected by x; he can express this by saying 'x is bad *for me*'.

This is by far the most common meaning attached to the idea of something's being bad for somebody, and perhaps the only one that occurs in normal discourse. But there is another, quite distinct, sense which appears to be implied in some philosophical usage: an event or state of affairs is sometimes said to be bad for a person, meaning simply that it is bad *from his point of view*. What is bad for him in this sense is simply what he considers bad. In this sense something can be bad for somebody even if it does not affect that person's health or well-being. His concern need not be for himself at all. All that is required is that one of the things he values be adversely affected; he can express this by saying: 'x is bad', *tout court*. In this sense your surfeit of lampreys can be bad for me, bad from my point of view, bad as far as I am concerned; and the more I value your well-being the more I will be concerned. In this sense, x can be bad for somebody other than the person who has or does x, or to whom x occurs, or who is affected by x, so that what is not bad for me in the first sense can be bad for me in the second sense. It is also possible that something be bad for me in the first sense and not bad for me in the second, injurious to my well-being but not bad from my point of view. I may deliberately overdo the lampreys in order that they be bad for me because it seems good from my point of view to harm myself physically or kill myself, or to make myself wretched.

In brief, the first sense I have identified may be said to concern well-being, the second value. In discussion of death and whether it is to be feared it is, I wish to argue, the second that is pertinent. It may be that one of the things I value is my own well-being, in which case the question of whether my death is bad for me (in the first, common, sense) is pertinent; if I value my own well-being, and if death is bad for me, this gives me a reason to fear death. But I may not value my own well-being. I may be indifferent to it; I may hate or despise myself and attach positive value to harming myself. In such a case, even if I believe that my death is bad for me, this gives me no reason for fearing death; it may, on the contrary, give me reason to seek it. It appears to be a tacit assumption of

Rowe's argument that, for the person contemplating his own death, his own well-being has positive value, and further that this value is the greatest and most important of all his values: what is bad for me in the sense of being detrimental to my well-being is also what is bad from my point of view. This assumption allows him to elide the difference between the two senses I have distinguished. But it is an illegitimate and false assumption, and making it encourages Rowe to ignore other possibilities; this is fatal to his argument. He argues as if 'My death will be bad' (*tout court*) and 'My death will be bad for me' were equivalent; they are not. I can perfectly well think that my death will be a bad thing, and therefore fear it, even though I have no tendency to think it bad *for me*. But this means that it is a mistake in the first place to describe the problem of death as the problem of whether death is bad for the one who dies.

One aspect of his thinking which allows him to conflate more easily the two senses in which something can be bad for a person is his conviction that both value and well-being reside in experience: on the one hand, what is valuable for me is either an experience or something which I experience, and on the other hand it is my experience that determines my well-being. What is intrinsically good for me is a good experience, and what is intrinsically bad for me is a bad experience. This can be summarized by saying that Rowe generally writes as if the sentences 'I have an experience x which is bad' and 'I have an experience x which is bad for me' were equivalent. Again, they are not. The first sentence refers to an experience to which I attach negative value, one which I would rather not have, such as a headache. This experience is bad for me only in the extended and attenuated philosophical sense that it is bad from my point of view. The second sentence, on the other hand, refers to an experience which has a deleterious effect on my well-being. Things which are bad for people are in general things which have bad effects on people, rather like Rowe's extrinsic evils. I may have a severe headache which I will certainly want to describe as a bad experience. But it would sound very odd to say that the headache is bad *for me*, unless I were claiming that it also had some bad effect on me, such as making me depressed. Seeing my wife killed by bandits may be a very bad experience, but it will not be bad *for me* unless it seriously impairs my ability to cope with life. Bad experiences are not in general bad for people at all,[13] yet these are precisely what Rowe seems to be isolating as intrinsic evils.[14] Intrinsic evils in Rowe's sense are not, then, bad for people; they are simply experiences that those who suffer them would rather be without, experiences that they count as bad experiences.

This is more than a minor linguistic point; it is important when it comes to understanding the rationality of fear. Rowe seeks to locate the justification of a fear in the belief that what is feared is bad *for one*. But it is not the case that I may rationally fear, i.e. have a reason to fear, only those experiences which are bad for me. I may also rationally fear having a bad experience, an experience to which I attach negative value. Fearing such an experience has nothing to do with believing that the experience will be bad for me. I may fear having another of my migraines, but not because I fear it will be bad for me. I fear it because it will be very unpleasant, because it will hurt; that is why I would rather be without it, and that consideration is enough to make my fear rational. Its being unpleasant does not make it bad *for me*; it simply makes it bad *from my point of view*. It is experiences which are bad from my point of view that are the proper objects of my fear. If I fear experiencing *x*, what is important in discussing the rationality of my fear is not the bearing of *x* on my well-being but the relation of *x* to my values.

Rowe's argument concerning the rationality of the fear of death has to be recast, then, in terms of experiences which are good or bad, not experiences which are good or bad *for me*. This is by no means a trivial adjustment, for the question is now revealed to be one unequivocally related to my values rather than to my well-being.

Up to this point I have followed Rowe in speaking largely of good and bad experiences. This is because, as we have seen, Rowe locates value in experience, however defined.[15] My death will not be an experience for me. If Rowe is right here it looks as if death still lies outside the realm of rational fear. If what has value is experience and death is not an experience, then death has and can have no value, positive or negative. It can be rationally neither good nor bad from my point of view. But we do in fact value things other than experiences. I will now argue that we are logically correct to do so, and that Rowe is wrong to connect the value of *x* with the experience of *x*, however experience is defined. To do this I will speak of the value of an occurrence, where an occurrence is any event, which may or may not be an experience and which may or may not be experienced.

In general we fear an occurrence if and to the extent that we think it may be a bad occurrence: not an occurrence bad *for us*, but an occurrence to which we attach negative value. On Rowe's account I can rationally fear my death only if it is possible that I may experience my death and if I believe the experience of death would be a bad experience (death as an intrinsic evil); or I can rationally fear death if I believe it will cause other, bad, experiences or deprive me of good experiences (death as an extrinsic evil). The plausibility of this depends on the general supposition that I can rationally fear the occurrence of x only if I believe it is possible that I may experience x and if I believe the experience of x would be a bad experience, or if I believe that x will be extrinsically bad for me. There are thus putatively two cases in which it is irrational for me to fear the occurrence of x: first, if I believe it is impossible that I shall at any time experience x; and second, if I believe that it is possible for me to experience x but do not believe that I would experience x as bad. In both these cases it is, on Rowe's principles, irrational for me to fear the occurrence of x, unless I believe that x may be extrinsically bad for me, that it will cause me to have bad experiences.

But it can easily be shown that this account is false. It is possible to justify fearing an occurrence x in both the above cases, even given that x is not extrinsically bad for me. Take first the case in which I believe it is impossible for me to experience x. Suppose I have young children whom I love. I have been something of a wastrel and with the onset of a fatal illness have come to realize that I have not yet provided as I should have done for the security of my children in the event of my death. It is now clear that I will die very soon, probably before I have the opportunity to make adequate provision for my children. I now fear that this may be so; I fear that my children will be impoverished by my death. If what I fear comes to pass, I will be dead when my children are impoverished; it will therefore be impossible for me to have a bad experience of either their impoverishment or any of its consequences; it cannot therefore be an intrinsic evil for me. It cannot be an extrinsic evil for me, either, since it neither causes me bad experiences nor prevents me from having good experiences. What will happen to them cannot be bad for me in any way; it cannot harm me at all after I die. Hence on Rowe's principles it is irrational of me to fear as I do. But it clearly is not. In these circumstances I can rationally fear that my children will be impoverished after my death. I can describe my fear coherently and give reasons for it. Perhaps I cannot be harmed after my death but, obviously, what I fear here is not that I will be harmed, but that those whom I love will be harmed. What makes this fear rational is that I value things other than my own experiences, in this instance my children. And I value them for their own sake; I do not value my children only because they give me good experiences.

Now take the second case in which on Rowe's principles it is irrational for me to fear x, that in which I believe it possible for me to experience x but do not believe that if I do experience it I will experience it as bad. I may, because of religious belief or ethical persuasion, highly value being a certain sort of person. Suppose, for example, that, though I am rich, I wish to be the kind of person to whom virtue is important and money relatively unimportant. If I am not yet such a person, or not to a sufficient degree, I strongly desire and strive to become such; if I am, I take great care to continue as such. I exert myself to cultivate values such as justice, courage, temperance, prudence, love of God and love of neighbour (a love which will make me generous with my possessions), and to regard money as secondary. Some people might regard these values as noble, others might see them as foolish; but they are perfectly intelligible as values and have no tendency to appear as irrational, strictly unintelligible aims. But if it is important to me to be a person who lives according to these values, it will be correspondingly important to me not to be a person who lives according to other, incompatible values. If I value virtue above all, what I may dread above all is becoming the kind of person to whom the accumulation of money is all-important. That is, if I value being the kind of person to whom money is unimportant I will correspondingly fear failing to become or remain such a person; I will fear becoming avaricious, if I see it as a possibility that I might become such (which I will do if I am aware of my own frailty). Such fear is the logical corollary, the negative side, of my positive values. In Rowe's terms, I fear becoming an avaricious person because, from my point of view, it is an intrinsic evil rather than an extrinsic evil. I fear it, not because of any consequences that might flow from being such a person, but in itself, simply because I very much do not want to be that sort of person, but desire very strongly to be an incompatible sort of person. As the value that gives rise to it is perfectly rational, so the fear to which it gives rise is a perfectly intelligible fear, even if it is one that not all share. Many of us want to be a certain kind of person and consequently fear, want to avoid, being another sort of person.

However – and this is the important point – I may be perfectly aware that if what I fear comes to pass, if I do become a person to whom money is all-important, I will not experience this state as bad. On the contrary, I may realize that if I do become avaricious I will delight all the more in my wealth for valuing it so highly. I will still respect myself and even be proud of myself. I will not criticize or despise myself for having so deeply failed to live up to my values, for they will not be my values any longer. My values will have changed, and it is precisely this possibility that I now dread. On Rowe's principles, however, this fear would be strictly unintelligible, for though I will be alive and often conscious if what I fear comes to pass, I will not experience it as bad. That it is on the contrary quite intelligible shows once again that Rowe's approach is false.

Rowe holds that we can rationally fear x only if the occurrence of x would be a bad experience for us (x is intrinsically bad for us) or if x will cause us to have bad experiences or not to have good experiences (x is extrinsically bad for us). But we can also rationally fear x, as the above examples show, if we believe it possible for x to occur and if the occurrence of x would be incompatible with our values. The more strongly we hold our values the greater may be our rational fear of x occurring. The greater the probability of x occurring the more it is rational to fear the occurrence of x. All this is true even if, necessarily, as in the above examples, we could not experience x as bad, or experience it at all. Once again, it is value that turns out to be central; as earlier it was value rather than well-being, something's being bad rather than its being bad *for me*, that was the correct concept to work with in understanding people's attitude to their experiences, so now it is value rather than experience which must be borne in mind in assessing the rationality of fear.

These considerations apply to the fear of our own death. As the general principle that we fear things necessarily because we believe them bad for us is false, so it is also untrue that we necessarily fear death because we believe it bad for us. We may rationally fear death, not because we think it will be bad for us, but because our future death is bad *from our point of view*. We may do so, as the above examples show, though we do not believe our death will be a bad experience or deprive us of good experiences. We will have such a rational fear if our death is incompatible with or detrimental to people or things that we value. *One* of the things we may value very highly is our own life, being alive, the sheer ability to act, relate and have experiences – good and bad – in the world.[16] If so, our death will be the end of something we value highly. In that case it is rational for us to fear our own death; we can give as the reason for our fear of death that it is the end of our life. If we value our own life greatly, it is rational for us to fear death greatly. Death is also unavoidable. In such circumstances we may rationally *dread* death. This is so, not because death harms us or deprives us of anything, or because we imagine that being dead will give us bad experiences. The Epicurean argument that fear of death is irrational since when we are dead nothing can harm us because we will experience nothing is entirely beside the point.[17] We fear death because we value life; we want very much to remain alive and dying is incompatible with remaining alive. We value acting in the world and experiencing the world, and we do not want our acting and experiencing to cease. This cessation is precisely what we dread. (It may be necessary to stress once again that we do not dread *experiencing* that cessation; or if we do, that is a different fear from dreading the cessation itself.) Jeff McMahan puts the point thus:

> The Epicurean simply denies what most of us believe. Death, he claims, cannot be bad for us because when it occurs we will not exist at all. But that is precisely what we object to: that we will not exist when we might otherwise be enjoying the benefits of life.[18]

If I fear death in this way I may or not express my fear by saying that my death will be a bad thing for me; though I confess it sounds very odd to me, for reasons explained above, to describe my death in this way. But this is a secondary matter; the question at issue is not whether my death is properly described as bad for me but whether it is rational to fear death. The above considerations show that it is.

IV

What is central in one's attitude towards death, then, is not calculation of possible good or bad experiences but values. Having good experiences may be one of the things that I value, but if I am halfway decent as a person I will value much else besides. I may value – love – particular people and institutions. If I do I will care about what happens to them, including what happens to them after my death. My own potential experiences, losses or injuries are simply irrelevant to these values. To the extent that I love another, I am concerned not with what is good or bad for me but with what is good or bad for him. I care not about what I might experience but about what he might experience, and about what sort of person he may become, what values he may come to hold.

One result of the foregoing discussion is that it is impossible to discuss whether death is a bad thing *in general*, as if everybody's death were bad for them or could rationally only be a matter of indifference to them, and as if the badness or otherwise of every person's death were a matter of brute fact.[19] On the contrary, the value of death varies from person to person. The badness of a person's death for that person depends on what he values, and on how what he values is or may be affected by his death.

At this point we can begin to see that Rowe's alleged dilemma, with which we started, is illusory and that it can after all make sense to speak of transcending death, even if we assume with Rowe and other modern writers that we in no sense survive our death. It is not true, as Rowe asserts, that either death is bad or it isn't. I can *make* my death bad from my point of view or good from my point of view, or indifferent, or a greater or lesser evil, by the values that I hold and cultivate. I cannot avoid my death, but I can transcend my death by making it into something I do not need to avoid. If I fear death I can make my coming death into something I need not fear. I can do this by cultivating values with which my death is compatible and by extirpating values with which may death is incompatible. I can, for example, cultivate detachment from my selfish ambitions and encourage myself to be indifferent to wealth and other self-centred considerations; I can die to self. Desire is perhaps essential to life, but I can live according to generous desires rather than self-seeking ones. This is not self-deception, a matter of closing my eyes to the brute fact of the badness of death. Nor is it a matter of coming to realize through argument that death is not bad after all and does not need to be transcended. Rather, by changing my values, and hence my way of life, I change the relation that my death bears to my life so that it is no longer the destroyer of what I hold dear. I can overcome death, not by escaping it, but by robbing it of its sting. This possibility is offered by several classical religious and ethical systems.

I can, then, value, not merely living, but living in a certain way. My overriding and all-embracing concern may be, for example, not simply to continue to live but to live a life of virtue, to be a virtuous person. If I am not yet virtuous, living in this way is a goal for me. Since I have a goal which I have not yet achieved, I am still importantly subject to death: there is a chance that it will come before I have become virtuous. I may then still rationally fear premature death, that is, that I may die before I achieve my goal. If I succeed in becoming virtuous my death, when it comes, will not be premature, and I can face death with equanimity (unless some other unfulfilled ambition supervenes).[20] The fact that I have lived in this way, that I have already constructed the kind of life I valued, makes my value safe from death.[21]

This approach to life has its downside. Depending on what my selfless values are and on the circumstances of my life, it may become impossible for me to continue to live in the way that I value, or it may become clear that I have definitively and irremediably failed to live in that way.[22] In such a case I can be prepared or even willing to die rather than to continue to live otherwise than I would wish. For example, I may place supreme value on living honourably, according to whatever code of honour I subscribe to. This may be so important to me that when I dishonour myself in a moment of weakness I willingly kill myself; here my suicide is an expression of a conviction that life without honour is not worth living.[23] To die in these circumstances is not to die happy, but to have lived in this way is to have lived a life in which the dread of death plays at most a small part, and so to have transcended death.

Much of the modern philosophical discussion about death assumes that people are totally self-regarding, that they have no values or loves or hates that transcend the limits of their own interests and their own lives. What a person considers bad he does so because he sees his own interests being badly affected by it. Thus, for example, Joel Feinberg writes:

> There is nothing a normal person (in reasonable health and tolerable circumstances) dreads more than his own death, and that dread, in the vast majority of cases, is as rational as it is unavoidable, for unless we continue alive, we have no chance whatever of achieving those goals that are the ground of ultimate interest.[24]

His main point, that dread of death can be rational, is one I have shown to be correct. But one wonders what notion of normality Feinberg is working with here. If it is a normative view of normality, if dreading one's own death more than anything else is being proposed as a criterion of normality, then his view of what constitutes a normal person strikes me as narrow and impoverished.[25] If on the other hand, Feinberg's remark is intended to express a statistical truth, it is doubtful whether he is correct. I recently saw it reported that more American women fear being fat than dying.[26] A possible implication is that some American women value thinness more than life. Perhaps some are prepared to die rather than become fat. If so, this is not a good approach to life. But still, it illustrates the point that there are things that ordinary people value above simply living, and so that there are things they fear more than death. Somewhat more nobly, many ordinary people have, it seems, feared harm to their loved ones or their country more than their own death and have been prepared to die to protect the people or things they valued.

Many people, perhaps most people, actually do care about, value, other people and other things, and they value them for themselves, not for what they can contribute to their own well-being. Indeed, valuing these other people and things for themselves often itself contributes significantly to the well-being of the one who values them. Holding such values can in certain circumstances give one reason to fear one's own death. If my death will be harmful to somebody or something else that I value, this also is a reason for me to fear dying. If I fear that my children will be impoverished by my death, that is also a reason for me to fear dying.[27] But this is a special circumstance. In general, if I have lived a life of love for others (so that, for example, I have properly provided for my children) they will not be harmed by my death, though they may be greatly saddened by it; so I need not fear that my death will harm them. To that extent my values will not be harmed by my death, so my death will not be an object of fear to me.

The fear of death can be rational, because we can give a reason for it (rather than simply a cause for it, by appeal to some alleged instinct for life, as Rowe does in the last part of his paper).[28] Given that most of us value at least our lives, our fear of death *is* rational, in the sense of being intelligible; the reason that we fear death is that we value our lives. This is not to say that it is always a sensible fear. My fear of death can be sensible if it stems from my concern not to leave my children impoverished. In this case I might be able to do something about it, to provide adequately for their future before I die. If I can do this my fear of dying, in so far as it is this altruistic fear, will disappear, and I can die content. But if I fear death simply because I value seeking and having enjoyable experiences or for other self-regarding reasons I am bound to be overtaken one day by what I fear. I can only hope that death will come upon me unawares so that I am spared the horror of facing my own extinction at close quarters, and this is a very uncertain hope.

V

There are values for which people give their lives, in the sense both that they devote their lives to them and that they are prepared to die in their pursuit. Let us call these values *ideals*. An example of an ideal is communism. A idealistic communist might spend his adult life working for the hoped-for revolution, and willingly give up his life in an act, for example a suicidal bomb attack, which he thinks will help to bring it about. He may prefer to live rather than to die, but see his own death as a price well worth paying to further the ideal to which he has devoted his life. Or again, an idealistic Christian may spend her life living by and spreading the Christian gospel and Christian values, and happily face death for doing so at the hands of a hostile tyrant. In this case her prospective death might seem not only a price well worth paying in pursuit of her ideals, but actually to have a positive value as a powerful witness to those ideals. Her death helps to bring about those values to which she has consecrated her life.

It is an important feature of ideals that they are often shared. Individual communists and Christians are members of movements, groups of like-minded people working towards broadly the same end. When the individual group member dies the cause does not die with him, and his death can be a contribution to the cause that will be carried on afterwards by others. This is an important difference between ideals and selfish or self-centred goals. I may devote my life to my own enrichment, where I pursue riches not because of their instrumental value to me, not because they help me get other things I value, such as comfort or power, but for their own sake; I see the possession of wealth as valuable in its own right and set out to realize this value. This is a selfish goal, and it is a feature of it that, however successful I am at achieving it during my lifetime, it dies with me. I cannot be rich if I am dead. If anybody is to pursue the goal of making me rich, this requires that I be alive. Of course I personally cannot pursue this value after I am dead, since I cannot then pursue any value; but neither can anybody else pursue it. I may during my lifetime enlist the help of numerous people in the project of making myself rich, but once I die these others cannot continue to work for the same end.

It is a feature of many selfish values that they die with the one who holds them. If I hold such a selfish value, then my death means the destruction of that value. If I value being rich, then when I die a state which I value, my being rich, will no longer obtain.[29] Since this state is something I value it is rational for me to anticipate its cessation with distress, to fear it. Since its cessation is certain when I die, it is rational for me to fear my death, as the moment of its cessation. Such values are, we may say, subject to death in a way that ideals are not. To live dominated by such values is to lead a life in which it is rational to fear death greatly. To live one's life according to an ideal, on the other hand, is to have little reason to fear death. To be converted, to pass from one way of life to the other, is greatly to reduce one's reasons to fear death; it is to render one's future death relatively innocuous, and to that extent to transcend death; to overcome the obstacle, to defeat the enemy.

Religions are ideals. A particular religion may or may not have much to say about death and what, if anything, happens to a person at or after death. Regardless of the actual belief content of a religion concerning death, its formal character as an ideal means that a person whose life is devoted to a religion has less reason to fear death as such than somebody who lives according to selfish values; he may exclaim with St Paul: 'O death, where is thy sting?'

NOTES

1. Ludwig Wittgenstein, 'Lectures on Religious Belief', *Lectures and Conversations*, ed. Cyril Barrett (Oxford: Basil Blackwell, 1966), 53–72.
2. D.Z. Phillips, *Death and Immortality* (London: Macmillan, 1970).
3. In this he follows Fred Feldman in his article 'Some Puzzles About Death', *The Philosophical Review* 100, no. 2 (April 1991), 205–27, reprinted in John Martin Fischer (ed.), *The Metaphysics of Death* (Stanford, California: Stanford University Press, 1993), 307–26, though Rowe's argumentation is free from the references to possible worlds which unduly complicate Feldman's article.
4. Epicurus's argument, in the translation used by Rowe (pp. 137–8), goes as follows:

   So death, the most terrifying of ills, is nothing to us, since so long as we exist, death is not with us; but when death comes, then we do not exist. It does not then concern either the living or the dead, since for the former it is not, and the latter are no more.

5. Rowe appears to concede this later when he acknowledges that 'Some will undoubtedly object that we have not given much content

to the idea of intrinsic value, and have stated no criteria for determining what things are intrinsically good, intrinsically bad, or intrinsically neutral' (p. 137).

6.   See 'Death' in Thomas Nagel, *Mortal Questions* (Cambridge:
Cambridge University Press, 1979), 1–10.

7.   Rowe is in fact at this stage in his argument about to modify this
characterization of extrinsic good, by allowing that something may
be extrinsically good if it prevents intrinsically bad experiences. But
this modification does nothing to weaken the link between intrinsic
value for a person and that person's experience; on the contrary, it
strengthens it.

8.   Of course an intrinsically good experience may still be extrinsically
bad for me if it causes a bad experience. For example, an intrinsically
good experience of drug-taking may be extrinsically bad for me if it
causes me to suffer in life through neglecting my work, or if it later
causes pain or illness.

9.   Note that this interpretation proceeds from Rowe's *assumption* that
'nothing can be intrinsically valuable for a person at a time if the
person is not alive and conscious at that time' (p. 137). However, in
the footnote attached to this sentence (note 4), Rowe appears to
present this rather as a matter of definition: 'A person's being conscious is ... a necessary condition for a state of affairs being intrinsically valuable for that a person. ... A state of affairs is
intrinsically bad for [a person] S just in the event that it consists in
S's being in some conscious state that is intrinsically bad.' There is
plainly some tension here; that S be alive and conscious cannot be
both an assumption and a stipulation. Although I am unhappy
with it as an assumption, it seems to me that treating it as a stipulation makes matters worse, since Rowe would then have the
problem of showing that what he defines as being *intrinsically bad
for a person* is also *bad for a person* as that is normally understood.
Unless he can show this (and he makes no attempt to do so), his
whole argument runs the risk of irrelevance, since for him the
philosophical problem of death is the problem of whether it is *bad
for the person* who dies.

10.   That Rowe must be prepared to countenance some very wide view of
experience is clear from his view that being happy is an intrinsic
good for a person (see p. 135 and p. 147 note 3). Although having
various experiences may contribute to somebody's happiness, being
happy is itself hardly an experience in normal usage.

11.   Not everything: I may fear that I *have missed* the train, or that it *is*
raining.

12.   We may want to add the possibility of something's being injurious to
a person's mental health or spiritual health.

13.   Stephen Rosenbaum, discussing the thwarting of desires, writes:

> The very concept of something being bad for one is in need of
> some careful examination. However, it seems plain that it is not
> generally correct that what thwarts a person's desires is bad for

that person. ('Epicurus and Annihilation' in Fischer, *The Metaphysics of Death*, p. 300, reprinted from *The Philosophical Quarterly* 39, no. 154 (January 1989), 81–90.)

Rowe does not discuss death as a thwarter of desire, but Rosenbaum's remarks are nonetheless pertinent to the present discussion: the experience of having my desires thwarted may be a bad experience, but it will not normally be an experience that is bad for me; indeed, it may be rather salutary. Rosenbaum's observation on the need for study of what it is for something to be bad for one finds justification here.

14. Thus he writes, offering a definition of what it is for something to be intrinsically bad for a person:

> A state of affairs is intrinsically bad for S just in the event that it consists in S's being in some conscious state that is intrinsically bad. For example, S's *being in pain* is intrinsically bad for S since it consists in S's being in a conscious state that is intrinsically bad. (note 4)

I have already referred to this note in another context. Here I would add two things. First, it is simply wrong to say that somebody's being in pain is bad for that person, even if he and everybody else concur that being in pain is a bad experience. It does not help to make this error a matter of definition. Second, there are difficulties with the idea that a conscious state might be intrinsically bad. Rowe would find it difficult on this basis to deal with somebody, such as a masochist, who claimed that a particular experience of pain was a *good* experience.

15. It is worth noting that Feldman, whom Rowe seems to follow to an extent, also seeks to determine whether death is a bad thing by assessing its affect on that person's welfare, calculating whether it is bad *for* her, rather than being that to which she attaches negative value. He also seeks to do this by attaching intrinsic goodness and badness to experience (pleasure and pain). However, unlike Rowe, Feldman focuses on experience in this way merely as a device to make his argument against Epicurus as weak and narrow as possible, yet still sufficiently strong (as he believes) to show Epicurus wrong. See Fischer, *The Metaphysics of Death*, p. 311.

16. As a matter of psychology, it may be that we are more likely to value life in this way if our experiences have been good, our relationships fulfilling, our activities successful. But this does not mean that what we really value is good experiences, fulfilling relationships and successful activities. To say this would be to confuse the cause of a value with its content or object.

17. This is not to say that it may not be an effective argument in Epicurus's own terms, if only good and bad experiences are in fact valued. But the argument does not show that experiences are the

only possible bearers of value. Part of the point of my own argument is to show that they are not.

18. 'Death and Value of Life' in Fischer, *The Metaphysics of Death*, p. 241, reprinted from *Ethics* 99, no. 1 (October 1988), 32–61.

19. Rowe appears to subscribe to something like this view. Thus he makes remarks such as 'If death were not a bad thing and we came to see that it is really not a bad thing, the problem of transcending death would simply go away' (p. 134); and 'If [death] really is a bad thing ... We can perhaps engage in some kind of self-deception whereby we gloss over the fact that it is bad, or get ourselves to think of it as not bad ... But this won't get rid of the badness of death' (ibid).

20. Thus, though there is an obvious biological sense in which death can be premature, a person's values enter into the question of what constitutes premature death for that person.

21. It is also possible to construct a goal which is not subject to the danger of premature death. Instead of making it my goal to live virtuously I can have the closely related goal of striving to live virtuously. Then my daily (and perhaps often failed) attempts at virtue will be not a struggle towards my goal but the living of my goal itself.

22. It is one of the interesting aspects of Christianity that according to its vision of life one can never during one's life fail irredeemably. Even in the last moments of a wasted life it is possible to turn to God in repentance and so to make a good death. This is not to make it true that one's life was good after all, but to accept the redemption by God of a wasted life.

23. And perhaps also a way of re-affirming my commitment to my code of honour.

24. 'Harm to Others', in Fischer, *The Metaphysics of Death*, p. 73, reprinted from Joel Feinberg, *Harm to Others* (Oxford: Oxford University Press, 1984), 79–95.

25. Unless Feinberg intends the phrase 'tolerable circumstances' to do a lot of work. He may allow, for example, that having behaved dishonourably is an intolerable circumstance. This does not, though, appear to be the spirit of his remarks.

26. This was reported in a documentary film, *The Famine Within*, about anorexia, shown on American television in November 1995.

27. Once again, that fear is not shown to be irrational by the consideration that I will not be around to see their impoverishment, and I would be offended by any philosopher – surely nobody else could make such a suggestion – who offered this consideration to me by way of consolation as I faced death.

28. See particularly p. 144. Here he quotes Jung, who speaks of death as 'that dark wall, which threatens to swallow up irretrievably all I love, desire, possess, hope, and strive for'; when he contemplates death, 'then all the wise dicta go into hiding and fear descends upon the sleepless like a choking blanket'. Rowe's point in quoting Jung is to give these words as an example of what a bad

experience the fear of death is, and it is a very convincing example. However, what Jung is plainly doing here is giving *reasons*, and pretty compelling ones at that, for his fear of death; he is showing that his fear of death is rational.

29.   Note that this is not true of fame. Instead of devoting my life to the pursuit of wealth for its own sake, I may devote it to the pursuit of fame for its own sake (I may perhaps pursue wealth as a means to becoming famous). I may enlist others, such as publicity agents, to help me. Though I cannot be rich after my death, I can be famous after my death, and others can continue to work to that end after my death. This no doubt accounts for why many people have pursued fame rather than wealth.

Part Six
Transcending the Human?

12
Transcending the Human[1]

Marina Barabas

'Transcendence' is a word which has largely disappeared from our discourse, and that is perhaps as it should be for so, it seems, has the *concern* with it from our lives. As for the *concept*, it subsists in the thin atmosphere of scholarship rather than normal – ordinary or philosophical – discourse; in theology rather than religion; in the unfamiliar Eastern or the esoteric Occult. The consequent difficulty in reaching the *issue* through ordinary language justifies, perhaps even necessitates, dropping it – unless one thinks, or feels, that there *is* an issue. In that case, however, one needs to recover the issue in the absence of language, perhaps even save it from the language. In the following I will nevertheless try to get some grip on the concept so as to attempt its analysis. If this fails I will try the more troublesome analysis of 'experience'. Ideally, of course, the two should come together in a better understanding of how *we speak* about what *we think and feel*. But that is to be hoped for rather than aimed at. Though 'transcendence' seems largely moribund, other members of the family, most noticeably the verb 'to transcend', have some life left in them and so offer an opening for an inquiry. We encounter 'transcend' in newspapers, in public addresses, in advertisements for vacuum-cleaners, not just in recondite journals or flyers for yoga classes. With this assurance of its respectable proletarian nature, we can set out upon the road of conceptual analysis, in the hope of either (dis)solving the problem or discovering one.

I PURSUING THE DIVINE

Human beings want to be immortal and ageless.[2]

As verbs go, 'transcend' packs a reasonable punch. Besides sounding good it's also a true verb in that, unlike 'suffer' or 'dream', it expresses active effort. To transcend is to *move*; what's more, it is to move *beyond*, and so not just away from but also towards something. And it is to move *purposefully*, and so not just to shift or fidget.

I move purposefully away from something because it's undesirable or bad; I move towards something because it's desirable or good. This locates the issue of transcending within the general context of value and the response to it. Put in terms of moving, we get good as goal, response as pursuit; put in terms of action, we get good as purpose, response as seeking to attain.

It further suggests that behind action lies *dissatisfaction* with what one has, *desire* to have something else; behind going lies *not wanting* to be *here*, *wanting* to be *there*. From the standpoint of the agent 'there' is *better*, 'here' is *worse*. 'Moving from worse to better' is, after all, constitutive of purposeful motion, of rational action.

But if so constitutive, then 'worse/not wanted' or 'better/wanted' are formal, that is contentless, terms which can be of no help in designating the goal. And how can we pursue, let alone 'attain what is fitting' without a 'clear target to aim at'.[3] Turning to the title – 'Transcending the Human' – for help, we get 'human' as that away from which to move, and so, implicitly, the 'divine' as the goal. Yet given the notorious protean tendency of 'divine' and 'human' to change their shape according to the mouth of the speaker, relying on them may be using the threadbare to patch a hole.

Yet perhaps not so: doubling the formal need not just double the useless; rubbing pieces of dead wood can produce an illuminating spark, even a warming fire. Under a certain treatment grapes yield wine, not just grape-juice; subjected to a right kind of analysis, concepts yield the 'clarification' of the *elenchos*.

So taking the expression 'Transcending the Human' we get the suggestion of human beings experiencing their condition as not (wholly) good, even undesirable, and straining away from it; conceiving some other, the divine, as better or more desirable, and straining towards it. We get the suggestion of men fearing and disliking certain aspects of their condition and desiring others conceivable from within but not part of that condition; and wanting to be rid of the former and possess the latter.

A conceptual analysis should record not just the intuitions of the speaker, but also the response of the listener. The response of an ordinary man to the idea of climbing out of the human because it's worse, and climbing into the divine because it's better, is likely to be: I don't know what you mean. This isn't a request for clarification but a polite way of saying 'Don't talk nonsense!' or, coming from a religious man, 'Don't blaspheme!' The first response would end our project on grounds of feasibility, the second on those of permissibility.

But with the divine at stake, we won't let this deter us. Instead we'll add these would-be-brush-off's to our collection of formal criteria and try to remember that our findings should make not just ordinary but also normative sense.

A vigorous development of these assumptions is offered by Martha Nussbaum in her article 'Transcending the Human', where she not only tackles the issue of transcending humanity, but also tries to recover it from the dead wood of scholarly irrelevance. She does this by presenting transcending as a real – albeit a fictional – choice:

> Odysseus tells Calypso, once again, that he's determined to leave her. Once again, she offers him a bargain that no human being, it seems, could refuse.[4]

On offer is the divine itself, this time substantively spelt out: 'human self-transcendence' of 'anthropomorphic perfection [viz.] the removal of constraints that make human life a brief, chancy and in many ways miserable existence', primarily those of toil, suffering, aging and death.[5] And since 'human beings want to be immortal and ageless' there is here no question of the desirability and so also none of the sense of the enterprise: 'The desire to transcend humanity and to take up the life of a god with a god is a perfectly intelligible and even a highly reasonable desire'.[6]

Indeed, *qua* negation of the not-wanted, the divine is, by definition, 'wanted', (and so) 'better'. And since the 'wanted' is offered as a gift,[7] there's here no problem changing wanting to willing, desire to choice. The logical tie between 'better', 'want' and 'choice'[8] makes it impossible for Odysseus not to choose the divine. And yet – inexplicably? mysteriously? – this is just what he does.

Having thus resuscitated a dead issue by turning it into someone's problem Nussbaum addresses her real task: to consign the issue to its proper place – the graveyard of misconceived human and philosophical aspirations.

Her argument is in three parts: (1) (sections i–iii) examine and approve Odysseus' 'choice'; (2) (section iv) considers and rejects the philosophical project of transcending humanity; (3) (section v) rejects the invitation to transcend human vulnerability by eliminat-

ing emotions. But since the choice of Odysseus remains central
we'll concentrate on it.

The question is thus: how *can* Odysseus – logically, psychologically – reject Calypso's gift? How can he not desire the desirable,
not choose the divine? In answer we're offered a new, *human*, logic
of choice: choice not of the better, but of what is 'simply ours':

> [Odysseus chooses] the whole human package: mortal life,
> dangerous voyage, imperfect mortal woman. He is choosing
> quite simply what is his.[9]

A yokel refusing to *choose*, stubbornly or fearfully clinging to what
is his, is of no interest. But Odysseus the *Polymetis*, the by-word for
intrepid resourcefulness, can't be so dismissed. His 'choice' thus
confronts us with the question of *true* value, of the *proper* object of
love: is love to be of what is *good* or of what is *ours*? If of ours, is this
because, *qua* measure of *good* and bad, it itself lies beyond measur-
ing, or because we owe it loyalty simply *qua* ours? The passage suggests the latter, the argument the former.[10]

Yet it quickly transpires that in 'choosing' the human Odysseus
does not stay with what is *simply* his, nor loyally stand by what is
simply *his*, but that he instead holds onto what is *better*. The
human is the proper *choice*, though it takes a man heroically
cunning to see through gods' false pretenses. We'd see it too,
Nussbaum hints, if we but heeded our narrative intuitions: 'the
affectionate reader's preference is likely to be for a hero who goes,
so to speak, where the action is, so that he can go and achieve
the things with which human heroism is usually associated'.[11]

Indeed more. Life with Calypso – this 'life of a god with a god' –
would, like Calypso herself, be 'boring and monotonous': it 'would
bring the story to the end'. It's not despite, but because of, their
constraints that humans are 'more interesting', the human couple
'more erotic'.[12]

Nussbaum now proceeds to ground our mytho-philic intuitions
philosophically and morally. Taking the example of athletics she
argues that it's an activity *constituted* by pushing against the limits;
then, extending this claim to activity in general, she argues that the
gods, 'lacking certain limits and defects which characterize human
life are strangely different',[13] their life 'just not comprehensible as a
life for a human being'.[14] *Qua* incomprehensible, the divine is also
unwantable: the unintelligible can't be desired. But what's at stake

is meaning as *value*, not just as logic. For life of and with Calypso is incomprehensible 'for a human being with human *virtues* and human heroism': the *good* of athletic contest lies precisely in pushing against limits. The argument for the interdependence of limits, efforts and value is now extended to virtues, to human actions and relations in general, still more broadly, to social and political life. Everything in human life depends for its meaning – in both senses – on our physicality, neediness, and mortality. The divine, just because it knows no want, lacks projects and so also efforts and virtues needed to attain them; it is without fine qualities and admirable achievements. In fact, boring and unadmirable. Odysseus thus chooses not what is his, but what is, at least for the humans, better. Indeed, as gods' habitual infatuation with the mortals suggests, man may be 'the measure of all things, human and divine', not just for men, but also for the gods.

Our true goal should be 'inner transcendence': pushing against the human limits from within, seeking the *better human* rather than the divine: improving and creating our world and ourselves in the world by thinking mortal thoughts, loving mortal beings and pursuing mortal ends. We are, with final irony, referred to Diotima for the lesson that 'it is only when one gives up on the aspiration to external transcendence … that one will begin to pursue (with good results for the world) the other sort'.[15]

There are several problems with this argument, starting with the example. Odysseus does not tell Calypso that he *wants* to leave but is told by her that he *must*. And he must because she must. Athena, tired of her favourite being held at Ogygia, uses Poseidon's absence to cajole Zeus into forcing Calypso to release Odysseus. Here there are no choices and so no bargains, let alone gifts. From above come commands backed with force, from below obedience laced with bitterness; those above choose what they want, those below do and suffer what they must. Odysseus, the hero of this article which holds up choice-propelled activity as that true good in whose name we thumb our nose at the divine, is, in the story, essentially a sufferer. He is not just *polymetis*, the resourceful one, but *pathetos*, the 'patient/suffering' one.[16] Indeed the main lesson of the *Odyssey* is that, for all its importance, careful choice and pursuit of projects is not wisdom; that for all the need of heroism for action, greater heroism still is needed to endure.

But though Odysseus doesn't have a choice, he's certainly glad to leave, and so can be said to choose it. For his life with Calypso is 'suffered' not because it's not chosen, but because it's forced upon him and because it's dreadful. He doesn't desire the (better) human over the (worse) divine, but *good human* life – as king, husband, father, friend – over unbearable *human vegetation* – as prisoner with days spent in speech- and activity-less solitude, nights spent performing amorous services to a no longer desired woman. Here deathlessness and agelessness don't mean divinity but the never-endingness of hell.[17]

The example can't be ignored, for, besides remaining the focus of the discussion, it also provides the specification of the divine: the purported *telos* of transcending. The divine is – Calypso: an ordinary woman with the ordinary needs of someone to love and something to do who, lacking both, spends her days outside a cave spinning cloths for no one to wear, her nights inside the cave dreaming of things being different – for ever and ever. The divine so described would indeed put an end to the transcendental *Wanderlust*. But then, so described, it could never have generated it. The argument against transcendence based on the prospect of living with and as Calypso would be a *reductio ad absurdum* were it not directed against a straw 'person'.

For it is not Calypso who uproots man from his natural habitat. She is a far cry even from the Olympic gods,[18] who in turn are worlds apart from that divine which has awakened the transcendental aspiration. But why? Aren't 'the gods ... better than us, worthy of our worship and emulation'? Since 'better' suggests a continuity between the things compared – here the human and the divine – we must see how the gods are better and so also what form of worship and emulation is – conceptually and normatively – possible. We're told that they are better in that 'They lack certain limits and defects that characterize human life', namely 'They are immortal ... healthy and vigorous ... always in their prime ... They have what they want without effort'.[19] This substantive characterization of gods' superiority confirms the suggestion of a continuity between the human and the divine: the gods are what we are, only better, they have what we want, only more so. This not only shows the divine as *ours* but, more importantly, as simplistically, that is *naturalistically*, ours: as the human minus certain naturalist (rather than for example moral or spiritual) undesirables. To the extent to which this is a true depiction of the Olympians, we can see why their contribution to the Greek transcendental awakening was something to *reject* rather than a *telos* to pursue. And to reject not as 'boring' or 'strangely different', but as *menschlich, allzu menschlich*.[20] Not only does the Olympian-, let alone the Calypso-divine, not contain any new values, but those that it contains are of the lesser kind.

The problem with the example is thus not its being directed against a straw man, but its *begging the question*. For underlying the focus on the choice of Odysseus are naturalist assumptions about value and the response to it, which in turn determine the substance and the logic of the argument. It's these assumptions, which locate value in Calypso and our response to value in our reaction to her, which need examining. Particularly so since these assumptions appeared claiming a conceptual status in our opening analysis of 'transcend'.

As we saw, Calypso is the embodiment of naturalist goods. The response to these is want: indeed it is only *qua* wanted that they are goods. This stringent intentionality – mutual constitutiveness of object and response – permits clarification of one through the other. We'll begin with (the experience of) want and see what kind of object it constructs.

Want has an internal and an external side. Internally it's a desire to have/enjoy or to avoid something. (It's an important feature of natural goods that the positive and the negative relation to them has the same logic.)[21] But since wanting implies being 'in want', that is lacking the good, want must turn into willing or become unsatisfied desire. This transforms the good, already assumed to be 'that at which all things aim'[22] (especially when, as with Calypso-value, it's in and of the world), into an object of the will. That is, where valuing means desiring, the desirous subject becomes the agent, the response to the good becomes pursuit – action in and of the world. In what was the first systematic philosophical development of this conception, Aristotle came to use the ordinary term *ephiesthai* – 'to aim at' or 'pursue'[23] – quasi-technically, virtually to define the 'practical'. *Ephiesthai* became not one, but *the* response to value; active response to value becomes desire-motivated movement in space.[24]

Once *ephiesthai* becomes the practical, that is the *response* to value *simpliciter*, it starts structuring the *recognition* of value and so also what *can* count as (relevant) value. The centrality of *ephiesthai* ensures that only a potential *object of pursuit* can be recognized as a relevant good. Hence the ease with which Aristotle disposes of Plato's Good: *qua* unpursuable it's *unpracticable*; *qua* unpracticable it can't be a relevant – ethical – *good*. From here it's but a step to either no longer seeing as good what is not a potential *telos*, or to forcing any value into the logical mould of a *telos*.[25]

When, as with Calypso-perfection, the good is not (logically) unpursuable but only unattainable, we get unsatisfied want. Unsatisfied want views those who are satisfied as (more) lucky. But 'more lucky' doesn't mean 'better'; it certainly doesn't make the lucky ones 'worthy of our worship and emulation'. One natural response to someone having what I want is envy; when he also has power over me, envy turns to fear and hate.[26]

But the external manifestation of want, as the Will, that is the transformation of the desirous subject into the agent, is but a consequence of the fact that want means being *in want* of the desired object. 'Being in want' implies the subject's imperfection;[27] while the transformation of wanting into willing promises some remedy of it. So with good defined as 'that which all things pursue', we get teleology in two senses: action as end-directed effort; successful action as the end of the effort. Success means *Aufhebung* as consummation and self-annulment. This is why perfection, construed as lack of lack, is for the modern Aristotelian[28] the epitome of the undesirable: life without activity, a story without a plot – an existence of dreadful boredom. Moreover, as we saw in connection with the dual sense of 'meaning', absurdity is threatened along with undesirability. For when the human is defined as essentially lacking, unintelligibility follows on removing that lack. Indeed, the 'transcendentalist' Greeks would be the first to insist that to de-*fine* is to de-*limit*:[29] that removing the limits means dissolution into the *apeiron* – into identity-less stuff. To talk of ignoring the limits is *ouden legein*: it is to talk of no-thing, nonsense.[30]

There are, however, different kinds of limits, and so also of transgression. Transgressing – or transcending – the limits involved in the Calypso-bargain is of the *nouveau riche* kind: innumerable dinners before innumerable TVs in innumerable rooms of innumerable houses, whose innumerable garages house innumerable cars – with no hunger to assuage or friends to feast, no work after which to relax, and nowhere to go in one's car. With none but natural wants on offer, 'transcending' means moving beyond the realm of meaning: sinking into senseless pleasurable undergoings.

The prospect of meaninglessness, however, doesn't deter us from overstepping limits even in the sphere of thought and speech, let alone of desires and pursuits. In the latter case, however, things are more complex: a mis-relation to the 'practical' – and so to value – is, after all, a mis-relation to *value*.

This transgression of the 'practical' limits takes different forms and invites different punishments. The most obvious is the transgression of immoderation: its punishment is sickness and, generally, the destruction of the very conditions of enjoyment. Its undesirability can thus be recognized by the subject himself given a minimal desire to continue in future as he is now, that is, a minimal concept of time and consequences.[31]

Nussbaum, however, is concerned with another dimension of transgression: the destruction of the *practical dimension* consequent on lacking lack. The real target of her attack is thus not transcendence but *modern hedonism*: the attempt to substitute enjoyment for happiness, sensuous satisfaction for activity. Here punishment is the loss of meaningful and structured practical life, of the thrill of activity and the happiness of attainment. But pointing to the prospect of structureless passivity will not convince a brain in the vat, not even a desirous subject, to exchange his existence of pleasurable input for a striving, perhaps a needy and anguished, life. If Nussbaum succeeds in convincing, this is not only because, unlike brains in vats, we recognize that present indulgence may carry undesirable future consequences, but because we also live our life as temporally and organically structured. More importantly, we recognize values other than those of enjoyment and so distinguish better and worse from more and less pleasurable. From within this 'enlightened human' perspective inactivity, however pleasure-filled, is a punishment not just because it's boring but also because it's unworthy.

Thus where the hedonist appeals to the subject's *actual* (present or future) desires, Nussbaum appeals to the *real* wants of an active human being. In both cases the rational individual (though rationality means different things for the desirous subject and for the human being) can see that he *has a reason* to refrain, that refraining is in his interest. But though in both cases this gives us a self-sufficient account, with motivation grounded in *self-love*, it also gives us an account where self-love seems the *only* possible motive. Indeed formally so: where the good is object of desire (the hedonist account), it can pull and push the desirous subject; where it is an object of want (Nussbaum's account), it can appeal to or attract the human agent. In neither case, however, can it *claim* or command: *qua* desired or wanted it has power but not *authority*.

Moreover, as we saw when we considered the relation between the good and the response to it, to define the good as an object of pursuit, makes pursuit the *only* response to it. Yet life as a single-minded, 'aggressive' pursuit of one's wants is not merely imprudently immoderate, nor ignobly passive, but rather ruthless and greedy. At this point we get a third transgression of limits, namely *hybris*. This crime is unrecognizable by the hedonist as well as the Aristotelian, for it's not a crime against *oneself*, but against the order of things. As wanting more and more, *hybris* is the vice of intemperance, the evil of greed; as readiness to go where it takes to get what one wants, it is the vice and evil of injustice and violence.

The initial 'conceptual analysis' portrayal of transcending as going or reaching for the better/divine is thus in difficulties: 'better' and 'worse' seem an inadequate reason, 'want' an inappropriate motive. It is not proper to climb over the fence because the grass is greener on the other side; to move out of the human out of desire for more and better human; to move (in)to the divine propelled by self-love. And if one does? If, perhaps by building a tower, one seeks an entry into heaven? Then he will fail, for such enterprise is nonsensical. 'Nonsense', however, as we saw, is not just a descriptive category: *ouden legeis* means 'Don't talk nonsense!' In relation to value, nonsense means culpable transgression: in relation to true value, *ephiesthai* translates into greed and violence, in relation to the divine into blasphemy and sacrilege.

Our dry sticks of wood seem thus to have generated a fire rather than a mere spark. That they ended up consumed by that fire is the sad consequence of their being beyond the call of duty. The analysis of the seemingly formal terms dissolves the problem. Or – the road ends here for the Naturalist. Should he feel that the journey was not worth the effort, he is right; but then, he should never have undertaken it.

Things, however, are more troublesome for one for whom there *is* an issue. For how, if not by analysing what *we* say or want, is he to proceed; how, if not through the idea of an end-directed effort, is he to make sense of activity and so of transcending? With 'analysis' discredited, he must turn to experience. Yet the absurdity of the very idea of *transcendental experience* seems a clear invitation – or command – to desist. To continue means to do without a clear starting point or a clearly delineated target and so also without activity as purposeful and energetic pursuit. Here 'value' must be teased, even constructed, out of unclear stutterings and hesitant pointings, out of intimations of space to enter and, as importantly, of *limits* to respect. Such enterprise demands a personal authentication of both the experience and the language: it demands speaking *as* 'I' rather than *of* 'We, the human beings'.

II   FLEEING THE IMPERFECT

I will discourse with myself alone and look more deeply into myself …[32]

But what does it mean to say that the I is the starting point (and the destination?) of this quest? And how is one to proceed? The above 'look more deeply' suggests differentiation between the I at, and the I below, the *surface*, as well as a need of *effort* to move from the – presumably apparent – to the – hopefully real – I. 'Look' further suggests the effort to be that of understanding, its goal being discovery. What Descartes found in looking within himself was his imperfection; what he discovered was God.

But while this challenges the hedonist's claim that all experience is (equally) real, and that value is whatever happens to be desired, it won't take us beyond the Aristotelian position discussed in Part I, which begins with the apparent imperfection – revealed in the experience of want as deficiency which one desires to eliminate, confirmed by the analysis of 'transcend' – only to warn us against drawing the apparent (hedonist and philosophical) conclusion of the divine as without want and striving. There we were asked to look past the concrete experience of want, to the narrative intuition; past appearance's suggestion that 'it is right to call him who wants nothing happy' to the deeper insight that 'In that case stones and corpses would be supremely happy'.[33] Which in turn allowed us to see past the apparent desirable of the divine as lacking lack, to the really desirable human as constituted by wants in whose pursuit we 'become deeper and more spacious'.[34]

The clash between the claim of 'surface' naturalism that 'the amount of pleasure being the same pushpin is as good as poetry', and that of 'deep' naturalism that 'it is better to be a Socrates unsatisfied than a pig satisfied',[35] highlights the distinction between value as desired and as desirable: between the experientially potent and the authoritative. But it also raises the question of the latter's validity against the former. In the end, we are told, it is those who *experience* both who legitimately make and validate the distinction: in the end 'the sole evidence it is possible to produce that anything is desirable is that people do actually desire it'.[36] The distinction between appearance and reality, want and authority, is thus that between mere and valid experience, mere and real want. This takes us a long way, but not the whole way.

It won't account for the experience of *moral* imperfection: experience of imperfection as ordinary as that of desire, yet internally, or experientially, constituted by the distinction between experience and authority. This experience is ordinary in that it occurs in ordinary people on ordinary occasions, and finds expression in ordinary language: 'I acted cruelly, treacherously, ruthlessly'; 'I was fully of envy, greed, malice' – these are as ordinary as bread, as common as dirt. And yet the experience is puzzling, extraordinary, mysterious.

Compare it with (the imperfection of) wanting. Like wanting, moral imperfection is experienced as a deficiency of a kind, namely of goodness. Yet it differs from want in respect both of 'experience' and of 'content'. In the case of want, value is determined by the (actual or potential) desire: for instance, death is not an 'evil' unless one desires not to die. By contrast, non-dependence on wants or experience seems internal to the experience of (moral) evil.[37] But to say that 'evil' is not defined through (not) want – that it's *experienced* as *not-experiential* – is to treat (im)perfection as a non-natural concept. Here 'perfection' seems to escape Xenophanes' (and our) criticism of construing the divine as 'anthropomorphic perfection', that is, out of the human. But by that very fact it raises the problem of the origin and authority of the non-experiential which brought Descartes to the innate idea of God; more generally, gave modern philosophy its major headache.

The problem is only aggravated by trying to deal with it through the *content* of the experience. Speaking of *deficiency* of goodness seems to re-introduce goodness as something wanted. After all, evil is what I want to be rid of, to lack goodness is to want it. The 'end' of eliminating evil seems to translate into the end of attaining goodness, thus positing the stance of *ephiesthai* as the 'practical' or 'moral' response. This seems logically so: the presence of a wanted object generates pursuit, and there can be no wanting without object/content. Such object, moreover, must be a clear and distinct *telos* to pursue. The experience of moral imperfection, however, seems deficient in both respects. In the above examples there is no 'end', let alone a clear and distinct one: attention is on what is, not on what might be. In this (first-personal)[38] experience, the *negative* remains irreducible: I'm conscious of the badness ('thickly' understood: ruthlessness, cruelty, envy) of my thoughts, feelings or actions. And though we may speak here of deficiency of *goodness*, this is not to suggest goodness as an end. Unlike in the Part I examples, the negative can't be turned into a positive with a simple negation sign (e.g. desire for immortality = not {not wanting to die}). To be appalled by my envy or treachery is not to be in pursuit of generosity or loyalty.

Indeed, far from goodness being an end, absorption in ends is the ordinary manifestation of the deficiency of goodness. Most forms of everyday badness mark my *commitment* to goods and ends: envy, meanness or ambition, manifest the importance I attach to goods; graspingness, ruthlessness or treachery, my resolute pursuit of them. Recognition of my badness is here a judgement on these ends, or on my involvement in them, rather than a criticism for not pursuing better ones.[39] To refrain from acting because it would be cruel or treacherous need not mean being motivated by desire to act compassionately or loyally. Such an assumption is indicative of simple logic and simplistic psychology.

One may be tempted to resolve the threat to intentionality contained in the claim that moral imperfection can't be spelt out in terms of special – moral – ends, by replacing particular ends with the End *simpliciter*, for example the Self. On this account the experience of moral imperfection, as it emerges in my absorption in particular ends, is an intimation that the real end or project is not the pursuit of particular projects, but of the Ideal Self.[40] By digging 'deeper' we thus discover the Self as the true or real good, with which to confront the apparent goods pursued by the self as given to immediate experience. This would solve the problem of intentionality: a meta-goal requires a meta-pursuit; as well as of authority: the higher *telos*, the nobler *ephiesthai*, legitimately challenges the lower ends and pursuits.

But intentionality is salvaged by this 'in-depth analysis' at the expense of the phenomena: these remain stubbornly negative. An envious thought, cruel wish, treacherous action, is felt as bad because of what *it* is, not for failing to be something else; my shudder at my so thinking, wishing or acting, is at my *so* thinking, etc., not at my failing to attain my *ideal* (generous, kind, etc.) self. Such 'positive' concern is not impossible but in these circumstances[41] it would be morally dubious. Transforming the negative into a positive would here be a *mis-* rather than a *re-*description of value.

Then the experience of moral imperfection is thus often the experience of what is – my thoughts, etc.; myself as so thinking, etc. – as simply bad, unacceptable, impossible. This 'simply', however, is far from simple. It offends against the fundamental naturalist credo of 'What is actual is possible'. How can that which 'is' be impossible; how can something be bad, let alone impossible, unless there be something – end, pursuit, ideal – *in virtue of which* it is such? How can there be good and evil unless it be such *for* someone? The logical, the psychological, the philosophical, even the moral, difficulty of making sense of these ordinary examples is but one aspect of the difficulty of making sense of the *impersonality* of good and evil.

But don't I, in judging, acting or refraining, do so in the *light* of something? and so in the light of some*thing*? and so for the *sake* of something? Yes, sort of. There is an engraving called 'The Grave of Napoleon' depicting, clearly and distinctly, two trees. Nothing else. And yet, right out in front there stands, clearly and distinctly, Napoleon: he is the *space*, the *form* between the trees. Once seen, Napoleon – the delimited emptiness – becomes the bearer of meaning.[42] The trees, their sturdy actuality notwithstanding, are now judged according to their suitability for the emergence of the right form, the right no-thing-ness.

And if they aren't suitable? If the actual generates the wrong form? To see one's thought, feeling or action as distorted is to see it as impossible: as *must not*. As the desired/desirable manifests itself 'practically' in want and pursuit, so evil is experienced as what must not be: *flight* is its practical form. Intentionality seems thus preserved: a non-natural object generates a non-natural response. Confronted with evil I flee simply because it's evil. But this intentionality fails to comfort, this 'simply' is, again, anything but simple. It expresses *ungrounded necessity*: the gravest offense to natural(ist) practical thought.

But what does this mean? How is necessity recognized and experienced? In the case of intention it seems easy: seen as cruel or treacherous – as impossible – the intention is annulled. Here necessity manifests itself as *negation* of (actual) ends, as annulment of *ephiesthai*. But a thought, feeling or deed; myself as thinking, feeling or acting – these are *in* the world and thus not annullable. This experience of 'impossible' as ineradicably 'actual' is shame and guilt: a central form of the experience that 'the facts of the world are not all there is to it';[43] an ordinary experience of transcendence.

This experience is no promise of a desirable heavenly habitat. Heavenly are the criteria of judgement; I, however, remain rooted in the earth. As such this experience is not a desirable addition to my collection of pleasurable or interesting experiences, nor an invitation to become 'deeper and more spacious', nor a flattering recognition of being more than human. This experience of transcendence is the anguish of being what one must not be, the impossibility of, the flight from, the actual.[44]

One filled with it approaches the heavenly gate as a fugitive, not as an economic migrant. He comes driven by *necessity*, in hope and prayer of a safe place, not because he chose 'there' over 'here' to improve the quality of his life. As fugitive he appeals to pity and, addressing Zeus the protector of the suppliants, hopes to by-pass the Moirai, the grim guardians of boundaries. Yet he need not fear them for he is not guilty of the *hybris* of desire-propelled transgression of limits. When he stretches out his hands towards the divine it's to supplicate, not to attain. Indeed, since his plea is to be brought into a *proper* relation to the divine – within the bounds of the permissible, of the true limits – Zeus' mercy coincides with the Moirai's justice.

But what if I don't find the heavenly gate, don't reach the refuge from the impossible actual? What if I recognize a 'must' without finding a 'can' – evil which I can't escape? This is despair: it too is an experience of transcendence.

But what does all this mean? Who drives whom? From and to where? Io is a touching heroine for an ancient tragedy, but hardly a modern role model.

To make some philosophical sense of these 'ordinary experiences' I want to consider Kant, whose entire work can be viewed as an endeavour to elucidate 'the facts of the world not [being] all there is to it', and whose conclusions shape most modern attempts to even express, let alone make sense of, the transcendental aspiration.

The nature of the concern – relation between fact and significance – calls for efforts both metaphysical and ethical. Plato, Kant's acknowledged great predecessor, devastated his metaphysics and lamed his ethics and epistemology by failing to account for mud and hair. Kant learnt his lesson and declared the very attempt misconceived. Not just mud, but earth, sky and stars; not just hair, but the face and the smile on it: all that is given to perception, to experience, is mere fact. Facts are all that can be *known*.

Restricting knowledge to the empirical does not deny the *existence* of 'reality' beyond 'nature', but only our ability to know it. Indeed, we do and must *think* such reality, we do and must use Ideas not derived from experience. *A priori* Ideas are natural to our Reason and necessary for the 'highest systematic unification of empirical knowledge'. As long as their use is 'immanent, negative and regulative', it is (though 'transcendental') proper. The transcendental is thus thinkable but, for beings like us who lack 'intellectual intuition', it's not knowable. Any attempt to step outside the epistemic into the ontological, to take these Ideas for concepts of real things, is 'transcendent' and 'for that reason ... delusion'.[45] However natural, overstepping the limits of experience, like any other limits, is punishable *hybris*. In the context of Reason we get the capital punishment of *ouden legein* as contradiction.[46]

To proclaim the empirical as the only knowable is to sever being from value, fact from significance. What is *merely* is. This denial of the knowability of value brought despair to many;[47] to Kant it brought freedom. A freedom of a kind emerges already in the distinction between the theoretical and the practical: things in the world can be known, but are not, as such, valuable or (practically) relevant.[48] A 'thing' becomes valuable not by being known but by being desired: value is generated by the subject.

But though value is dependent on the subject, *he* in turn is dependent on his own, *inner*, nature, and so is unfree. Freedom means independence from events as such, be they external or internal, physical or psychological: freedom means *acting* as opposed to *undergoing*. It is this contrast between, on the one hand, *events* – that which 'is' or happens in the domain of (natural) necessity – and, on the other, *action* – 'ought' and the domain of freedom – which yields the 'practical' as the *ethical*.[49] Above I as *subject* confronted the world, here I as *free* subject confront myself as *natural* subject. This, however, means dualism and so also a potential conflict between I as 'is' and I as 'ought'. Yet though potentially painful, this conflict is no mere tug of war: in any engagement between 'is' and 'ought', 'ought' has inherent *authority*, the relation is *hierarchical*, the driving and the being driven *legitimate*. This distinguishes the position both from hedonism and from Aristotelianism: the confrontation of 'is' by 'ought' is a declaration of war against Naturalism.

This brings in yet another level of freedom. As the term 'practical' suggests, and as the contrast between I as 'is' and I as 'ought' confirms, the I in both its forms is the *Will*. *Qua* 'is' or desire, the I is given to experience; *qua* 'ought', however, it is not given or discovered, but *created*. Kant turns away from Descartes' effort of looking and the hope of discovery, and transforms the price of conflictual dualism into the prize of that highest form of freedom – self-determination.

We'll now consider the philosophical steps taken by Kant to erect his ethics on the ruins of traditional metaphysics, and to raise the phoenix of free – transcendental – I out of the ashes of transcendental reality.

The denial of value's accessibility by experience makes it startling to find Kant begin with experience. Yet what else can he do, having rejected Plato's Forms and Descartes' Innate Ideas as transcendental delusions? So he starts with the subject observing things around till desire lights on one of them, transforming it from a (theoretical) object of experience into a (practical) object of desire. When this object is within one's power, desire, as we saw in Part I, turns into Will, want into pursuit, subject into agent.

But though it is I who bestow (practical) relevance on a 'thing' – the first degree of freedom – yet I don't choose my desires, am in fact myself moved *by* them, and so am, in that sense, unfree, *determined*. What's more, *qua* desirous I'm driven by largely pleasure-constituted self-concern. Its brute factuality and self-centered hedonism makes desirousness unacceptable as the identity of a being capable of the idea of freedom and respect. Fortunately the facts of me are not all there is to me.

For unlike an animal I do not just go after, but 'pursue', what I desire. That is, I *think* the desired state of affairs as to be realized by my *action*: I act on a *maxim*. To want is to think 'f so as to attain (desired) X'; wanting is thinking oneself as so, that is, purposefully, f-ing. But this idea of purposeful action, and so the thinking of any concrete maxim, involves a dual criterion of rightness which inheres formally in 'I will' as 'true' does in 'I think'. In its first form – as requirement of *efficacy* – the criterion is analytic and so presents no problem: to will the end is to will the means.[50] But in its second form – as requirement of *lawfulness* – it involves a 'must' which is neither analytic nor grounded in any, external or internal, 'fact'. To think it is to think an *a priori* (synthetic) imperative: the make or break of metaphysics.[51]

But however difficult this requirement is to render and justify philosophically, there is nothing abstruse about it. The question 'Is what I want to do right (*qua* lawful)?', expressed as, for example, 'Should/may I f to attain X?' (where 'should' means lawful as obligatory, 'may' as permissible) is both ordinary and, ordinarily, easily answerable. And yet it's puzzling. For 'Law' analyzes into ideas of necessity and universality – neither of them derived from experience – and so emerges as itself an *a priori* Idea of Reason. Yet, unlike Descartes' Innate Ideas, this Idea has no substantive predicates: it offers no perfection to think or imitate;[52] unlike Plato's Forms, it offers no object to contemplate: it's empty of content, a *mere* form.

The content, indispensable to practical Reason, comes from desire for things in the world: the sensuous Will. In rational beings, desire, as we saw, becomes the Will by being thought as a (material) maxim: 'f to attain X'. But, as we also saw, 'May/should I?' – the idea of law – is internal to the thinking of 'f!'. Thus (the very thinking of) the material maxim involves the need that it fit in to the *form* of the law: that it answer to the Idea of necessity and universality.[53] The actual desirous I makes possible, but simultaneously falls under the judgement of, the formal Ideas of Reason. Without the trees there'd be no form; but it's the form which determines the suitability of the trees. Their unsuitability, the unfittingness of the maxim – the intended *ephiesthai* – results in its *annulment*. Annulment not on grounds of undesirability but of *impossibility*: want is silenced by *necessity*, rather than another want. This necessity, though ungrounded in nature, is recognized as authoritative over nature. Exercising one's natural Will thus involves submitting it to the Idea of law. But since this is *a priori*, in so submitting I move beyond, transcend, my nature.

Nor are we, like Io, merely *driven* from our natural pursuits. For since the form inheres in the substance of my Will, it is *I*, not some other, which drives the I. Moreover, rational necessity presupposes being *thought*, that is, freely *accepted*,[54] and so, strictly speaking, I'm not driven at all. Lastly, since thinking means here thinking the *law*, that is, *legislating*,[55] I'm moved by *my law*, that is, I move of my own will.

Indeed, Kant offers more than the, however voluntary, exile from my sensuous home, more than the *Aufheben-annulment* of my activity. He offers a *new* home: the *Aufheben* as transubstantiation of activity. This is clear when the maxim passes the test and the desired action is performed as *permissible*, that is, as sanctified by Reason; clearer still when it's performed not just as (permissible) desired but as *right*, that is, under the Idea of law. Though less obvious, the case is logically the same when I *reject* a maxim as contravening the law. In either case – of acting or refraining – the *cause* is Idea; in both cases I step outside the nexus of natural causality and enter the noumenal sphere. And I do so not by sneaking in or begging for refuge, but openly and confidently. Whoever *can* enter the noumenal realm, *may* do so. And he does so as an active member. The noumenal is the realm of activity.

The activity, moreover, is that of thinking *qua* legislating, that is, of *creating*. The ontological argument ignominiously driven out of 'I think' by Kant is now re-instated with new glory in 'I will'. The *a priori* Ideas which in the speculative domain were merely regulative and negative appear in the practical positively and constitutively: as *immanent* rather than transcendent.[56]

Furthermore, the domain of practical Reason not only identifies thinking with legislating, but also with executing the law: I thus enter not only as a legitimate legislative member, but as an equal with all other members: God included.[57]

Indeed, not just equality with, but divinity itself, is on offer. For every adoption of a maxim – every assumption of 'I wish' into 'I will' – is a *decision*: an experienced free act, an autonomous, specifically, *first*, cause. The divine attribute.

To sum up: the very experience of wanting tells me, without kibitzing from Innate Ideas or Platonic Forms, that wanting is not all there is to it. The very act of wanting drives me to submit to the formal test of Reason, pushes me beyond itself into the noumenal. I move out of natural want into rational necessity; out of determination into autonomous freedom; out of the passivity of the passions into the creative membership of the Kingdom of Ends. I don't transgress eternal bounds – be it by *hybris* or by God's mercy – for there are no noumenal facts to be discovered or appropriated, no heaven to climb into. Transcending means not moving from the lower to the higher realm, but from the lower to the higher *self*; it does not mean *moving into*, but *creating*, the Kingdom of Ends and *myself* as its member. To speak here of 'noumenal facts' is to mark the 'discovery' that the important facts are not *discovered but created*: that they aren't *data* but the product of activity (*facere*).

Here then is a coherent account of an experience of imperfection and an intoxicating cure for it. Yet finding myself thus exclaiming, 'bliss is it to want, but to will is the very heaven!', I wonder whether the account does justice to the experience; whether the cure is not too sweet to be wholesome.

We can begin by asking whether the account is not too strong. For if wanting has built into the recognition of its inadequacy, that is, of the hierarchy between the actual and the authoritative, the (sensibly) wanted and the (rationally) willable, then how do we account for Reason's failure to assert itself, for the frequent cases of *wrongdoing*? Indeed, if its transcendence is built into every desire, where is my freedom? Kant offers one answer to both worries. The fact that the rational requirement is internal to the experience of desire does not guarantee that it will *prevail*: authority is not power. But though I can disobey the command of Reason I can't *ignore* it. Like the law of the land, the law of Reason does not become *irrelevant* when transgressed but changes into the punitive mode. In the moral domain punishment is the painful recognition that I have disregarded my own law. This pain is but another way of *acknowledging* the law and, paradoxically, the most tangible 'experience' of the non-experiential – of the noumenal. The painful recognition/ response to my imperfection would thus provide a good starting point for another look at Kant's construal of perfection.

The general response to something going badly for someone or something is regret and pity. Both, however, are logically out of place in an account wholly centered on free *action*; morally out of place in an account proudly centered on *free* action. Since the only relevant – 'practical' or *ethical* – response is to dis-value freely caused by me, guilt and shame seem the only response left. Of the two, guilt is more promising, for not only is it a deeper concept and one of traditional significance to non-naturalist ethics, but Kant is also merited with advancing moral consciousness by re-orienting it from shame to guilt. This he's thought to have done partly by making intentional agency – what *I did* rather than just caused – the sole focus of moral response, partly by making the subject the sole legitimate judge of his conduct, thereby freeing him from moral dependence on others.[58] So examining whether the pained response to acting against Reason's command is what we know as guilt – that 'ordinary' experience of transcendence – is a good test of the fidelity of Kant's account to the ordinary experience of imperfection.

So described – as pain at going against my own Reason – it doesn't sound much like guilt. Guilt ordinarily understood seems to involve pain at (1) my doing; (2) irreparable harm/evil to; (3) someone or something (reality). Since the three are inter-related, changing any one of them affects the others. Kant focuses on (1): 'I intend/act'. But as we saw, the I gains its new, creative, significance at the expense of reality. Whatever 'is' *merely* is. As object of (speculative) thought, 'it' is practically, and so also value-, irrelevant; as 'desired' it's practically relevant but without *inherent* value since its relevance and value are *relative* to my want. The desired object is thus a mere *thing*.[59] A thing can be *damaged*, but not, properly speaking, harmed. It's only when 'It' is *significant* ('reality', rather than mere 'nature' or 'thing') that we can speak of harm or evil being done to it. Connectedly, the response to damage (leaving aside its consequences for me), is at most regret. A 'thing' can't sustain even the response of pity, let alone guilt. Guilt manifests my taking seriously *what* (harm or evil) I did and so also that *to which* I did it; just as pity manifests my taking seriously what has been suffered and so him who suffered it. But taking seriously is just what's precluded by the claim that whatever is not a subject is *a mere* object.

Guilt, then, seems possible only in relation to a subject. And *qua* response to harm or evil I did to another, it relates me to *other subjects*. Yet this too is troublesome. For the claim that only phenomena are given to experience applies not only to 'things' but also to subjects. And though 'I want', as it turns from 'I desire' to 'I will', transposes me from the experienced to the non-experiential, this goes only for the first person. Another subject is for me an *object* of experience – and so not value. But, Kant asserts,[60] I can and must *think* him as I think myself, that is, as a rational *subject*. But does this yield the right kind of 'other'? Kant's indifference to language makes him unable to account for people speaking to one another;[61] more generally to recognize the central condition of (what could be called) a noumenal *relation*: the mutual give-and-take between thinking, feeling, speaking beings, with all its potential for good and evil. But it's precisely here, in the second person,[62] that we ordinarily *experience* the other as substantive value. With no access to 'you', Kant remains in the third person: the other remains an object – albeit a special, namely *subject-object* – for me to view, think about, and take into consideration.

What kind of subject is that? The requirement to think the other as I (relevantly) think myself, yields the other as an *autonomous*

Will. The response appropriate to him under that description is *respect*, expressed primarily in *refraining from* interfering with his practical rationality – his thinking and willing; secondarily (though in experience primarily) in recognizing him as a *limit on* my action – an End to my ends.[63] Morally speaking the other thus emerges as a do-not-touch, as what is *not* to be engaged with. The basic moral relation to another – respect – is thus *negative*.[64] Positive engagement with another *qua* noumenon is, Kant seems to assume, practically impossible; were it possible, it would be impermissible. As rational subject, that is, as one capable of sustaining a serious moral response, the other can't be engaged with. But if he can't be engaged with, then he also can't be harmed, can't have evil done to him. In relation to the other as a noumenal subject, guilt therefore can't arise.

Engagement is possible, inevitable, even obligatory, at the phenomenal level. Though Kant rules out concern with another's *perfection*, he prescribes concern with his well-being as a phenomenal creature, that is, his *happiness*. Since the other is here also conatively construed, this means concern with his ends and pursuits. But even here the negative predominates: the primary expression of my respect/concern is *not* interfering with his legitimate actions. The move from refraining to positively furthering another's ends is grudging and awkward. Grudging because even at this level autonomy (here meaning non-dependence on others) seems the highest good; gratitude (Kant tends to speak of 'debt') an evil to avoid. Awkward because both psychologically and philosophically Kant cannot salvage happiness from the natural trash of *ephiesthai*: an aggregate of satisfied desires and interests. So described, happiness – mine or another's – can neither claim nor sustain moral concern. More relevantly here, its *loss* can't be taken seriously. Once again we get the rent between 'reality' which can't be harmed, and 'nature' whose harm can't be taken seriously. That's not to say that I can treat lightly what I do to another. As a responsible agent I must take steps to repair what harm or damage I caused; when that is irreparable, I pay damages. But as the shift from 'subject' to 'agent' indicates, the 'guilt' at work here is *legal*, rather than moral: a requirement on *action* rather than demeanour.

The autonomous first-personal thus goes beyond preserving the moral subject from determination by another (heteronomy): it *prevents* him from being claimed by the other, from taking the other seriously. This rules out moral responses – many of them essentially first-personal – which involve seriously relating to another, of which guilt is perhaps the most important one.[65] Guilt as ordinarily understood now drops out of the moral domain to be replaced with a response to *myself* as failing or imperfect. And while (not the least because of Kant's impact) many philosophers are today tempted to describe this self-relation as guilt,[66] doing so goes against that ordinary experience of imperfection, which we hoped Kant would elucidate. The problem with guilt raises a more general one: can we sensibly speak of transcending given this emphatic focus on the self? Doesn't transcending involve moving beyond the *self*, towards something which is both *other* and *value*?

Since in a sense Kant would be the first to agree, how does he reconcile value as other with value as autonomy? The answer is: *dualism*. Unlike most of his modern followers who work with one self at a lower and a higher stage (prudential deliberation or reflection being the means of progress),[67] for Kant the sensuous and the rational Will are two distinct protagonists, each with its own object (state of affairs vs. form); under its own description (pleasant vs. lawful); with its own necessity (hypothetical vs. categorical); with its own response (want vs. reverential obedience). The starting point of the moral story, as we saw, is the experienced, that is, the sensible, Will. This self experiences Reason as radically *other*. This is because Reason's *impersonality* – validity irrespective of wants and interests, and essential non-possessibility – puts it in sharp *contrast* to desire, the most emphatic I-experience. What's more, as a *limit* on my pursuits, Reason is in *conflict* with the desire- and pursuit-constituted sensible Will. Heeding the command of Reason is thus *experienced* by the sensible I as moving away from the self towards the *other*. Since, moreover, the command of Reason is experienced as authoritative or *legitimate*, heeding it makes this a movement towards value, that is, transcending.

Still, doesn't this 'other', however valuable, destroy my self-determination; isn't this transcendence at the expense of autonomy? Not if we remember that this 'other' is *my* thinking the maxim (un)lawful, that it's (*my*) *law* legislated by my rational self. The two selves meet in the experience of *dignity* – my absolute value as autonomous source of the law – and in *reverence* – the awed obedience to this law. But though as 'person' I *have* intrinsic autonomy and absolute value, yet I can act counter to them. We are back to imperfection, and the appropriate response to it.

Reason's character as *law* turns every 'surrender' to desire into a *transgression*. Such transgression is by definition unlawful, and so *wrong*. But is it, as such, also *evil*? Evil, like guilt, seems to require an *object:* someone harmed. And while Reason, *qua* 'other', is an object of a kind, it is not an object such as can turn wrong-doing into evil. Evil requires a *substantive* not just a formal object, and that means one which is *vulnerable* to substantive harm. Reason, however, can't be harmed. But am *I* not harmed? Perhaps, but in that case the 'other' disappears, and the *self* returns as the primary object of moral concern. Besides, what kind of harm is here possible? As long as the relevant description of the mis-deed is 'disobeying (my own) law', or 'surrendering to sensuality', the harm in question is to my *dignity as a rational being*. The harm befalling the self is thus baseness or ignobility, its imperfection is not evil but weakness and shortcoming. Where before guilt was inappropriate owing to the self being the object of moral concern, it now becomes inappropriate owing to the nature of what is done. For the response suitable to my baseness or loss of dignity is not guilt but *shame*.

Thus, far from eliminating shame from moral consciousness, Kant seems to put it at its very centre. His innovation lies in giving shame a different object and context, which he does by replacing honour – concern with how others judge me – with dignity – concern with how I judge myself.[68] This solves the problem of heteronomy. But the worry about shame taking up central moral space is not heteronomy but *moral mediocrity*. First because shame is the response appropriate to misdemeanour rather than felony; second because it is *self-* rather than *other*-concerned. Shame is morally inadequate, and so inappropriate, in response to evil or serious harm, because, regardless of the source of judgement, that judgement is a response to *my* loss of face rather than to what *I did*.[69] Where guilt asks 'How could I have done *that*?', shame asks 'How could *I* have done that?' We're back to the first-personal – only now it's personal in the wrong way.

The issue of badness and the response to it can be clarified by taking a closer look at the Kantian self. It is, we saw, emphatically the dual *Will* – traditionally the 'soldierly' part of the soul. Soldierly too seem its concerns and values: overcoming selfish pleasure and convenience in pursuance of duty; respect for law; dignity. The worst thing for a soldier is acting shamefully or dishonourably, losing his honour (dignity). The moral task too has a military feel to it: the content of the Will, like a well-conceived military plan, is clear and specific: it seeks to fit into a maxim 'to f so as to attain X'.[70] With the maxim – *intended action* – determining both the scope and the nature of moral attention, we lose outside reality except as space for my pursuits.[71] Even more importantly, we lose all *inside* reality except as it pertains to the intended action. Thoughts, feelings, emotions – the very things which (at the opening of this Part) seemed to awaken us to our imperfection and to the facts of the world not being all there is to it, disappear as bearers of moral significance. Having lost guilt, we now lose a good deal of shame too.

And we lose it without argument. For the identification of the self with the Will, that is, with (ideally) intentional action, makes thoughts or feelings in their own right, still more oneself as thinking or feeling, logically *unrecognizable* and so morally *irrelevant*. For the Will can't *recognize* anything as its task unless it's *do-able*: 'will' implies 'can'. Behind this conceptual point lies the normative concern with responsibility, and so with my (moral) identity as a free and autonomous subject. Thoughts and feelings, however, can't be willed, and so, it seems, lie beyond responsibility and with it also beyond moral significance. But don't I experience them as evil and so as morally significant? Faced with the prospect of losing freedom and autonomy, dignity, and the membership in the noumenal realm where I'm on first-name terms with the divine, it's all too easy to concede that thought or feelings, which at first seemed so crucial a feature of value- or transcendental experience, are in fact *mere* experience. And so, however loudly they clamour for attention, however successful they are in *grabbing* it, they don't and can't *claim* to be moral: they're merely 'pathological'.[72]

The above becomes clearer once we realize that what Kant in fact accounts for is not the experience of imperfection as such, but its easiest, albeit central and important, form: *temptation*. Temptation, moreover, which is both logically and morally of the simplest kind: desiring to f while thinking it wrong.[73] Such temptation involves a sharply experienced dualism: conflict between want and right, force and authority, 'is' and 'ought'. These are, *ex hypothesi*, situations where it's clear what *ought* to be done, and where, therefore, the task lies at the level of *doing* rather than *thinking*, of Will and strength rather than discernment.

This (soldierly) concentration on strength and doing stems from the presupposition built into the Will and so also into temptation, namely the *givenness* of the situation. The Will – deliberation and decision – becomes active when 'confronted' with the practical situation constituted by the alternatives of doing/refraining. Temptation, a specific form of the conative, is the experience of being pulled by a desire for something while simultaneously recognizing its inadmissibility (or the recognition of a duty in the presence of a desire not to do). The subject experiences both 'alternatives' as 'there' or 'given', his task being to come to terms with them. In Kant this is further underwritten by a static Hobbesian psychology which ascribes the same nature to all and so portrays all as facing the same situation; and by his faith in the equal ability of all to overcome their nature. This treatment of the moral situation as a practical problem *confronting* the would-be agent prevents Kant from appreciating the role of *judgement*, that is, the moral and epistemic work involved in *recognizing*, or *constructing*, a moral situation. So, paradoxically, though he centers on Reason Kant has little to say about 'thinking'; though a founder of modern rationalist ethics he has no place for wisdom; though he hinges all on law he's largely unconcerned with justice.[74] Nor is this accidental or avoidable. For wisdom goes beyond clarity and consistency, requiring a substantive and nuanced engagement with what 'is'; justice goes beyond not-transgressing, demanding an interactive concern with a substantive other. Both thus presuppose a reality capable of *claiming* one, that is, reality not as mere facts, but as embodiment of value. But by placing all the weight on free action, Kant loses the activity of 'attending to' or 'making sense'; fearing to fetter the Will by the given of Reality, he locates it within the given situation. That is, he fails to realize that the Will, like a good soldier, acts only when confronted by a task of (not) performing an action under a specific description, and that it lacks the wherewithal to look outside the situation, to question the description.

These various stands – metaphysical and moral rejection of Realism, concentration on the Will, Hobbesian psychology – prevent Kant from considering moral perception, thinking, and learning, and so encourage his indifference to *what* is being done to *whom*, that is, his *formalism*. They also strengthen, and are in turn strengthened by, his focus on temptation. For temptation is, *logically*, a situation constituted by the desirability-cum-wrongness of an action/state of affairs, that is, by the task of resisting desire; while, *experientially*, it often feels like a curiously contentless tug of war between 'want' and 'ought', where it's the force rather than the content of the desire which counts. As regards this force (and so also the effort needed to resist it), it may make no difference whether one desires an after-dinner cigarette or an after-dinner adultery, nor whether one desires it for pleasure, or to prove oneself, or to destroy another's happiness. Temptation is a battle between two forces and battles, once launched, are decided by the strength rather than the cause of the antagonists. Moreover, once a battle is underway, attention shifts inevitably to the battle-field. Where, as in our case, the battle is between the sensible and the rational self,[75] the self becomes the sole focus of interest.

But we, and even the human (by contrast to the conative) subject, distinguish a true battle from a keep-fit exercise, a proper from an improper self-concern. We do so by considering what is *at issue* in the battle, that is, *what* one is tempted to do, the *reality* being affected for better or worse. Here, however, reality means not an experience of an aggregate of inert data, but an experienced claim. We saw Kant trying to account for this experience, while avoiding all reference to reality, by using the idea of the Moral Law grounded in the rational Will, but experienced as an imperative – as a claim – by the sensible Will. But how can formalism, recognized and accepted by Kant as the price, avoid becoming *narcissism* unless there's something which *substantively* matters?

Kant would say that I – *qua* person – matter. Leaving aside the dubiousness of the *self* as the primary object of moral concern, let's see *how* I matter. When the moral is a conflict between Desire and Reason, we get only one story – that of a battle – with two endings: *failure* – being overcome by Desire/not acting according to Reason – and *success* – acting according to Reason/overcoming Desire. And while it's analytically true that success and failure matter to the subject, yet their objective importance depends on *what* it is he succeeds or fails in. The importance of failure, Kant suggests, is that it *harms* me as a rational being. But for 'failure' to translate into 'harm' there must be a self vulnerable to harm, and so susceptible to change. Changeability, however, is precluded psychologically by Kant's Hobbesian construal of human nature, logically by his conative construal of the self, its 'life' an aggregate of concrete episodes. The psychological and the logical, as so often in Kant, merge with the moral: the construal of the practical as autonomous rational freedom, and the faith in morality as a domain of equal opportunity, presuppose my ability to face every situation afresh. This means that what I do today cannot and may not determine my self at any other time. Within any 'practical' situation (conative) 'I' pops up like a Jack-in-the-box, equipped with the same burden of his sensuality and the same means of overcoming it. Failure may evoke the cry 'How can I sink so low?!' but not 'What have I done?', not even 'What have I done to *myself*?' There is here no 'myself' to which anything – harm or good – can be done.[76] The imperfection of failing to overcome myself can't be experienced as anguish at having harmed or done evil, but at most as a smarting at my weakness, as *shame* at my loss of dignity. Here again we see that the problem with shame as a central moral response is not its threat to autonomy, but its exclusion of anything but a mediocre self-concern.

The problem becomes clearer in the case of *success*. The winning of the battle is the conquest of the sensible by the rational I achieved by my strength and endurance. As such it is *my victory* experienced with *pride*. But since pride is a dubious candidate for moral demeanour it's not surprising to find Kant playing it down. He seeks to undermine the suggestion of 'mine' – and so of pride – by construing 'victory' impersonally, to wit, as being necessitated. But, as we saw, the Will, especially when embattled, is the most emphatic experience of the I. The consequent psychological difficulties in avoiding the possessive stance become insurmountable in the absence of a *substantive* object of concern on *whose* behalf one fights the battle. The formal law of Reason may command, but it can't provide an object of love. Only love, however, can silence the self and pride.

Even this, however inadequate, logical apparatus for resisting pride-grounded self-concern disappears once Kant's heirs abandon the idea of the independent reality of the noumenal and its authority over the sensible. Without the *a priori* synthetic Idea of law we can't make sense of impersonally determinable right and wrong, thereby losing the 'substance' of Kant's formalism. Right and wrong become reflective cohesiveness of beliefs and commitments grounded in one's (or society's) wants and interests rather than in correspondence to the law. *Coherence* replaces *correspondence*; integrity as 'being of a piece' replaces integrity as fidelity to the Ideal; consistent prudence replaces the noumenal/supra-natural. The facts of the world are now all there is to it, and if at times they come in conflict, this 'imperfection' is at most unfortunate, hopefully redeemable. The moral battle is between short- and long-term wants, that is, between desire and prudence. Victory – the attainment of perfection – is experienced as proud, if somewhat joyless, satisfaction. Kant eliminated love from morality and denied any-thing outside the subject the ability to claim reverence, thereby depriving morality of the whole range of 'psychological' responses through which we experience and express our recognition of em-bodied value. Kantianism stripped of the noumenal loses reverence too, having now nothing capable of sustaining it.

In Part I transcending was portrayed as a search for perfection understood as a pursuit of human desirables and avoidance or elimination of its undesirables. Part II began by pointing to another, though equally ordinary, experience of imperfection, that of moral badness. Moral imperfection, we suggested, is frequently experi-enced as simple unacceptability of what is, rather than as a goal of being something else. The 'transcending' here occurs in the recogni-tion of the impossibility of what is: the unacceptability of the present reality providing the 'proof' that 'the facts of the world are not all there is to it'. We emphasized three features of this experi-ence: the replacement of 'want' by 'must'; the dominance of the negative categories; the connected difficulties in construing the active relation to one's badness in purposive terms, which we sug-gested resulted in 'moral activity' manifesting itself in hopeful, fearful, even anguished, humility rather than in pursuit.

We turned to Kant in the hope of a philosophical rendering of this experience. We saw his focus on necessity- rather than want-motivated activity; and the connected recognition of the anti-purposive demeanour of morality. Both lead to the portrayal of the moral 'transcending' the natural ends not in pursuance of ends of its own, but in *obedience* to the formal criteria of Reason. Yet when that Reason, i.e. the moral protagonist, is the Will, activity begins to take the form of pursuit. So the moral Will, as that which negates natural (desire-driven) pursuit, turns out to be itself engaged in an – albeit negative – *ephiesthai*.

What's more, the purposive construal of activity implies good as purpose or end. So the anti-*ephiesthai* character of moral activity brings with it the good as an (anti-)end. The return of value as end and of effort as pursuit re-introduces the criteria formulated by the founder of conative ethics, Aristotle. As a rational expenditure of effort, pursuit, and so also anti-pursuit, must be, in principle, feas-ible, that is, its end must be, in principle, attainable. This makes success and failure constitutive of moral activity, and pride and shame of the demeanour of the moral protagonist. This, as we saw, is true of Kant and perhaps helps to explain the similarity between his moral subject and Aristotle's virtuous man. It simultaneously helps to explain his difficulties with what we argued to be crucial features of the experience of moral imperfection. For hope or humility, let alone anguish and supplication, are alien to the Will.

But there was something else which Aristotle, attentive to the promptings of the conative stance, noted: one can't walk on for ever; the effort must come to an end. Kant agrees: after all, morality is an encounter between Desire and Reason, ending with the conquest of one over the other. Except that – another such encounter is just around the corner. And while this is a source of comfort when one *loses* the moral battle, it's less acceptable when, in a moment of victory, I know that there's another time, and that my present victory cannot guarantee the outcome. Failure can't harm me, but, for that same reason victory can't safeguard me. From this perspective the moral life, as a series of independent conative episodes, appears as 'one damned thing after another'.

To a moral subject this is frightening – or humbling; to a Will-centered moral philosopher it is unacceptable. Besides, as a matter of experience, and for Kant also of theory, there seems to be a continuous (noumenal) Self *whose* episodes these are. This Self is, of course, *practical*, and thus (for Kant) the Will. But *qua* Will it requires goal or end. This End, however, transcends particular (anti-) ends, just as this Will transcends particular acts of (moral) willing. And as these acts are episodes of negative *ephiesthai* – repression of natural ends in obedience to the rational command 'Be ye therefore perfect' – so the End of the Self as a whole is Perfection itself. From being a limit *to* my ends/pursuits, Perfection emerges as my End: the *telos of* my pursuit.

But this Perfection is unattainable and so can't be the End. But there's unattainable and unattainable. While Aristotle's target – Plato's Good – is so logically, never being intended as an End or object of the Will, Kant's perfection is unattainable only contingently: due to our being burdened by sensible nature. That is, it's unattainable because it lies 'ever so far'. But the factual insurmountability of imperfection gives way to the *thinkability* of perfection. To think Perfection is to recognize it as my task, and since '"ought" implies "can"', this posits 'ever so long' to attain that which lies 'ever so far'. My imperfection posits my duty to transcend it, which in turn posits, *en passant*, my dutiful right to possess myself of yet another divine predicate: immortality.[77] But now immortality is transformed from the end prayed for to a distasteful means to an end; from an object of hope to the dreadful fate of Sisyphus: endless striving, 'walking on for ever'.

We noted earlier how Kant's cure for overcoming the *hybris* of limitless pursuit – obedience to the limit of Reason – threatened to produce the *hybris* of pride. Now we find added to it an invitation to, once again, overstep limits – this time of nature. With this double *hybris* marking the curing of imperfection, one may find oneself preferring the sickness – even if it be 'Unto death'.

III   GREETING THE BEAUTIFUL

Joy (pure joy is always in the beautiful) is the feeling of reality.[78]

A different expression of something beyond, and yet a condition of, experience is found in Wittgenstein's musings about his book *The World as I Found It*.[79] This book, he notes, lacks one thing, namely the *I* who is 'finding' the world. That which does the finding cannot be itself found: it is not *in* the world. Not being 'in the world' the I – the metaphysical subject – *transcends* the world. This, however, seems transcendence on the cheap: the I as simply the Not-it, the subject as simply the Not-object. Thus – namely negatively – construed, the I seems of no value or concern. It's a mere, even if a 'transcendental', *datum*.

But something else is missing from the book: namely the *world*. For only temporal and spatial sequences of events, not the world, can be 'found'. The transcendental subject may be got on the cheap, not so the transcendental object.

This, after all, is the point of Kant's theoretical philosophy. Perception (and the experience based on it) is realist, indeed naively so: it *finds* its object. The object perceived is the same for all (normal, rational, language-using, etc.) beings: a public, empirical, static *datum* or fact.[80] As such it is beyond ordinary doubt.[81] But also beyond concern. For as that which merely is, it has no value. Being indifferent *an sich*, it is so also *für mich*. To acquire relevance it must lose its 'isness' – its 'theoretical' status, which it does by becoming 'practical' *qua* desirable or useful. But while this makes it relevant or valuable *für mich*, it doesn't make it so *an sich*. The absolute separation of 'is' from 'value' gives us the world as either a conglomerate of (practically irrelevant) objects, or of (want-relevant) 'things'. Neither *qua* object nor *qua* thing can it sustain the response of concern. And that is a conceptual point. Value lies not in the world, but in the (rational willing) subject.

Wittgenstein goes with Kant in elucidating value through the *willing* subject,[82] and in construing the 'true' willing subject as transcending the 'apparent' one. But whereas in Kant this involves transcending the material into the formal, personal desire into the impersonal law, want into necessity, Wittgenstein goes one better: true willing, he claims, means *surrendering* willing altogether. This requires acceptance of the 'world as I found it', that is, abandoning action. By surrendering interaction with things in the world I come to *view* things 'from the outside': *sub specie aeterni*, and so as a *world*, as a *transcendental object*. Kant offers transcendence as *ephiesthai* under rational description; Wittgenstein as active surrender of *ephiesthai*: as *perception*.[83]

Yet why should this 'transcendental object' be of any greater concern than the above transcendental subject? Wittgenstein suggests that the view from the outside is 'aesthetic' and thus *concerned*: its object is *not-indifferent*. Moreover, stepping out of the world means surrendering demands on it and becoming independent and invulnerable to it. This makes the subject safe and so happy; and happiness and goodness are one. The transcendental object seems thus to give us also the proper transcendental subject: 'Ethics and aesthetics are one'.[84]

In the following I want to consider the idea of the 'transcendental object', and its implications for the subject. I agree with Wittgenstein that such an object is given to perception rather than to the Will/agent. But I disagree with him in three important respects. (1) I don't believe the world *sub specie aeternis* to be constructable by *my act* of negating my Will; that is, I want to emphasize *perception* and so argue for the priority of the object. (2) I'll argue that the perception of a non-indifferent object is *practical*: a responsive recognition of value; that is, I wish to re-consider the theoretical–practical dichotomy. (3) I'll be suggesting that such perception involves me in the world and so, far from rendering me invulnerable, opens me to *suffering*, that is, I reject the idea of the perceptibility of the transcendental object from the outside, and of the transcendental subject as out of the world.

(1)   Perception

Let's try again the route of analysis – of experience as well as concepts. But where Wittgenstein speaks of the 'aesthetic', and of aesthetic experience, we'll stay with the more ordinary 'beauty' and the experience of beauty.

Normally we speak of *perceiving* beauty. The concept of perception, as we saw, commits us to – naive – Realism: the object is found, not constructed. Yet, to perceive the object as beautiful is to perceive it as *important*, as significant, or precious: as anything but an indifferent *datum*. The implicit value of the object strengthens the Realism, transforming it from naive to *emphatic*. For meaning is revealed or discovered, rather than 'constructed', or 'up to me'. A frequent factor in the experience of beauty is surprise, and a sense of the object as vibrantly, indomitably, and incalculably 'other'. The idea of beauty thus suggests a direct or non-mediated experience – (let's say) perception – of value rather than '*datum*': of (let's say) reality rather than nature.

Its perceptual character protects beauty against the standard sceptical treatment of 'moral' values: the claim that they're a mere cover for some interest – be it of an individual, the strong individual, the ruling class, the society, the species, or nature as a whole. The sceptics would agree that without some idea of goodness and virtue, 'the centre cannot hold, everything gravitates downwards', i.e. that *belief* in (so-called) values is essential though the values themselves are unreal.[85] This sceptical argument, which distinguishes the first-person moral fool from the third-person rational knave, can't be used against beauty. Tied as it is to perception, beauty is confined to the subject both in being 'private' and in lacking 'objective' value. It *serves* no purpose; it *has* no value. In perception we have two options: to see or not to see. And given the realism implicit in perception, 'I don't see' translates into 'There *is nothing* to see'.

But while its perceptual character protects beauty against scepticism which can be levelled against moral value, it also seems to condemn it to irrelevance. For *qua* perceptual beauty is *not-practical*; *qua* not-useful it's *useless*.

And yet, *qua* perception of *beauty*, it's a perception of *value*, and so *not irrelevant*. But before considering the 'relevance' of beauty, we'll briefly look at what's meant in this context by perception, and the kind of object it takes.

An obvious answer to the question of why we speak of *perception* of beauty is that beauty *is* perceived, i.e. that we reach it centrally through the senses. To put it the other way: the natural world is beautiful. And yet, even as revealed to the senses, beauty is not an object of *sense*-perception; 'perception' is here not a faculty contrasted with the intellect or with the conative/emotive/affective.

Indeed, the experience of beauty resists the language of faculties: beauty is 'perceived' by the unified and harmonious self: by the spirit. So perhaps it's truer to say that we speak of 'perception' to convey that the experience of beauty is a direct and unmediated experience of the 'other', that is, to express its Realism. If this is true, then anything which is thus – namely, directly – experienced may turn out to share logic of beauty.[86] The experience might thus not be confined to the sense-perceptual domain. Hence my saying above 'let's say perception'.

But the claim that beauty is perceived by the unified and harmonious self, makes questionable the contrast between reality and nature – hence my saying 'let's say reality rather than nature'. The perception of beauty involves gladness in the object, and this precludes the rejection-*cum*-assertion stance underlying the distinction between nature (appearance) and reality. To perceive something as beautiful is to perceive it as *kosmos*: a harmonious and sufficient whole. That which is *kosmos* is at peace with itself and with the outside: it does not assert itself by denying something else. He who perceives it is satisfied with it: at peace with it and himself. Such a one is temperate, just, not tempted to exceed limits – without *hybris*. In experiencing beauty one wants nothing from it, but also nothing from oneself: one wants neither to use it nor to transcend oneself. Being at peace silences not just concern to attain the desirable, but also to attain one's higher self; it seems to silence the practical: *ephiesthai*. And so also transcending? Not quite.

To begin with: experience of beauty is experience of the *other*. In that sense it involves going beyond, transcending, the self. But isn't this transcendence on the cheap? – the quasi-logical point that the eye is not a part of the visual field?[87] Not if we remember that beauty *matters*, and that it does so *qua* 'object' rather than 'thing', that is, perceptually, rather than conatively. The experience of beauty thus involves transcending that perceiving (or theoretical) I whose object is a 'mere object', as well as the *wanting I* whose object is the (desirable) 'thing'. The emphasis on the object differentiates this not only from Kant's account of transcendence as movement to the higher Will, but also from Wittgenstein's suggestion that we 'construct' the object by withdrawing from Will and action. However necessary such withdrawal may be for the contemplative stance, it is not sufficient: I can't *create* beauty simply by not viewing something as 'merely useful'. Beauty is *discovered* and, when discovered, *it* is of concern. Being 'of concern' (relevant, important, precious) means that it is the object which calls upon and sustains the attention, not the attention which creates the object.[88]

One way of putting this is to say that the object must be of interest: the I/eye must be *interested*. Here we get transcending the world of 'objects' and of 'things'; and with it also of the (merely) perceiving, and wanting I. But does this make transcendence the condition of every 'lover of sights and sounds'? We could argue that 'sight' or 'sound' is, by definition, not a meaningful or significant 'whole', and so not a suitable object. But transcendence 'by definition' doesn't seem very satisfactory either. We can, however, argue that a sight or sound holds my attention only as long as it *happens* to do so; as long as it happens to please, amuse or interest me. So while the interested, unlike the perceiving, I/eye sees the object as relevant and, unlike the wanting I, sees it as relevant without seeking to use it, yet the object's relevance or value remains dependent on what it does 'for me'. The perspective of the *interested* eye remains self-concerned. The interesting is a false pretender to beauty in particular and value in general; interest is the false pretender to contemplation in particular and concern in general.

The beautiful is experienced as of concern to *me* because *it* is of concern, that is, as unconditionally important, as value *an sich*. This is not to say that it's valuable in the absence of anyone valuing it; only that it is valued in its own right. And that it is *to be* so valued by me: as value *an sich* it is a value *für mich*. Sight and sound may grab me, but beauty *claims* me.

Or rather, as reality beauty grabs me, as value it claims me. This makes beauty a *datum*: but a *datum* in the sense of something gratuitously given, that is, a *gift*. If we speak here of transcendence we do so without suggesting the *effort* of transcending. One is not just beyond the sensuous, but also beyond the legislating I; not just beyond appetite, but also beyond reason. The I which perceives beauty is harmonious and unified: it is the spirit; the eye which perceives beauty is the *loving* and joyful eye. Both as harmonious and as loving, the I/eye wants nothing from the object: the object is of concern without reference to 'mine'. Here we get the impersonal tied to what substantively matters; experienced as glad, rather than imperative, importance.

Whether beauty shocks into surprised gladness, fills with joy, or with more gentle contentment, it evokes the response of acknowledgment or *greeting*, and the desire to remain in its presence, to cling to it. All these belong to the meaning of *aspazdesthai*: a word used by Plato in the perceptual/affective as well as in the epistemic context.[89] *Aspazdesthai*, greeting or welcoming, I want to suggest, is a *practical* stance.

It's an important, 'analytic', point that this stance is only possible towards an object of *positive* value. Similarly with joy: 'All joys come from paradise,' says Rabbi Pinhas and, having perhaps attended the same school as Socrates, he adds: 'jests too, provided they are uttered in true joy'.[90] The analytic point can be expressed in terms of intentionality: the response requires a certain kind of object, and so heralds its presence. If joy, then beauty; joy; therefore beauty. Simone Weil links the response, the object and the value more emphatically: 'Joy (pure joy is always in the beautiful) is the feeling of reality. Beauty is the manifest presence of reality'.[91]

But this raises some questions. There is firstly the – rather awkward – suggestion of transcendence as *experienced*, that is, immanent. And that both at the subject-level – *aspazdesthai* being the experience of transcending the I – and at the object-level – beauty being reality experienced as precious, as not of the world.

This in turn is connected with the following: to say that one is grabbed by reality and claimed by value is *descriptive*. *Aspazdesthai* is a *response* and so has no reason or motive, certainly no purpose. Lying thus beyond the Will it seems to lie beyond 'ought'. If there is a necessity here, it's not experienced as an *imperative*. But doesn't the exclusion of the conative eliminate freedom and responsibility? If it does, and if *aspazdesthai* involves moving into the divine sphere, and so exceeding the limits, gods have only themselves to blame. Having created beauty and creatures capable of perceiving it, they can't blame them for responding. Put differently: though *aspazdesthai* be yet it involves no *act* of transcending and so nothing for responsibility to attach to. *Qua* 'response' *aspazdesthai* is an *obedient* activity, not an autonomous action.

But *eo ipso*, the gods blame us for *not* responding. The dismissal of the conative seems to lose us the general idea of *effort*. I can't *make* myself see or respond, and so can't be held responsible for (not) seeing or responding. And yet greeting is the *proper* response. Failure to perceive beauty is a failure to perceive *value*; failure to perceive value is failure to respond to, to acknowledge, to give it its *due*: it's a failure of *love* and *justice*. This re-entry of the normative suggests either that we are out of the perceptual sphere, or that the 'perceptual' is 'practical' in yet another, more disquieting, way. Above I suggested that *aspazdesthai* doesn't involve *hybris* as 'unlawful transgression'; now, however, the absence of *aspazdesthai* suggests *hybris* as failure to honour, as *disrespect*.

'Respect', like *aspazdesthai*, involves the descriptive and the normative, though the latter more emphatically. This is because where *aspazdesthai* directs us to the object, 'respect' looks to the subject, and so to the possible source of shortcoming. Respect is what I *owe* to value. The emphatic subject-slant of respect makes it the cornerstone of modern ethics, the main expression of our (inherently imperfect) relation to value. This explains (see Part II) its negative feel, its being experienced largely as a *silencing* of the self.[92] Such silencing is only needed when something goes wrong with the perception of the object. The important thing is the object, the 'visual field'. When, however, something goes wrong with the eye, attention turns to it. This is why failure of *aspazdesthai* may be experienced by one who still sees well enough to know that there *is* something to see, as respect, that is, as a recognition that there is something wrong with his eye.

But the positive and the negative go together. When I'm stopped in my tracks by the song of a bird or a 'host of daffodils', I *honour* them by my glad attention. But this attention involves, among others, a *suspension* of my pursuits. The presence of beauty thus puts a brake on the efficient flow of my *ephiesthai*. I stand and gape, the embodiment of ineffective agency of – practically speaking – foolishness. And when I don't, when I rush by too preoccupied with my goals or myself, then my not not-stopping, not-seeing, can be viewed as a failure of both love and respect. We argued above against the claim that *qua* perceptual, beauty is non-practical and useless. Now, however, beauty emerges as a *threat* to the practical, as emphatically useless.

(2) The practical

The demand of respect – the experience of constraint – is stronger when it's *dishonouring* rather than failure to honour which is at stake. Above we had disrespect in spirit: the practical character of perception; here we have disrespect in what is more straightforwardly action: doing which accidentally, in the course of my other pursuits, or intentionally, harms or destroys the object. The song of the bird ends when I cut down its tree or when I kill it for my dinner; the daffodils can be trampled as I take the shortest route to my destination, or destroyed in being turned into a bouquet. This possibility of actively destroying takes us more directly to the second concern: to *ephiesthai*, to *praxis*.

As we saw above, respect – constraint imposed on the subject by the object – is only available to one who is open to value. Only such a one can recognize that 'useless' means here *not-to-be-used* or destroyed. For one entirely constituted by *ephiesthai*, for the rational efficient agent, respect is a foolish scruple, *aspazdesthai* a nonsensical self-indulgence, and that both as a matter of fact, and norm. 'He who does not hear the music thinks those who dance mad'.[93]

In setting us dancing, beauty puts an end to our purposeful *walking*. As response to what is not of this world, *aspazdesthai/* respect puts an end to pursuit of things in it, and to the virtues pertaining to such pursuit: deliberation, prudence, efficiency. Here, temperance as prudence or careful weighing of desires and their cost confronts temperance as wanting nothing from the object.

And yet not quite. For beauty inheres in and illuminates things in the world: the beautiful is *lovable*. If above one became imprudent in allowing beauty to interrupt one's pursuits, one now becomes a fool when, loving, one drops one's projects and attainments, the very structure of one's life. As love, *aspazdesthai* is not just imprudent but mad; it not only endangers the attainment of one's particular goals, but upsets the overall balance of one's needs and interests.[94] The challenge posed by love to efficiency and prudence is the big theme of the *Phaidros*, where Socrates is delivered, by the beauty of Phaidros and their surroundings, of two discourses, both of them nonsensical: one blasphemous, the other mad. The blasphemous one describes how to pursue and take possession of beauty, the mad one how to poise oneself for beauty to take possession of one.

In the *Symposium* Phaidros – remembering or anticipating these discourses – juxtaposes *philia* – membership in the natural (family and social) world into which one is born – against *eros* – a relation created by the particular individuals. As something created, that is, as a *factum* rather than a *datum*, *eros* responds to criteria of value: honour rather than advantage. Love thus creates a *touchstone* for our natural ends and attachments. As such it may not only end our ends and shatter our attachments, but may even dis-attach us from life itself.[95] The madness of such voluntary sacrifice of one's desires and possessions, even of life itself, is a far cry from the divine conceived as endless enjoyment of the good things of life.

But youth is foolish: it takes the older Pausanias[96] to point to an inherent difficulty. To love is to desire, and to desire is to seek to *possess*. Unlike the *formal* moral law, beauty illuminates – imbues with value – particular things in the world; unlike the *negative* moral law, which puts an end *to* our ends-seeking pursuits, beauty's desirability makes it an end *of* our pursuit. Beauty beckons and we, earthly creatures that we are, take the beckoning as an invitation to stop looking and to reach out for it.[97]

But by taking hold of it we change it from being *in* the world to being *of* the world. Pausanias doesn't get beyond distinguishing two 'drives': one seeking to possess under the description of use and enjoyment, the other under the description of honour and virtue; one for a time, the other 'for ever'.

The idea of two loves – one to be resisted or transcended, the other to be surrendered to – is further developed when Eryximachos gives it a cosmic application:[98] all disorder and sickness is due to the *hybris* of unlawful love, to intemperate and unjust transgression of proper limits. Where relation between things – love – is respectful of limits, there the whole is *kosmos*: healthy, harmonious and beautiful.

Aristophanes[99] applies the normative idea of love as creating wholeness – 'all' is not *kosmos* unless it's 'whole' – to the human condition. We are sick and needy because incomplete; love is yearning for what would complete and heal us. Love manifests itself as a yearning when the needed good is absent; as glad clinging when it is present. 'Glad clinging' we have met already – *aspazdesthai*. But yearning is – well, it is desiring what one lacks: it is *ephiesthai*.[100]

Ephiesthai now emerges as the general condition of the soul *lacking* (wanting) its good. But whereas before *ephiesthai* – construed as pursuit – determined the logical structure of the good, turning it into an end, now the good determines the response, that is, the form of the *ephiesthai*. But also – that being another side of intentionality – depending on which part of the soul we focus on, we get different (construals of) the good. When the focus is on the Will, the good becomes the end of action; when it's recognized that nothing in the world is 'the good', attention may shift to oneself as judging and bestowing value on 'things' in the world: to oneself as the (higher) Will. When, on the other hand, attention is on the perceptual/affective, then the soul's object is something to greet and rejoice in when present, to *long* for when absent.

But things are still more complex. For beauty is experienced as what is *precious* yet *distinct* from me. This 'preciousness-yet-otherness', raised in our discussion of 'emphatic realism', is often experienced as a *pain* of distance. Here the object does not evoke *aspazdesthai* but, experienced as *absence*, it evokes the restlessness of *ephiesthai*. This is in part the protest of the I at becoming a mere 'eye', the pain of the feathers breaking through the hardened surface of the wings. And since the pain is associated with looking, it's natural to seek to end it by destroying the distance needed for looking, that is, by *seizing* the object. Here we get the transformation of the *ephiesthai* of perceptual activity, or longing, into the *ephiesthai* of desire to possess turning to action in space. The weakness of our wings tempts us to move horizontally towards the object, rather than remain poised at a distance from it.

The temptation to touch, possess, mark and even mar, is the 'natural' response to beauty: it is the 'natural' face of love. It's clearest in children who want to eat all that is 'of concern' to them, and who, in their splendid impartiality, find all that comes their way of concern: for them the world is a sequence of delicious morsels.

The 'natural' response – the desire for (the possession of) the precious – is the response of the lower part of the soul. When felt as somehow wrong and resisted by, however inarticulate, a need to stand still, to view, to honour, then we can speak of the struggle between two selves, two loves, two forms of *ephiesthai*: between the two modes of the practical. And when the latter prevails, however briefly, when one consents to the I remaining the eye, and consents and clings to the precious as essentially 'other', then we can speak of transcendence as completion of the process of transcending. When beauty is experienced with gladness, when there is no pain and no struggle, then we may speak of transcendence without transcending.[101]

Two basic ways of experiencing the other as precious can be mentioned here: inanimate reality under the description of beauty; human beings under the description of (dia)logos – all that can be addressed to and received from another in thought and speech.[102] In the first case love takes the form of *aspazdesthai* as the greeting of glad acknowledgement, in the second as the greeting of *philia*, of friendship. This new *philia* which replaces that of 'natural attachments'[103] raises, sometimes insistently, the question whether love is of what is ours or of what is good. Aristophanes, in claiming that we could be made 'whole' by clinging to another human being, moves beyond the *philia* of natural attachment, but also beyond the *eros* as desire to possess another for oneself. What is now sought is *oikeiotes*: intimacy, oneness. And yet even when this is attained, his couple stands bewildered, for their coming together seems not to have healed their incompleteness. And so, filled with inarticulate yearning, they wish to be welded together, for ever to cling to one another, to lose their separate identity and become one indivisible whole. This, however, Diotima suggests, is the wrong medicine, for it is only by clinging to, intimacy with, the *good* that wholeness can be secured.[104] But this new intimacy – this fellowship with, respect for, the good – does it not exile one from the intimacy with the world? Does it not amount to *disrespect* for the world? Granted that this can't be punished by the gods as the *hybris* of unlawful entry into their domain, might it not be punishable by men, as unlawful abandonment of *theirs*: as the *hybris* of arrogance? This, however, raises issues which cannot be examined here.

(3) Doing and suffering

So far we have considered the mystery of beauty's immanence: its being in the world and given to the senses; and of the effort required in relation to it: glad or yearning recognition of its preciousness-yet-otherness. To experience a thing as valuable *für mich* because it is so *an sich*, and so precisely not *für mich* is to experience the *impersonal* – this time in its substance and particularity. Simone Weil thought that beauty was a trap set for the carnal part of the soul – the I – to seduce it into allowing the I-annulling impersonal to enter into it.[105]

There is, however, another feature of beauty's straddling the this- and the other-worldly. We said that *qua* value beauty is unconditional, and suggested that 'unconditional' is a central meaning of 'transcendental'. But 'unconditional' and 'transcendental' are often understood as what is not in the world in the sense of not being subject to change and destruction. The *Symposium* seems to offer a clear, historical, certainly a crucial, formulation of this idea. For if what we love is the good, and if the good is not in the world, then it follows that only the indestructible is worthy of respect and, consequently, that all that changes and perishes is not. To the extent to which the changeable does matter to us, it *grabs* rather than *claims* us. And that which grabs without claim must be resisted. The perishable thus descends from being not worthy of love to being unworthy of love, from there to being worthy of contempt, finally to being that which must be resisted.

But if 'unconditional' means valued independently of what it does for me – impersonal rather than unchangeable, precious rather than imperishable – then embodied beauty is unconditional: it has a right to claim. So far we considered the response to that claim at the level of perception – viewing in the right spirit – and of active surrender of pursuit. But in so far as it is in the world, beauty is also fragile and perishable. And its fragility and ephemerality do not lessen their claim on us but become constitutive of it. When the precious is fragile, *aspazdesthai* becomes *tenderness* and *pity*: 'Dear daffodils, we weep to see you pass away so soon.' Tenderness and pity are to the response to value *qua* precious. Indeed, more strongly: to see something as fragile is to see it tenderly and *thus as precious*. Here again the Greeks thought and felt more lucidly than we do. *Aidôs* means respect, but also that which is *due* to one who is helpless. The helpless are to be respected – they're *aidiôs* – not because of some inalienable 'value' which they possess *despite* their helplessness, but *on account of* their helplessness.[106]

So the fragile, like beauty and value in general, imposes *constraint on my action*: it forbids me to do anything which might harm it. But *qua* harmable, it also imposes an *obligation to act* on its behalf when it is threatened with harm. Here *ephiesthai* as deliberation, decision and effective agency, is in place. But not as expression of my 'freedom', but as obedience: action is here a *response* to the need of the object, not a 'first cause'. Such action is simply another expression of concern for the other. When things go well with its object, love takes the form of non-interfering glad acknowledgement. When, however, its object is threatened, love takes the form of protective, or restorative, action. And as *aspazdesthai*, which views the particular embodied thing as precious, requires being *in* the world, so even more does *ephiesthai* – acting on behalf of the object – require being in, *interacting with*, the world. Transcendence in the first case means concerned attention – active passivity; in the second it means acting in obedience to the demands of the object – passive activity.

But the fragile can, despite all my efforts, be destroyed. The form taken by love when its object is destroyed is *grief* or *suffering*. Grief thus seems the third form of the response to value.

Like guilt, grief is the pain at the destruction of value. As the possibility of destruction tells us that the unity of 'is' and 'value' is 'in the world', so pain tells us that we too are 'in the world'. So we transcend from wanting and using things to contemplating, protecting, and grieving for them. *Sub specie aeternis* seems thus to have brought us back into the world with vengeance: with *suffering*. The Moirai, the grim protectors of the frontiers between the human and the divine, are first silenced when men become intimate with gods by loving the same things; now, however, they are outraged as god becomes intimate with man, by sharing in his suffering: as Zeus turns from protecting the suppliant to being one himself: *Zeus aphiktôr.*[107]

Simone Weil sees human beings as shipwrecks tossed around by waves.[108] Each has a rope thrown to him from above, and can grasp it with different motives. One may hope to use the rope to escape the waves. This, however, can't be done. Another seeks to use the rope to steady himself against the buffeting of the waves. He may soon discover the opposite to be the case: the new alignment prevents him from going with the waves, turning him instead into a point of resistance. His loss of pliability means not only that the waves hit him *harder*, but also that he now experiences them as *force*: where before he was merely passive, he now *suffers*, where before he merely suffered, he's now *offended*.

But if he can hold on without bitterness or pride, then he will learn the meaning of a new tension, he will learn to distinguish the horizontal from the vertical, the necessary from the good. The cost of this may be the vertical draining the horizontal of value. When this happens the horizontal becomes incapable of sustaining his love, leaving him unable to look anywhere but upwards with gladness. Such a one 'like a bird gazes upwards, and neglects things below'.[109]

He may, however, learn to read the horizontal through the vertical: to find good in what is necessary and consent to it under that description. He may, while lucidly distinguishing the 'good' from 'ours', come to love what is ours under the description of the good. This – the return to the cave – is the highest form of transcendence. Is this 'transcending the human'? or 'finding the divine in the human'? What work does the distinction do here?

NOTES

1. I dedicate this paper to the memory of Dr Paul McLaughlin.
2. Martha Nussbaum, 'Transcending the Human', in *Love's Knowledge* (Oxford: Oxford University Press, 1990, pp. 365–91), p. 368.

3. Aristotle, *Nicomachean Ethics* 1094a.
4. Nussbaum, 'Transcending the Human', p. 365.
5. Ibid., p. 371.
6. Ibid., p. 365.
7. The passage speaks of 'bargain', but since *acceptance* is all that is wanted from Odysseus, 'gift' seems more appropriate.
8. When, as here, 'wanted' is synonymous with 'good', the question of *akrasia* does not arise.
9. Nussbaum, 'Transcending the Human', p. 366.
10. The difference is due to the article's moving between three standpoints: the hero's, the reader's and the philosopher's. Odysseus, the agent, is said to choose the human out of loyalty; we, the readers, wish him to choose it also because it's more interesting; we the philosophers come to recognize that the human is built into the very idea of value.
11. Nussbaum, 'Transcending the Human', p. 366.
12. Ibid., p. 367. The article as a whole relies crucially on concepts like 'admirable' and 'interesting'. And while 'admirable' goes back to Aristotle, 'interesting' is a recent newcomer to the philosophical scene. Its claim to the status of a central moral criterion (indeed a general philosophical criterion, as can be seen in, for example, the work of Richard Rorty) must be noticed and should be justified. We need to know whether 'interesting' constitutes merely an *'interesting* moral agent', or an *'admirable* moral agent', or a *'moral* agent' *simpliciter*. And what about human being? Is one who is boring merely boring? or unadmirable? or non-moral? or immoral?
13. Ibid., p. 371.
14. Ibid., p. 366.
15. Ibid., p. 382.
16. Indeed, it is suggested (e.g. Od. I. 62) that the name 'Odysseus' comes from *odysomai* – I grieve.
17. Here (V, 176–85) is Homer's description of Odysseus at Ogygia:

> ... tears succeeding tears / Deluged his eyes, while, hopeless of return, / Life's precious hours to eating cares he gave. / Continual, with the nymph now charm'd no more. / Yet, cold as she was amorous, still he pass'd / His nights beside her in the hollow grot, / Constrain'd, and day by day the rocks among / Which lined the shore heart broken sat, and oft / While wistfully he eyed the barren Deep, / Wept, groan'd, desponded, sigh'd, and wept again.

18. The Olympians differ in at least two important respects from Calypso.
      (1) They live in *society* and so partake of many of the activities and virtues presented by Nussbaum as peculiar to humans. Nussbaum's claim that the gods lack political dimension derives from her modern – welfare, physical well-being, oriented – standpoint, rather than from Aristotle. Indeed the Olympians, as free of bodily needs and given largely to speech-activities, are closer to Aristotle's political ideal than

are the humans. When Aristotle denies the political dimension to the divine he is thinking of his god – the *solitary* unmoved mover – not of the chatty gregarious Olympians. Calypso, like Aristotle's god, is alone; unlike him, however, she is *lonely* rather than solitary.

(2) As described by Nussbaum Calypso is possessed of 'unchanging good looks' but not of *beauty*. By contrast the Olympic goddesses are portrayed as beautiful. Their beauty is beheld even by the emphatically this-worldly Homeric heroes with glad awe rather than desire: as a *sui generis* – divine or non-natural – attribute. Nussbaum also ignores beauty in her discussion of athletics, concentrating instead on effort, on pushing and achieving. Yet without *to kalon* as the central perceptuo-ethical category we lose not only Plato, but also Aristotle, for without *to kalon* his insistence on doing and attaining acquires a bourgeois Protestant-ethic feel to it.

19. Nussbaum, 'Transcending the Human', p. 371.
20. Xenophanes, the first (Western) thinker to express the transcendental idea, does so precisely by attacking the Olympic gods. After mocking their humanness (Diels, *Fragmente*, 'Xenophanes' B11–16), he proceeds to construe the divine through ideas completely alien to the Olympic conception: oneness, mystery and goodness (ibid. 23–6). We find the same ideas in Aischylos; he, however, in view of their supra-natural character, thinks that their recognition requires suffering, stepping out of the ordinary life. For Plato god's goodness is the hinge which bears (or creates) all further attributes (*Republic* 378ff).

    It's noteworthy that Nussbaum's attack on the entire Western transcendental aspiration lacks a single passage, or even an accurate paraphrase, of anyone who felt its call and tried to come to terms with it.
21. So, for example, to fear/not want death, toil, etc., is to desire their *negation*, i.e. to desire *not* dying, *not* toiling, etc. Part II argues that this is not true of non-natural goods.
22. Thus the opening of *Nicomachean Ethics* (1094a):

    Every art and every investigation, and likewise every action and choice seems to aim at some good (πᾶσα τέχνη καὶ πᾶφα μεθοδος, ὁμοίως δὲ πρᾶξίζε καὶ προαίρεσις ἀγαθοῦ τιϑὸς ἐφίεσθαι δοκεῖ).

23. (Liddell and Scott) – *ephiesthai* ... B. Med. ... II. c. gen. to aim at (Aristotle). Aristotle uses other terms, e.g. *zdetesthai* – to seek – or *diokezdesthai* – to pursue, go after. But *ephiesthai*, just because it means 'aiming' as well 'pursuing' or 'going after', implies consciousness and epitomizes our rational-active nature.
24. Thus e.g. *De Anima*, III, 432a:

    The soul in living creatures is distinguished by two functions, the judging capacity which is a function of the intellect and of sensation combined, and the capacity for exciting movement in space.

and ibid., 433a:

Appetite and practical thought [are] the producers of movement
[in space]; for the object of appetite produces movement, and
therefore thought produces movement because the object of
appetite is its beginning ... That which moves, then, is a single
faculty, that of appetite.

25.   Aristotle, *Nic. Ethics*, I, 4; 1096b:

For even if the goodness predicated of various things in common
really is a unity or something existing separately and absolute, it
clearly will not be *practicable* or *attainable* (*prakton oude ktêton*) by
men; but such is the good which we must seek.

So also in *Metaphysics* (988b), Aristotle accuses Plato of not recognizing
the Good as object of pursuit, that is, as something for me to *cause*. Plato
would reply that the Good he was interested in was not an *object of*, but
a *limit on*, pursuit. For this view of value see Parts II and III.
     Aristotle, recognizing that Plato's Good is logically unsuitable for
ephiesthai, i.e. as not *prakton*, demands its renunciation. But the mood
of renunciation is alien to his modern followers. Taking *ephiesthai* as
the only active recognition of value, they assume that for anything to
be a good it *must* be *prakton*. So for Nussbaum (sec. iv) Plato's view of
philosophy is not 'learning how to die', that is, a judgement on one's
pursuits, but one desirable pursuit among others. This allows the
question to arise of whether philosophy is *better* than the other pursuits: 'Is the life of philosophical contemplation, or rather the life
devoted to the maximal *attainment* of this, in which all other *pursuits*
are viewed as merely supportive or instrumental, the best or highest
life?' (383, my emphasis). This portrays Plato as doing what he so
scathingly rejects in the *Phaidôn*: bartering pleasure for pleasure. I
don't discuss this here since the criticism of this construal of Plato is
implied in the general criticism of good as object of desire, and of activity as desire-propelled pursuit of it.
26.   *Phthonos* – envy and jealousy – is an important feature of the
Olympic religion. It is one form of recognizing the difference
between the high and the low. Men often envy gods' *eudaimonia*,
and begrudge their power; the gods watch jealously lest men's
good fortune turn to hybris; at times they view that good fortune
as itself hybris. The elimination of *phthonos* from the relation
between men and the gods is a crucial feature of the transcendental tradition. The Greeks accomplish it largely by eliminating force
from gods' dealings with men, replacing it with necessity; and by
eliminating fear and resentment from mens' relation to gods,
replacing it with consent. Plato is consciously undermining the
Olympian 'grammar' by explaining the creation of the world
through the fact that the Creator is '*good*, and in him that is good
no *envy* arises ever concerning anything; and being devoid of envy
he desired that all should be, as far as possible, *like unto himself*'
(*Timaios* 29e).

27. Thus, for example, Plato, *Symposium*, 200ff.
28. I say 'modern', for Aristotle differs from his modern followers not only in placing *to kalon*, a non-natural good, at the heart of his account, but also in craving the cessation of *ephiesthai*. This appears as a frequent methodological remark (for example, warnings against *ad infinitum* – 'one cannot walk on for ever'), as well as in the substance of his account: for example, his ending *Nicomachean Ethics* with the contemplative life; his construal of god as unmoved mover. His unmoving god differs from the Olympians as well as from Plato's god. The Olympians move in pursuit of 'ends', Plato's god, however, moves without end – in a circle: he walks on for ever.
29. (Liddell and Scott) – *horizdo*: Divide, separate from, as a boundary; (2) to bound. II. mark out by boundaries; III. limit, determine ... 2. define.
30. On the dependence of substance ('matter', the uncertain, the infinite) on form or limit (*peras*), see Plato, *Philebos* 25ff; Aristotle, *Met.* IX 1050a; XIV 1091a, etc.
31. Nussbaum's treatment of temperance as a consequential concern for one's bodily well-being rather than as respect for impersonal limits is marked by her substitution of 'moderation' for 'temperance': thus for the gods:

> moderation will go out too, since for a being who cannot get ill or become overweight or alcoholic, there is not only little motivation to moderate intake, but also little intelligibility to the entire concept. (374)

32. Descartes, *Philosophical Writings*, Meditation III (London: Nelson, 1954), p. 76.
33. Plato, *Gorgias*, 492e.
34. Nussbaum, 'Transcending the Human', p. 379.
35. J. Bentham, *Principles of Morals and Legislation*; J. S. Mill, *Utilitarianism*, Chapter 2. Mill's differentiation between higher and lower pleasure is an attempt to free Utilitarianism from Bentham's sensual hedonism and to bring it closer to the Aristotelian position.
36. Mill, *Utilitarianism*, Chapter 4.
37. This is not intended as an argument, but merely to point to the fact that the subject himself *experiences* the first as subjective, the second as objective. Of course the experience does not validate itself.
38. Things are different in the second and third person, where goodness can be experienced. The asymmetry between the first, second and third person is as important a feature of moral experience as is the asymmetry between the positive and the negative which I am exploring here.
39. So, for example, Raskolnikov (Dostoyevsky, *Crime and Punishment*, Chapter 1), having successfully concluded his dress rehearsal for murder, is suddenly filled with abhorrence:

> Good Lord, how disgusting it all is! And will I – will I really. ... No! It's impossible! It's absurd! ... And how could such a horrible idea have occurred to me?

This is not thought in the light of some positive, though perhaps till now forgotten, ideal, nor in conceiving a new plan to replace the old one. It simply expresses Raskolnikov's experience of his plan (and of himself having it) as 'disgusting', 'impossible', 'absurd'.

40. Perhaps the clearest formulation of this view is developed by the British Idealists at the end of the last century. But we get something approaching such a view in certain renderings of Aristotelian ethics, when good human life is presented as fundamentally pursuit of the project of becoming a virtuous moral agent.

41. I say 'in these circumstances', for I do not mean to deny the importance of positive moral ideals.

42. Kierkegaard, *The Concept of Irony* (Bloomington, Indiana: Indiana University Press, 1965), p. 56. Kierkegaard uses the example for a different purpose.

43. Wittgenstein, *Notebooks 1914–1916* (Oxford: Blackwell, 1969), p. 74.

44. The experience of 'must not' without the corresponding 'can', of the imperative indifferent to the ability to fulfill it, can take the form of cry for help: '... And lead us not into temptation, but deliver us from evil. For thine is the ... power ...' This is a very different route to God from that taken by Descartes (*Meditation* III, p. 85):

> ... how could I understand my doubting and desiring, i.e. my lacking something and not being altogether perfect – if I had no idea of a more perfect being as a standard by which to recognize my own defect?

Wittgenstein rejects this 'philosophical' route, this inference from imperfection to perfection, in favour of the experienced cry for help:

> People are religious to the extent that they believe themselves to be not so much *imperfect* as *ill* ... Any half-way decent man will think himself imperfect, but a religious man believes himself *wretched*. (*Culture and Value* (Oxford: Basil Blackwell, 1980), p. 45; Wittgenstein's emphasis)

45. Kant, *Critique of Pure Reason*, 'Appendix to the Transcendental Dialectic', A 643/B671ff; for the final summary see 'Transcendental Doctrine of Method', A707/B735ff.

46. See 'Transcendental Dialectic', A293/B350ff, for the description of the various 'contradictions' Reason gets into when it tries to generate positive content, or discover how things are. The most famous is Kant's dismantling of the ontological argument: the rejection of the move from the (necessary) thinkability of God to His existence.

47. Thus young Heinrich von Kleist, after reading the *Critique of Pure Reason*, writes to his fiancée (22 March 1801):

> ... We can never decide whether what we call truth is really the truth or whether it only seems so to us ... Oh, Wilhelmine, if this thought does not pierce your heart, at least don't laugh at one who

feels wounded in his most sacred inner self. My only, my highest, purpose is sunk, I have none left.

This experience is thought by many to have contributed to his later suicide.

48. A similar thought is expressed in the *Tractatus*, 6.41:

> In the world everything is as it is ... *In it* there is no value – and if there were, it would be of no value.

49. Thus for example *Lectures on Ethics*, 'Proem', p. 1:

> Philosophy is either theoretical or practical. The one concerns itself with knowledge, the other with the conduct of beings possessed of a free will. The one has Theory, the other Practice for its object. ... Practical philosophy being the philosophy of action, is thus the philosophy which provides rules for the proper use of our freedom.

50. See Kant, *Groundwork*, Chapter 2 (Berlin: Walter de Gruyter, 1968), pp. 417–19. The claim that willing the end implies willing the means formulates the hypothetical, that is the *grounded*, imperative: its necessity follows either from a given desire (problematic hypothetical imperative) or from my overall desire for my well-being as a sensible being (assertoric hypothetical imperative).

51. Proving the possibility of *a priori* synthetic judgement is the overall task of philosophy. But whereas 'theoretical' *a priori* judgement is validated by experience, in its practical form, as free causality, it runs *counter to* experience. After all 'ought' depends for its meaning on the possibility of not being. See for example *Groundwork*, pp. 419–20.

52. The idea of perfection as the *telos* of our striving was part of Kant's native, Leibnizean, tradition, and one of his two *bêtes noires* (the other being British Naturalism). He criticizes it either as being tautological, and so incapable of providing a true end, or, when substantive, as threatening our autonomy (see for example *Groundwork*, pp. 442–3).

53. The basic test is that of universality: the first Categorical Imperative. In its other two formulations the Categorical Imperative tries to bring out different aspects of the Will: its ground, i.e. that its 'end' is the Will itself rather than any particular object of the Will (the 2nd formulation); its freedom, i.e. the need for the law to be autonomously legislated (the 3rd formulation).

54. Thus for example *Groundwork*, p. 420:

> Everything in nature works according to laws; only a rational being has the power to act *according to his idea of laws* ... and only so has a *will*. (Kant's emphasis)

55. See for example the discussion of autonomy in *Groundwork*, pp. 432 ff.
56. *Critique of Practical Reason* (Akad. Ausg., p. 240; Beck's translation, Library of Liberal Arts, 1986, p. 139):

Is our knowledge really widened in such a way by pure practical reason, and is that which was transcendent for speculative reason immanent in practical? Certainly, but only from the practical point of view.

Or (ibid.):

The a priori ideas (of immortality, freedom and God) are here not just immanent but *constitutive* for they are the grounds of the possibility of making real the necessary object of pure practical reason (the highest good).

57. Only in willing as thinking, of course, not as acting. For I differ from God as not omnipotent (*Groundwork*, p. 434). But Kant guards against vulnerability, and so against lessening our equality with the divine in the moral sphere, by excluding agency from it. The moral 'action' is completed in the act of (committed) Will; the consequent (successful or failed) 'realization' of my Will in the outside world is at most an epilogue to the moral story.

58. The Kantian criticism of the pre-modern moral consciousness as 'shame'-based (which has long dominated classical scholarship, see for example A. W. H. Adkins, *Merit and Responsibility* (Oxford: Clarendon Press, 1960)) is directed firstly at the subject's moral dependence on the judgement of others, secondly at the failure to recognize that guilt requires responsibility, which in turn presupposes free agency. The latter in particular is underlying in our difficulties with the Greek tragedy, most clearly with *Oedipus Rex*.

59. See *Groundwork*, pp. 429ff.
    Also H. J. Paton, *The Categorical Imperative* (London: Hutchinson, 1945), p. 106:

    ... things proper (as opposed to actions) appear to be good only as means to the ends which constitute my happiness ... Broadly speaking, I find my good in *activities*, rather than in *things*. (my emphasis)

60. The 'argument' for the second categorical imperative begins (*Groundwork*, p. 428) with: 'Now *I say* that man, and in general every rational being, exists as an end in himself...' (my emphasis). For the move from thinking myself to thinking another as subject or person, see p. 429.

61. Indifference to speaking marks most Kant-influenced ethics; noticeably the discussion of 'moral dilemmas', where the agent tends to be portrayed as deliberating on *behalf of*, yet hardly ever *speaking to*, another. Sartre's example of the youth deciding whether to join the Resistance or take care of his mother is a good example: he talks to Sartre, but not to his mother.

62. Martin Buber has emphasized the second-, as opposed to the third-person, relation: the relation to 'you' rather than 'it'. Though he means this as a criticism of Kant, Buber himself underplays language

and, in an even more significant agreement with Kant, suggests that a third-person relation precludes a recognition of value. (I argue against this in Part III.)

I also disagree with Buber's (connected) suggestion that the second person is all that's needed for a proper, moral, relation. Most forms of evil (as opposed to e.g. harming) require relating, however perversely, to the other as a you, as a (serious) 'subject'.

63. This pun on 'end' is not available to German, which has *Zweck* for 'end' as purpose, *Ende* for 'end' as 'terminus'.

64. *Groundwork*, p. 431:

> This principle of humanity, and in general of every rational nature, as an end in itself (a principle which is the supreme *limiting condition of every man's freedom of action* ... (my emphasis)

65. For an excellent discussion of the combination of the extreme solitude of guilt with an intensely personal involvement with the (harmed) other, see Rai Gaita, *Good and Evil: An Absolute Conception*, esp. Chapter 4 (London: Macmillan Press, 1991).

66. Thus, P. Ricoeur, *The Symbolism of Evil* (New York: Harper & Row, 1977), p. 7:

> 'Guilt', in the precise sense [is] a feeling of the unworthiness at the core of one's *personal being*. (my emphasis)

Similarly, Christine Korsgaard, *The Sources of Normativity* (Cambridge: Cambridge University Press, 1996), p. 104:

> Reflection does not have irresistible power over us. But when we do reflect we cannot but think that we ought to do what on reflection we conclude we have reason to do. And when we don't do that we punish ourselves by *guilt* and regret and *repentance and remorse*. (emphasis added)

67. This goes particularly for modern American Kantianism (especially as influenced by John Rawls) which tends to merge Kant with Aristotle (thus for example Korsgaard in *The Sources of Normativity*: 'We could rank different sets of values according to their tendency to promote human flourishing'). But in general few contemporary thinkers would be willing to assert the independence and absolute value of the noumenal domain and the corresponding non-value of the natural. Even fewer would take the next step to argue that on any particular occasion there is but one right thing to do for anyone, anywhere, all else being 'wrong' both epistemically and morally.

68. Kantianism has come recently under criticism precisely for denying moral significance to shame and with it to the significance of our social nature – our constitutive relation to others (e.g. B. Williams, *Shame and Necessity*, Berkeley, Calif.: University of California Press, 1993). But the Kantian subject is no less prone to shame than the

Homeric or the Humean one. The difference is that he's not ashamed
before another, but before himself. But the important question
regarding shame is not so much that of audience, but what it is an
appropriate response to, that is, its logico-normative scope.

69. Thus, for example John Rawls, *Theory of Justice*, Chapter 65:

> Shame [is] the feeling that someone has when he experiences an
> injury to his *self*-respect or suffers a blow to his *self*-esteem. ...
> Regret is the general feeling aroused by the loss or absence of what
> we think good for us, whereas shame is the emotion evoked by
> shock to our self-respect, a special kind of good. Now both regret
> and shame are *self-regarding*, but shame implies an especially inti-
> mate connection with our own person ... (my emphasis)

70. To f so as to attain X is, as we saw, the material maxim generated
by the sensuous Will. But since the rational Will is formal, it relies
for its content, and thus also for its (logical) boundaries, on the
material maxim.

71. Even when Kant explicitly brings in the (outside) other as a positive
value, he ends up spelling out its significance through the I. Thus, for
example, in what is perhaps his most moving passage, at the conclusion of the *Critique of Practical Reason* (pp. 288–9; Beck, p. 166):

> Two things fill the mind with ever new and increasing admiration
> and awe, the oftener and more steadily we reflect on them; the
> *starry heaven* above me and the moral law within me. ... I
> see them before me and associate them directly with the
> *consciousness of my own existence*. ... The former view of a countless
> multitude of worlds *annihilates*, as it were, *my importance* as an
> animal creature ... The latter, on the contrary, infinitely *raises my
> worth* as that of an intelligence by my personality in which the
> moral law reveals a life independent of all animality and even of
> the whole world of sense. (my emphasis)

72. So, for example, Kant's treatment of the command to love one's
neighbour (*Groundwork*, p. 399) is but a spelling out of 'ought' (i.e.
command) implies 'can':

> For love as an inclination cannot be commanded; but beneficence
> from duty, when no inclination impels us ... is practical and not
> pathological love. Such love resides in the will and not in the
> propensities of feeling, in principles of action and not in tender
> sympathy; and only this practical love can be commanded.

73. I argued earlier (p. 190) that intention is the easiest case of imperfection, since when seen as 'impossible' it's simply annulled. Such annulment, however, is not possible with thoughts, feelings, let alone
already performed actions. What's more, Kant centers on those cases
of temptation when something desired fails the test of Reason,

thereby becoming impermissible, and assumes that this has the same logic as not wanting to do one's duty. And since he denies the possibility of conflict of duties, and assumes that anything which is not a duty is a mere desire, the only conflict he can envisage is that between Sensuality and Reason.

74. So in his critique of virtue-ethics at the beginning of *Groundwork* (p. 394), justice is missing altogether, while wisdom is transformed into prudence.

75. The problem with wisdom and justice (see note 74) can also be expressed thus: Kant can only make sense of virtue understood as my fighting against my (low) self: that is, courage and temperance. And since courage was of little concern to the urbane 18th century, Kant concentrates on temperance understood as subduing desire. The concentration on the self also helps to explain the logical priority of duties to myself.

76. Existentialism concentrates on this side of Kantianism.

77. *Critique of Practical Reason*, p. 220; Beck, p. 120.

78. Weil, *Notebooks II* (London: Routledge & Kegan Paul, 1976), p. 360. This entire Part leans heavily on the work of Simone Weil, particularly the essays collected under the title *Intimations of Christianity Among the Ancient Greeks* (London: Routledge & Kegan Paul, 1978).

79. In the following I consider merely one strand of Wittgenstein's thought, and even that not in a scholarly spirit. Nevertheless, as can be seen from his continued preoccupation with it (see, for example, 'A Lecture on Ethics' in *Philosophical Occasions 1912–1951* (Indianapolis: Hackett, 1993)), this strand was important to him.

80. Though it is a 'fact' in the original sense of the word, that is, a *construct* (*facere*), yet it's *experienced* as a fact *qua datum*. For though experience is 'constructed', the subject is not actively engaged in, or even conscious of, such constructing.

81. Descartes makes it clear that sophisticated *reasoning* is needed to introduce doubt, and that *Will* is needed to maintain it.

82. *Tractatus*, 5.631; *Notebooks 1914–1916*, p. 80: 'The thinking subject is surely an empty illusion. But the willing subject does exist.' Similarly, *Notebooks*, p. 77: 'But can I conceive a being that can only represent [*vorstellen*] (e.g. see), but not will? In some sense this seems impossible.'

83. These thoughts preoccupy Wittgenstein way past the *Tractatus*. So, e.g., *Culture and Value*, pp. 4–5 (1930s) where he reflects on the importance of a 'perspective' for finding something valuable *an sich*:

> A work of art forces us, so to speak, to see it in the right perspective; but without the art the object is a piece of nature, like any other. ... But it seems to me that there is a way of capturing the world sub specie aeterni other than through the work of the artist. It is, I think, the route of thought which flies, as it were, over the world and leaves it as it is – observing it from above, in flight.

84. *Tractatus*, 6.421. For a more detailed attempt to work out these ideas, see *Notebooks 1914–1916*, especially pp. 76–7. E.g.:

Is it possible to will good, to will evil, and not to will? Or is only he
happy who does not will? To love one's neighbour – let that mean
willing ... And yet in a certain sense it seems that not willing is the
only good.

(The German *wollen* means both 'will' and 'want'.)

As late as 1929, in his 'Lecture on Ethics', Wittgenstein links the
two experiences of the world as a transcendental object (wonder at
the world) and of oneself as a transcendental subject (feeling safe).
Though he speaks of them as separate, in his mind or 'experience'
they are clearly connected.

Similarly the above reference to *Culture and Value.*

85. Those who reject moral norms despite their usefulness, such as
    Nietzsche or Callicles, argue often from a quasi-*aesthetic* standpoint.
    They work with the ideal of 'nobility', of value as what 'shines
    through', which on being seen cannot but be admired.

86. Hence our speaking of 'seeing' or 'insight' to express understanding;
    no less important, though less developed in Western philosophy, is
    'hearing'. The big issue here is the one addressed by Plato in the
    Symposium through the 'ladder': can one 'see' and 'love' that which is
    available to the intellect (or rather, to the spirit under the description
    of intellect)? Put differently, is Kant right in claiming that we lack
    'intellectual intuition'?

87. See *Notebooks 1914–1916*, p. 80; *Tractatus* 5.633.

88. This is clearer when (*Notebooks 1914–1916*, p. 83) Wittgenstein tries to
    use the concept of contemplation to distinguish 'thing' from 'world'.
    He suggests that by 'contemplating' (for example) a stove I transform
    it from being 'one thing among the many in the world' and *make* it
    into a world. But (1) Thus used, '*kontemplieren*' does not mean con-
    templation as a glad attention to a thing of beauty, but rather an
    effort of concentration, an exercise of *Will*. (2) When, as here, atten-
    tion is directed primarily at the self, it can only find *my world*, not
    the world. 'My world' may be an attainment, but it has no independ-
    ent value and so can't *claim* me. My attention can't 'make' the stove
    beautiful; the stove as created by it can't sustain the response of
    contemplation. (3) Such an experience and such a world is essentially
    unshareable and solipsistic.

89. (Liddell & Scott) *aspazdesthai*: (1) to welcome kindly, bid welcome,
    greet. (2) to embrace, kiss, caress. (3) to follow eagerly, cleave to.

    Gerard Manley Hopkins speaks in the same spirit (*Wreck of the
    Deutschland*, V): 'For I greet him the days I meet him and bless when
    I understand.'

90. Buber, *Tales of the Hassidim* (New York: Schocken Books, 1991),
    vol. I, p. 135.

91. *Notebooks II*, p. 360.

92. See Kant's various discussions of reverence; see also the already cited
    Conclusion of the *Critique of Practical Reason*.

93. Buber, *Tales I*, p. 53.

94. This can be expressed, up to a point, in the Kantian language. As glad
    acknowledgement, *aspazdesthai* can be said to threaten the authority of

the hypothetical *problematic* imperative (pursuit of particular ends); as love, *aspazdesthai* threatens the *assertoric* imperative (concern with happiness, that is, with the overall balance of ends). The problematic imperative expresses the rationality of specific desire and the obligation of agency; the assertoric imperative expresses the rationality of one's overall being as sensuous, the obligation of happiness. The latter – prudence – stands authoritatively to the former – desire. The categorical imperative stands authoritatively to both.

95. *Symposium*, 178a–180b. Contrast between *eros* and natural attachments through the idea of honour: 178c–d; acceptance of death: 178d; Alcestis – explicit contrast between *eros* and *philia*: 179b–c.

    For *eros* as severance of 'natural' ties, see also Genesis 2:24: 'Therefore shall a man leave his father and his mother and shall cleave unto his wife and they shall be one flesh'.

96. *Symposium*, 180c–185e.
97. Homeric hymn to Demeter 8–16 (S. Weil, 'God's Quest for Man' in *Intimations*, p. 1ff.):

    And narcissus ... was brought forth as a snare for the maiden [Persephone] with the rosebud face by Earth ... And she made it bright and marvelous; all were awed at the sight ... [Persephone] began to tremble, and stretched out both her hands to seize the beautiful toy. Then the earth with its wide paths gaped open ...

98. *Symposium*, 186a–188e.
99. *Symposium*, 189c–193e.
100. (Liddell & Scott): EPHIESTHAI ... B. Med. ... II. c. gen. to aim at (Aristotle); *to long after, desire* (Plato).
101. The divine souls, and the soul of man in moments of purity, are *carried* by the revolutions of the heavens, once they reach its top. Here there is no effort. But the imperfect soul with its heavy black horse must exert itself to stay at the right level. The need to secure the necessary balance leads to an inevitable preoccupation with oneself; such, *akosmos*, a soul may thus spend more energy looking after itself, than in looking around it. It may even mistake the necessary condition – maintaining the balance – for its proper task; may even get proud of its skill in doing so. Here we get the Kantian portrayal of 'transcending' as its own end; of integrity and consistency as the main virtue.
102. This is unacceptably oversimplified, most noticeably in leaving out animals.
103. At the end of his conversation with Phaidros (*Phaidros* 279b–c) Socrates prays to the gods for the gift of harmony within himself and with the outside. But he has been granted one gift already, as emerges when he turns to Phaidros with: 'Do *we* need anything more, Phaidros? For me that prayer is enough', and receives the reply: 'Let me also *share* in this prayer, for *friends have all things in common*.' This dimension of deepened friendship endows Socrates' simple closing words – 'Let us go' – with great beauty.
104. *Symposium*, 205e: '... love is neither for half, nor for whole, unless it is good ... what men love is simply and solely the good'. Here Diotima

not only rejects Aristophanes' account, but seems to mock him by doing so using his term – *aspazdesthai*.

    Similarly the move from Genesis 2:24 to Mark 3:31–5: 'Who is my mother and my brethren? ... whosoever shall do the will of God, the same is my brother, and my sister, and mother.'

105.   Weil, 'God's Quest for Man' in *Intimations*, p. 3:

> The soul in quest of pleasure encounters the divine beauty which appears here below in the form of the beauty of the world, as a snare for the soul. By the power of this snare God seizes the soul in spite of itself.

106.   For a discussion of *aidôs*, see Gilbert Murray, *The Rise of the Greek Epic*, (Oxford: Oxford University Press, 1960), pp. 83–90; also S. Weil, 'Zeus and Prometheus' in *Intimations*, p. 71.

107.   S. Weil, ibid:

> The supplication of a sufferer comes from God himself, and one cannot push the sufferer away without offending God. The Greeks stated that thought by an admirable expression: 'Zeus suppliant', not 'Zeus, the protector of suppliants'.

108.   'The Pythagorean Doctrine' in *Intimations*, p. 194.
109.   *Phaidros* 249d–e.

13

Transcendence, Genealogy and Reinscription

Michael Hodges

Professor Barabas has argued in a very rich and useful discussion that we cannot understand what it would mean to 'transcend the human' in terms of prudence or practical wisdom for, in such terms, the ideal would be simply an unbroken string of satisfactions which would finally be quite boring. She has also argued that if we understand transcendence in terms of the ethical – at least from Kant's point of view – we will be committed to a 'hierarchically structured dualism'; but 'few...would be willing to assert the independence and absolute value of the noumenal domain' (p. 227). I am in broad agreement with her on these two points.[1] In fact, I have argued in some detail that the early Wittgenstein's own views fall prey to the same sort of argument that she develops in Kant's case.[2]

Having examined the meaning of transcendence from the perspective of self-interest and ethics, she turns to aesthetic experience, particularly the experience of beauty. In what follows I will argue against Kant's dualism as conceived by Barabas and show how that same argument applies to the Wittgenstein of the *Tractatus*. Then I will attempt to assess her claims about the experience of beauty by bringing them into relation with Kierkegaard's discussion of Abraham in *Fear and Trembling*.

The account of the self that is implicit in Kant's ethics is, in the final analysis, incoherent and, I believe, so is a very similar account found in Wittgenstein's early philosophy. In order for ethics to be anything but an illusion Kant needs a distinction between the self as object – phenomenon – and the self as moral subject – noumenon. That is, he needs what Barabas calls a 'hierarchically structured dualism'.[3] Since the self as phenomena cannot not be free, it cannot be a moral agent. Only the self noumenally understood could

possibly be free, for as we know, the category of cause and effect is
a priori valid for, and only for, phenomena. But the difficulties here
are obvious. What sense can it make to talk of a noumenal *self*?
How is it possible, for example, to identify certain events – mere
phenomena – as the *actions* of a 'particular' noumenal self as
opposed to another? More particularly, what sense could it make to
talk of multiple selves? There is simply no way to individuate anything noumenal. It would seem that Kant would, at best, be committed to a sort of moral solipsism. But, of course, that would
destroy the very thrust of his ethical views, for there could be no
sense to 'the other' as moral subject and so 'the other' could not
constitute a limit for my actions. When Kant, in the third formulation of the Categorical Imperative, says 'so act as to treat humanity,
whether in thine own person or in that of another in every case as
an end, never only as a means,' he seems to naively assume that
there is one and only one moral self for each human being –
phenomenon. But such an assumption is devastating to his critical
philosophy.

The idea that there might be different 'transcending subjects' –
different noumenal subjects – would seem to undercut the unity
and objectivity of the world of phenomena. In the first *Critique*
Kant argues for what he calls transcendental idealism and empirical realism, but if Kant admits sense to the idea of individuated
noumenal subjects there will be as many non-overlapping worlds
as there are such subjects, and the problems of skepticism and
solipsism rear their ugly heads again. In short, it would seem that
the thrust of the critical philosophy requires that it make no sense
to talk of 'different noumenal selves' and the thrust of the critical
ethical philosophy requires that it does. Kant cannot have it both
ways. It would seem that there are good reasons why it is difficult
to find someone today who is willing to take seriously the idea of
the noumenal. Of course, it may be possible to avoid such objections by 'naturalizing' Kant's 'hierarchically structured dualism'
but to do that would force Kant or his interpreter back to the
prudential model of transcendence already rejected by Barabas.[4]

I have argued that Wittgenstein also falls prey to this sort of -
criticism because his ethical view in the end presupposes distinct
moral subjects or ethical wills.[5] Perhaps the way to develop the point
here is by noting a certain ambiguity in a claim that Professor Barabas
makes. She says that for Wittgenstein, the world as 'transcendental
object' 'is given to perception, rather than to the will/agent'.[6]

But this is both true and false. After all 'the world' is not given to perception at all. A particular scene is given on a particular occasion of perception. 'The world' as the totality of facts is 'given' only to the metaphysical subject and the same distinction applies to the will or self as agent. While it is quite correct to say that the world as transcendental is not given to the will *as agent*, it *is* given to the will *as ethical*. In Wittgenstein's early thought 'will' must be considered at two levels. There is the engaged will, desiring this, wanting that and setting about to effect change in the world; but this will – what I call 'the empirical will', following Kant – is ethically irrelevant. In this sense the world as transcendental object is not 'given to the will' any more than the world as 'transcendental object' is given to the individual subject situated in the world. After all,

> The philosophical self is not the human being, not the human body, or the human soul, with which psychology deals, but rather the metaphysical subject, the limit of the world – not a part of it.[7]

Only that will which wills the world as a whole – from outside – can be the ethical subject. Such a will is not and cannot be an item in the world and it is not an agent. 'It is impossible to speak about the will in so far as it is the subject of ethical attributes. And the will as a phenomenon is of interest only to psychology'.[8] Just as the so-called metaphysical subject 'shrinks to a point without extension' leaving only the reality co-ordinate with it, so does the will on the ethical side. But apparently there are different ways of willing the world as a totality.

> ... if the good or bad exercise of the will does alter the world, it can alter only the limits of the world, not the facts – not what can be expressed by means of language. In short the effect must be that it becomes an altogether different world. ... The world of the happy man is a different one from that of the unhappy man.[10]

The 'happy man' wills the world so that will and object coincide – so that what is willed and what is are one and the same. This will shrinks to a point without extension but it does not 'disappear', for the world of the happy man is a different world. It is suffused with happiness or beauty. Wittgenstein says in his *Notebooks*, 'The work of art is the object seen *sub specie aeternitatis*; and the good life is the world seen *sub specie aeternitatis*. This is the connexion between art and ethics.'[11] For Wittgenstein, as for Professor Barabas, aesthetic experience is a form of transcendence, but for Wittgenstein this involves a way of experiencing the world as a whole, not individual items in the world. The world as transcendental object is thus revealed to or presupposed by both the logical and the ethical parts of the *Tractatus*, for just as 'the world' is never an object for any particular subject but only for the metaphysical subject, so 'the world' is not the object of a particular will but only of the will as ethical will, that is, the will as transcendent.

Now all this would seem to commit Wittgenstein to 'a hierarchically structured dualism' just as with Kant and so one would suspect the same incoherence that was discovered in Kant and I think that Wittgenstein is guilty of. He is guilty of confusing psychological transcendence – a possible attitude for a particular will – in which the world appears as an aesthetic object to be appreciated, with the logical or metaphysical transcendence of the metaphysical subject.[12] For, of course, it is a fact about a particular will that it wills the world as an aesthetic object and as such, it is a fact that has no value. It can only 'have value' if it stands outside all facts, but then what could it mean to *speak* of such a will? If, after all, it is impossible to speak about the will as ethical then Wittgenstein should have followed his own injunction to pass over in silence what cannot be said.[13] Thus we must naturalize the transcendence on the ethical side, but in so doing it becomes just another strategy of a particular will and so fails to be transcendence in the relevant sense. Wittgenstein seems to be bound up in the same difficulties that we found in Kant. Either his view presupposes an unacceptable dualism or it offers no real alternative to the original model considered – that of prudence.

I now turn to Professor Barabas' discussion of beauty and specifically to her claim that 'its perceptual character protects beauty against the standard skeptical treatment of "moral" values: the claim that they are a mere cover for some interest – be it of an individual, the strong individual, the ruling class, the society, the species, or nature as a whole'.[14] But as she argues, since beauty 'serves no purpose', 'has no value', such accounts must fail. It is by no means clear exactly what is meant by the 'standard skeptical treatment' here or which philosophers she has in mind, but, in any case, there are two questions confused in her claim. (1) What is the analysis of the concept or experience of 'beauty'? and (2) Under what conditions, natural, historical or individual, does a concept such as 'the beautiful' form? For Barabas, it is part of the analysis of the concept or experience of beauty that 'it [beauty] serves no purpose'.[15] But from this claim, it does not follow that there are not purposes or interests implicit in the formation of that concept. Concepts such as beauty have histories and arise out of particular concatenations of circumstances. And as Wittgenstein has pointed out,

> if anyone believes that certain concepts are absolutely the correct ones, and that having different ones would mean not realizing something that we realize – then let him imagine certain very general facts of nature to be different from what we are used to, and the formation of concepts different from the usual ones will become intelligible to him.[16]

While Wittgenstein here speaks of the circumstances of concept formation as 'certain very general facts of nature' he also goes on to 'compare a concept with a style of painting' where the question of human history clearly emerges.

After all, Nietzsche was not interested in the 'analysis of the concepts of good and evil'. That he could leave to Kant or Hegel. He was interested in the question 'What historical forces conspired to produce such a set of concepts and what interests were served and what violated in that formation?' And he tells a story of powerful interests at war with each other. That we can ask the second sort of question means that whatever the analysis of a concept may be, there is still room for a further evaluative question. Should we continue to operate with that concept in light of what forces were at work in its formation and specifically what is excluded by its deployment? This question reinscribes the experience of beauty within the domains of either the ethical or the prudential depending on the nature of the 'should'. If what is experienced as beautiful is historically conditioned, the very existence of such experience is open to question.

It would, of course, be possible to remove the possibility of any critique here by claiming *contra* Wittgenstein that certain concepts are the absolutely correct ones having a non-historical, non-worldly basis. However, such a move would seem to commit one to just the sort of 'hierarchically structured dualism' that Barabas thinks no one is willing seriously to consider today.[17] Short of this, we must reject her contention that 'if *aspazdesthai* involves moving into the divine sphere and so exceeding the limits, gods have only themselves to blame. Having created beauty and creatures capable of perceiving it, they cannot blame them for responding.'[18] If we substitute for the gods here the historical conditions of concept formation, then consciousness of those conditions creates the possibility of transformation and with it the possibility of blame for continuing on our given path.

There is a second way to approach the issues raised in the previous discussion which does not require us to accept the legitimacy of genealogy as a philosophical method and for that reason may be less controversial.[19] Professor Barabas attempts to locate the experience of beauty outside of the ethical because, as she says, 'to say that one is grabbed by reality and claimed by value is *descriptive*. *Aspazdesthai* is a *response* and so has no reason or motive, certainly no purpose. Lying thus beyond the Will it seems to lie beyond "ought".'[20] Again she says, 'if *aspazdesthai* is transcendence, it yet involves no *act* of transcending and so nothing for which one can be held responsible.' But this is a surprising claim, for one might very well be held responsible for spending too much time in the art gallery and not enough time helping the poor and unfortunate masses. That is, we might very well judge not the value of the experience but its value as part of a larger whole. Surely that cannot be excluded.

In fact, questions of both prudence and ethics can be reintroduced at this point. While it may be unfortunate, it may also be a matter of practical wisdom to plow up that field of flowers to provide a field for growing corn. Or it might be necessary ethically to tear one's self away from the gallery and get back to the operating room in order to save lives.

It is worth pointing out that some contemporary performance art is aimed at this very issue. For example Chris Burden's work calls into question the separation between the aesthetic and the ethical or prudential. In one work the audience is seated before a television set which shows Mr Burden himself seated in front of a gun pointed at him and set to go off in a fixed period of time. Part of the situation is that we are told that Mr Burden is actually located behind a screen at the back of the stage on which the television set rests. He is in the hall but the audience's view of him is mediated by the television. How are we to react to this 'work of art'? Shall we maintain our usual aesthetic distance? Certainly the scene transfixes one. But in the meantime Mr Burden may be shot and die. Should I intervene? Does Burden have the right to impose such a problem on me in the name of Art? Perhaps I should let him die. After all, it would serve him right. If I do intervene, will I disrupt the 'work' or become a part of it? Do such questions make any difference in the face of the impending death? Here the neat line between aesthetic experience and ethical or prudential experience is intentionally challenged or called into question, but these or similar questions exist at the horizon of all aesthetic experience.[21]

Perhaps the way to put the matter here is that aesthetic experience may be an experience of transcendence but it is not an experience that transcends. There are, at least, two perspectives that one can take on such experiences. From within the experience it can be described as a form of transcendence which displaces other claims and limits their authority, but such an experience can also be situated within the larger field of human experiences in which it must make out its own legitimacy. In this larger field its claims become only some among others.

It is worth noting before we leave this topic that what Professor Barabas says about beauty can be said for any all-intrinsic value. Each is 'good for nothing', having no purpose. In fact, each is a purpose insofar as we seek it for its own sake. No compelling argument can be given for its value – it just is good, right, beautiful and if you don't see it you miss seeing something important, valuable etc. It is your failure, not that of the object. Surely this is how it is from within the experience. And yet, where there is radical disagreement, 'giving reasons must come to an end'. There is a gap between reasons and actions or experiences.

There is one form of experience that is conspicuous by its absence in Professor Barabas' discussion, especially in light of the general topic and the form of her argument. That is religious experience. I say this because her argument bears a striking resemblance to Kierkegaard's famous discussion of Abraham in *Fear and Trembling* in the following way. She moves from the prudential to the ethical terms and finally turns to a form of experience in which there is a 'suspension of the ethical' but for her that occurs in the experience of beauty, not in the experience of God's command. This omission is even stranger because the account of temptation that she gives would seem to rule out the possibility of describing Abraham's situation as a temptation.

She says that to be tempted 'just is to want to f under some description of (mere personal) want and to feel obligated to not f under some description of (impersonal) right or good'. But if we accept this account then Abraham was not tempted, since it is certainly false that he wanted to f under some mere personal description. He does not want to kill Isaac under any description, much less a personal one. And as Kieregaard argues, the highest moral obligation is that a father should not kill his son. If one can only be tempted by things personal over against the ethical, then how are we to understand Abraham and the transcendence that he brings into the world? Perhaps this religious transcendence offers us a mode of transcendence that will resist the sort of reinscription that I have argued for in relation to the beautiful?

It is the burden of Kierkegaard's argument that Abraham cannot be understood in either ethical or prudential terms. Any attempt to understand his willingness to sacrifice his son in terms of self-interest turns him into a monster willing to trade his son for his own eternal bliss. And Kierkegaard also insists that the highest ethical expression of the situation is that a father has an obligation not to kill his son. There simply is no overriding ethical principle at hand. Thus it would seem that in the experience of Abraham we have an example of a form of transcendence in which the believer comes into relation with someone or something that is 'higher' than anything human and in that relation the individual is transformed in a way that is beyond human capacity. Abraham, in his relation to God, transcends the human.

Must we accept such an account? The very same difficulties arise here as in the case of Barabas' analytic of the beautiful. On the one alternative, we might accept Kierkegaard's description of Abraham as the knight of faith but call such a possibility into question by means of a genealogy of the religious à la Nietzsche. We might reject Abraham as a model in light of what other possibilities of experience are destroyed by the dominance of the religious. I do not need to develop such a path here for Nietzsche has already done so.

Let me turn to the second approach. As was shown with Barabas' analytic of the experience of the beautiful, we must distinguish between the description of the religious experience from within and the question of the legitimate place of such an experience in a full human life, and this second question allows us to reinscribe religious experience within either the ethical or the prudential.[22]

Let me try to develop this point in relation to Abraham. When the story begins for Kierkegaard we hear that 'God tempted Abraham saying ...' The story begins from a transcendent perspective. It is an unquestioned assumption of Kierkegaard's treatment that it is God who speaks to Abraham.[23] We are not authorized to call this assumption into question. The experience as described already contains, one might say, half of the absolute relation to the absolute, namely the Absolute.[24] The only issue is whether the other half – Abraham's half – will be forthcoming. And for him the only language in which that issue can express itself is whether he will do the will of God or sin.

Now in this context it is a well-known feature of the story that Abraham himself cannot know that he will not be required to sacrifice Isaac. If he does know that, his actions are mere sham and play-acting. He would not have given up Isaac at all. If he did know then he would not have been called out of the ethical at all. There would be no 'suspension of the ethical'. But can the same thing be said for the rest of us as readers of the story? Isn't it essential to the point of the story that we know how it turns out? If we are to take this as a story about faith – true faith – can we suppose that Abraham does sacrifice Isaac? Suppose, for a moment, that the story ended with a bloody description of the evisceration of Isaac. Would this be included in the biblical canon? Would it be taken as the 'Word of God'? With this question we locate ourselves outside the story and demand that it meet certain ethical or prudential stand-ards. Of course, we do not need to pass judgement on God *per se*. Rather we can refuse to believe that God speaks in this story. We reject the story of Abraham as a story about an absolute relation to the Absolute. It is this possibility that relocates the experience of tran-scendence which defines the character of Abraham within the larger field of experiences, if not for Abraham, at least for the rest of us.

I do not mean to suggest that the ethical takes priority over the religious or the aesthetic but rather to point out that each can 'stand in judgement of the other' and insofar as the debate between them is broached, there will be no neutral ground from which to settle the question. As I have argued, the possibility of moral argument presupposes *de facto* agreement. It cannot generate that agree-ment.[25] It is the burden of Kierkegaard's argument to show that the ethical and the religious are incommensurable and that from the perspective of the religious there can be no question of authority. The religious is constituted by a relation to intrinsic and immediate authority – an absolute relation to the Absolute. But without a prior hierarchy which somehow ranks claims from competing domains, we can only speak from within a structure of claims which claims for itself absolute authority. For one within the grasp of the beautiful or the religious there can be no room for the question of authority, but for one outside that grasp there can be no question of its legitimacy. It does no good to insist that the Bible must be true because it says that it is!

Perhaps there is something to be learned from the way these different discourses take hold of us and situate other claims. Professor Barabas lets us see how from the perspective of 'being grasped by the beautiful' other sorts of claims on us fall away. Their authority is experienced as contingent and secondary and we have seen that the reinscription of the experience of the beautiful within the ethical or prudential produces the same effect for it. I have argued that the same is true for Abraham and religious experience. From within the experience of an absolute relation to the Absolute, every other claim, even the ethical, loses its validity. But the possibility of the reinscription of that discourse within another interrupts any claim to validity beyond the discourse itself. This interruption contains a possibility of transcendence which has not yet been examined. It is the experience of contingency of, and therefore the possibility of the absence of, all structures of meaning.

If the validity of a claim is a function of the discourse or language-game in which it has a place then, of course, within that sphere there can be no question of its application. For Abraham the experience of God just is that of an absolute relation to the Absolute. For one grasped by the beautiful there can be no question of carrying on in the some old way. However, the possibility of an interruption of that language-game by reinscription also shows the limit of such claims. And, as David Wood has pointed out, this limit can be read in two ways. On the one hand, it guarantees validity within the sphere of its application. But 'another reading of the appearance of these limits is possible: that they represent the return of the repressed, the re-emergence of the aporetic dimension. ... Limits of validity mean: beyond this point, unintelligibility, contradiction, aporia.'[26] The movement to guarantee by limitation also requires that the intelligible occur within an horizon of unintelligibility or non-meaning.

It is very difficult to remain clear at this point, for such 'non-meaning' is not just the open-ended possibility of imagining 'the interruption' of one discourse in the process of reinscription. For while, as we have seen, that is clearly possible, we are always left within a structure of meaning. To describe such a possibility is to remain within the structures of meaning even as it involves the substitution of one discourse or language-game for another. What seems to come into view is a much more radical possibility – the absence of meaning altogether. The experience of the beautiful, to take Barabas' case, shows the contingency of the claims of the ethical and the prudential, but the possibility of reinscription shows the contingency of the claims of beauty as well, and it is this contingency of meaning taken as a pervasive feature of all structures of meaning that concerns us here.

There is an obvious sense in which such a condition – the absence of all meaning – cannot be articulated. It can only 'seem to come into view' because, of course, any articulation of such a view will involve the deployment of some structures of meaning and will thus 'paper over' the backdrop of non-meaning in the context of which all meaning already exists. This possibility is experienced in the contingency of meaning – in the displacement of language-games when we imagine first the event of being grasped in which other claims are displaced and then in the reinscription in which even the being grasped is displaced. But this 'experience'[27] is a possibility which cannot strictly speaking be given voice. 'The absence of meaning' can have no language. There may be much that we are tempted to say in the face of such an experience but nothing can force itself upon us here. Nothing can be accurate to the 'experience' itself.

How then should we speak in the 'presence' (intentional bad choice of words) of the absence of meaning? This absence of meaning is what is on the margin of all structures of meaning. So it is other to all structures of meaning – it is the radically other to all structures of meaning.[28] By 'radically' here I mean to focus attention on the sheer absence of meaning as opposed to mere difference in meaning, although it is in the possibility of difference that absence interjects itself. It should be obvious, in one sense, that there can be no way to 'speak' at this point for all speaking will involve the invocation of structures of meaning which are exactly what has been called into question by the in-breaking of the radically other. We are left speechless. But speech should not be taken in a narrow sense here. No actions follow from this 'experience' either. No lifestyles are implied. No political agenda is suggested. No attitude modification is recommended. In each of these cases we would involve ourselves in structures of meaning. Even literal silence would fare no better. If one does not speak, that not-speaking will happen on an occasion and will thus be a not-speaking about whatever the occasion suggests. That is, my not-speaking will also be drawn into structures of meaning. One cannot therefore speak or remain silent in relation to the radically other. One cannot act or remain inactive either. Does this mean that one is unchanged or indifferent here? I will try to argue that there are some lessons that can be learned even if nothing is forced upon us. To see how this might be I will follow out one response to the 'experience' we have been focussed on.

Some may be tempted to speak in religious terms at this point.[29] After all, it is just God that is at the limit of all human structures of meaning – always outside and beyond the grasp of human thinking. In fact it might be argued that such an experience of the radically limited character of human meaning is just that experience that funds an awareness of the divine. This is not an unfamiliar line of development.

Now, on the face of it, an appeal to some structure of meaning, for example, the language of God, would seem to be an attempt to paper over the rift. What I mean here is that that language, at least, as it has functioned in the past, has been used precisely to deny a limit to structures of meaning. The appeal to God has been used to reject the contingency of meaning and to invoke a perspective from which meaning is grounded in the eternal. *As such* it functions to reject the very experience that it takes as its point of departure.

And yet, it might be argued that we cannot determine this limit of meaning in an anti-theistic nor even anti-ontological sense either. And this is certainly correct if these are taken in any positive sense at all. Of course, such notions as 'anti-theistic' and 'anti-ontological' invoke structures of meaning just as much as do 'theistic' and 'ontological'. But there are seeds of real confusion here. One cannot argue from the absence of determination to any positive claim at all. In a sense that absence allows for *any* speaking but it requires none. Hume's question in the *Dialogues Concerning Natural Religion* becomes relevant here. What difference would there be between atheist and theist? If language fails us then that is the insight and nothing more. What this means, on the negative side, is that no deployment of language here can be judged from the perspective of accurate representation. There is nothing to represent. What does it mean to believe in or deny the existence of 'a "something"' – and even this is too much – that is radically other to all structures of meaning? Wittgenstein says in another context, 'So in the end when one is doing philosophy one gets to the point where one would like to just emit an inarticulate sound. – But such a sound is an expression only as it occurs in a particular language-game [structure of meaning] which should now be described'.[30] On the representational model this would appear to be what the theist and the anti-theist have in common – the uncontrollable urge to emit an inarticulate sound.

That is why there is something wrong if the original claim about anti-theism is taken as a defense of theological talk. It seems to win by theft what it could not get in a fair encounter because it leaves the debate between theist and anti-theist within the domain of the representational model. In that context there is simply nowhere to go. Wouldn't the only legitimate move be to follow Wittgenstein's famous advice and admit that what we cannot speak about we must pass over in silence? We would, then, know that any religionist or anti-religionist who loudly insisted on his or her point was inconsistent and disingenuous and the rest of us could, at least, live with those who remain silent.[31] But actually no one expects either party to remain silent and this presents us with a new problem. What drives the religionist, or anyone who would speak at this point, to speech?

The desire to employ a language of divinity or any other language cannot be forced upon us by the 'very nature of the case', for the case that we are considering is that of the 'absence' of all natures. So that desire must arise from another source and the particular content of a discourse spoken in the absence of meaning must be borrowed from other domains. In short, how this experience will be taken up is a function of what 'structures of meaning' are available to the speaker. In this recognition the issues have been transformed from classical metaphysical/ontological matters to questions of ethics and/or politics. In other words, we, who are observers and not participants, must take up the languages of the religious life in a new way.[32] We must ask what values are embodied herein. Which aspects of human life are highlighted and which forced into the shadows? What political and social agendas underlie the urge to speak at this point and in this way? In other words, we must turn away from the transcendental *per se* and ask what place such speakings have in life. To refuse to take up religious language in this way is quite literally to condemn oneself to silence. Otherwise, there is simply nothing to say.

NOTES

1. I have discovered that Professor Barabas is quite willing to accept such a hierarchy and in fact sees the need for such as the thrust of her analysis of both the ethical and the beautiful. Needless to say I do not agree with her on this point. My contention is that her argument involves an attempt to draw an ontological conclusion from a claim descriptive of language or experience. I do not believe that such moves can be made as will be clear from my remarks.
2. See my *Transcendence and Wittgenstein's* Tractatus (Philadelphia: Temple University Press, 1990), especially Chapters 5, 6, and 7.
3. There are, of course, other interpretations of Kant but it is not clear that they would avoid the problems that Barabas raises without falling into a 'naturalized' version of Kant's position.
4. See pp. 206–7.
5. See my *Transcendence and Wittgenstein's* Tractatus, especially Chapters 5–8.
6. See p.208.
7. *Tractatus*, 5.641.
8. Ibid., 6.423.
9. Ibid., 5.64.
10. Ibid., 6.43.
11. Wittgenstein, *Notebooks 1914–1916* (Oxford: Blackwell, 1969), p. 83.
12. The details of this argument are presented in Chapter 6 of *Transcendence and Wittgenstein's* Tractatus.
13. *Tractatus*, 7. Here I leave out of account those interpretations of the *Tractatus* which construe it as literally 'saying nothing' – interpretations by Conant and Diamond – not because I don't find them plausible but because I am not sure how to think them through in terms of the ethical view of the *Tractatus*. In any case, it should be clear that Wittgenstein's early position will be plagued by the sort of objections outlined here only if it can be interpreted as 'saying something'.
14. p. 209.
15. Ibid.
16. *Philosophical Investigations* (Oxford: Blackwell, 1953), II, p. 230.
17. But which she is willing to accept.
18. p. 212.
19. I don't mean by this comment to reject or call into question my previous discussion but simply to offer an alternative approach.
20. p. 212.
21. It would be possible to reject such examples as having nothing to do with beauty, but such an approach would, at least, owe us an account of beauty or be open to the charge of begging the question.
22. It is of great importance to keep in mind that the questions that I am proposing cannot be Abraham's questions, for he is within the sphere of the religious. But, of course, there may come a time when other matters occur to him.

23. It would be more correct to say that the unquestioned assumption is that of Johannes de Silentio, but I will not broach the issues of the pseudonymous authorship here.

24. Notice that, according to this experience, absolute authority in such a way as to give it unrestricted priority to all others would seem to require us to endorse another example of that 'hierarchically structured dualism' so unpopular today. Of course, if that is not a problem, another arises, for if ethical experience requires a dualism so must the experience of the beautiful and now also the religious. How many selves will there be? Four? Or will each 'mode of experience' require one more?

25. See my 'The Status of Ethical Judgements in the *Philosophical Investigations*', *Philosophical Investigations* 18 (1995), 99–112.

26. David Wood (ed.), *On Paul Ricoeur: Narrative and Interpretation* (New York: Routledge, 1986), p. 5.

27 I am here put in mind of Wittgenstein's reference to three 'experiences' of transcendence in his 'Lecture on Ethics', *Philosophical Review* 75 (1965), pp. 3–12. He speaks of 'experiences' that cannot be put into words. Here we seem to have found another.

28 I think that it is possible to come to this 'experience' by way of the contingency of each and all language-games. In Part II of the *Philosophical Investigations* at p. 230, in a passage quoted earlier, Wittgenstein seems to countenance such a possibility.

29. One might be tempted to speak in a variety of ways – of mystery, of wonder, of the beauty of the world. Each of these language-games might be invoked and, no doubt, others. The religious response is here taken as an example. It is an instructive example because of the pervasive nature of this response in our cultural history. Why that is so is, of course, an interesting and perhaps answerable question.

30. *Philosophical Investigations*, p. 261.

31. Of course, I do not speak here of literal silence. There can be much use of religious language in the act of worship, for example, but that speaking is not to be taken up on the representational model.

32. Here I refer to those of us who would think about, not simply deploy, a particular language. If you will, this accounts for Kierkegaard's distance from Abraham, but the point also applies to those who deploy but also want to step outside and come to the defense of a way of speaking.

Part Seven
Voices in Discussion

14

Voices in Discussion

D. Z. Phillips

The papers in the symposia led to discussions to which I have tried to do justice in what follows. The reactions to these discussions, however, are mine and I do not claim to summarize different points of view in ways which would always be acceptable to their proponents. That is one reason why I have not attributed the various voices in this afterword to specific participants in the conference. Where similar points were repeated at various times by different participants I have not hesitated to bring them together in a single 'voice' where I have thought this philosophically or stylistically advantageous. Nevertheless, my hope is that the end result will give a fair indication of the discussions which occurred, and that this record will enhance the collection.

'Voices in Discussion' was written immediately after the conference from notes I had taken throughout it. I am also grateful to those participants who gave me their formal replies to use in these discussions as I saw fit. The discussions take no account of modifications or changes in the papers which occurred between the conference and the publication of this collection.

Voice A

I was asked to begin this conference with a general discussion of the epistemological issues posed by the notion of transcendence. Let me make it clear that by 'transcendence' I mean ontological transcendence, something objective, absolute, complete. Some people call it 'God'. My fellow symposiasts react to the notion in different ways. Some, while denying the notion in this form entirely, want to keep a use for the transcendent and the divine. For some this use is secular and for others it is religious. For some its rejection is tied to a denial of survival after death, while for others that survival is crucial since it brings to fulfilment a process of human development which otherwise, for many, would end in wretchedness and misery.

I want to argue that transcendence in the sense I am attacking is the desire for Nagel's 'view from nowhere', a desire to see things as they are and not simply through the lenses of our perspectives and practices. On this view, there is an internal connection between transcendence and truth. But this ideal is an illusion. There is no God's-eye view of everything. We need to replace this search for Truth with a capital 'T' with the knowledge we work with, a knowledge which enables us to distinguish between innovation and banality.

To B this sounds like Rorty, but I disagree profoundly with Rorty's emphasis on language. Although he emphasizes free enquiry, what interests him primarily is alternative forms of language. This is why Freud is so important to him. My emphasis, on the other hand, is on our creative artifacts and the pervasive influence they have in our culture. It is these which enable us to progress. These are the nuclei of our culture. I'm thinking of artifacts such as the clothes button, the wheel, concrete as opposed to stone bridges, and so on.

B likes my historical emphasis, but thinks I lapse into an instrumental naturalism, and make *that* my new god. What I do want to say is that there is something about *Homo sapiens* that drives them on to create artifacts. There would be no culture without them. An artifactual culture is our very oxygen. We couldn't exist without this high level of innovation. We live with a dangerous tension between this need and corporate authorities which hinder the conditions in which it can flourish.

But none of this needs the notion of Truth with a capital 'T'. B urges me to consider what 'truth' comes to in different contexts, but why not simply abandon the term and replace it with 'knowledge'?

Voice B

I am indeed sympathetic to A's aims of exposing the emptiness of 'the view from nowhere', and to abandoning the metaphysical notion of Truth, but I disagree with the conclusions which he thinks are entailed by these aims. One should not be led to speak in a general way about the valuelessness of truth. We can ask what a concern for truth comes to in various contexts without invoking the metaphysical notion of Truth.

In *Philosophical Investigations*, para 136, Wittgenstein says that 'p is true' simply means 'p'. He is not, as some have thought, advancing Ramsey's redundancy theory of truth, because he goes on to speak

of the relation between a proposition and truth. He criticizes correspondence theories which simply say that the proposition must 'fit'
the truth. He insists that we must pay attention to the ways in which
saying something (the propositions, if you will) are *interwoven* with
a concern for truth. What this amounts to in particular contexts will
depend on *how* you discuss the truth or falsity of what is said.

A wants to get rid of the correspondence theory of truth, and I
sympathize with this. But he offers, as substitutes, reliability or
enhancing our performative capacities. But this is equally vacuous.
Think of ordinary examples such as testimony in a law court. The
correspondence theory of truth may run into all sorts of difficulties
here, but that is no reason to jettison a concern for truth. The witness
is asked, 'Is this what happened?' and replies, 'Yes, that's how it
was.' We can't substitute any talk of 'passing for truth' or 'consistency' for this. If we do, we'll miss what a concern for truth comes to
in this context or the context Havel found himself in, where he knew
his captors would misconstrue and misuse what he said.

Voice C

I want to say 'p' entails 'p is true'. Isn't A led to deny this, only
because his criterion of truth is too stringent? He refuses to call 'p'
true if there is a *possibility* of its not being true. Of course, if that
possibility is realized we cannot say 'p is true'. But the possibility
itself does not prevent us from doing so.

Voice A

I don't want to allow your talk of 'truth' at all.

Voice C

But people believed the earth was flat.

Voice A

No one ever believed it. Greek and medieval scientists didn't
believe it.

Voice D

Do you allow us to say something can be reliable, but not true?

Voice A

It all depends what you mean.

Voice E

Look, the Ptolemaic system was wrong. They thought they knew, but didn't. Don't you need to bring in truth here?

Voice A

You have two different scientific methodologies. I object to saying, 'They *thought* they knew, but we *know*.'

Voice E

Are you going to say, 'It was knowledge, but it was false?'

Voice F

The examples of large-scale scientific differences allow you to speak of different methodologies. If you want to resist the notion that 'the facts', or the concept of 'factuality', is simply 'given' in science without taking into account the relation of scientific models to description, testing and so on, I sympathize with that. But this should be a prelude to a discussion of what 'truth' comes to in science, not a reason for jettisoning the whole idea. But, in any case, what of simple cases where I'm asked whether a room has chairs in it and I reply that it has?

Voice A

Here you are talking about 'truthfulness' and we certainly want that. It involves respect for one's interlocutor, fairness, the distinction between knowledge and belief, attention to evidence, and so on. But talking of 'truth' is of no help and is not involved.

Voice G

Think of what 'caring for the truth' may mean in different contexts by thinking of what its opposite would involve. In the courtroom it would involve lying. In intellectual enquiry it would involve being careless and slipshod. In science it would involve wishful thinking, rather than securing actual results. Plato contrasted really understanding something with a knack which simply enabled one to go on without understanding.

Voice A

I can agree with everything you say up to the point where you insist on bringing in truth.

Voice H

But why ask us to give up the distinction between truth and lying, distinctions which, in some cases, were hard won? You seem to be in the grip of the very 'view from nowhere' that you think you are free from. The distinctions we make are not 'once and for all' distinctions. Contexts change in the way you suggest. But ordinary distinctions and concerns about truth can be expressed without being committed to a general theory of truth, and without claiming that 'truth' is the only game in town.

Voice A

It seems as though you all keep offering me examples and I keep rejecting them. It is not that I reject the importance of the contexts you mention, but I ask whether what you want to say is served best by a notion of truth. For example, I am not denying the way some of you want to talk of propositional knowledge. I simply deny that it is fundamental, because it presupposes so much that is not propositional.

Voice E

If your arguments convince me, am I not thinking that they are true?

Voice A

I'm not interested in convictions. What you will think is that I am truthful, that I'll stand by what I say, and that I have treated you seriously as an interlocutor. What really interests me is the way our artifacts help us to transcend where we are. This is the kind of transcendence I can recognize.

Voice E

But isn't it a very odd use of 'transcend'? You may want to say that Velcro *superseded* the zip-fastener, but would you say it *transcended* it? Aren't you assuming, without arguments, that an ambition for transcendence *must* involve us in something like Nagel's 'view from nowhere'?

Voice A

I certainly think you must select examples and spell them out. I *would* say that concrete bridges transcended stone bridges when I think of the enormous cultural consequences.

Voice B

I still want to say that A presents us with a false dilemma: we either have to regard Truth as the 'view from nowhere', or give up speaking of truth altogether. But think of the circumstances in which different people have emphasized the importance of truth. George Orwell said that one of the worst evils of fascism was its systematic destruction of truth. The study of chemistry for Primo Levi saved him from abandoning the concern for truth. Kierkegaard, in *Purity of Heart*, emphasizes truth, and the terribleness of living a lie. This was connected with the importance of freedom from self-deception.

Voice A

I'm not confident about these ordinary notions of truth. Are these notions true? I repeat: we need truthfulness, respect for evidence, and so on. What I doubt is whether those who speak of 'living in truth' can actually provide a robust notion of 'living in truth', certainly not the kind of ontological transcendence I mentioned at the outset.

Voice I

I do have an ontological conception of transcendence, and any religion without it is a form of naturalism. The choice between transcendence and naturalism is a major theme in this conference. I have defined the Transcendent as that putative reality, limitlessly important to us, which transcends the natural or physical universe. The natural or physical universe includes human brains and hence all religious ideas, emotions, linguistic and other behaviours and social interactions that are (on a naturalistic view) continuously dependent upon the functioning of human brains. For naturalism, the Transcendent, whether conceived of as God or Brahman or the Dharmakaya or the Tao and so on, is an idea in human minds, and is thus dependent for its existence upon human cerebral activity; so that before there was human life, and again after human life has ceased, there was and there will be no God, Brahman, Dharmakaya, Tao, etc. So naturalism holds that the only reality is the physical universe plus (if this is regarded as non-physical) the mental life that is produced by and is wholly dependent upon the functioning of those bits of the physical universe that are human brains. And the central question to which I would love to hear a straight answer is whether Stephen Grover's or D. Z. Phillips' form of religion without transcendence presupposes naturalism as thus defined.

My guess is that J will not give a straight answer to this question. Instead, he will say that religious language says what it says and nothing else will substitute for it. To transcend the natural is to be unconcerned about how the world goes. In being indifferent to the world, according to J, one is transcending the natural. But is he not forgetting something? On a naturalistic philosophy the believer, including her refusal to curse God, and including all her thoughts and attitudes and emotions, is herself an item in the inventory of contents of the natural world. So the natural world has not been transcended. All that has happened is that one bit of the natural world is reconciling itself to the hard knocks that come to her from the rest of the natural world by using religious language about a loving God who is to be trusted through thick and thin. But of course, according to naturalism, this loving God transcending the natural world does not exist, and the reconciling thought is a piece of self-delusion.

Voice J

J asks for a straight answer from me, but one can only give straight answers to questions which are well-formulated. His does not tell us anything at all about what exists. He thinks that I must say that unlike the things which science is interested in, God does not appear in the list of existing things. All that follows is that we use the term 'God' in a different way from that in which we use 'colour' or 'the spin of an electron'. God's existence does not depend on the existence of believers and cannot be equated with an idea in the brain. But J wants a list of what things are 'out there'. Bernard Williams believes in such a list. What remains only exists in the human understanding, for example, colours, moral properties and God. This absolute list, as A would say, is unintelligible.

Are objects coloured? Of course they are. What interests us is what saying that consists in.

Voice I

I think this line of argument, which surfaces frequently, is an irrelevance. Appeal is often made to Wittgenstein's point that the conflict between a realist and an idealist about whether the chair or the table really exists is an idle dispute, because in practice both mean the same thing when they say that there is a chair in the next room. That is something that, I would have thought, most of us in the philosophical community assimilated some years ago. But it is completely irrelevant to the difference between what the Pope means or what you or D. Z. Phillips mean when God is referred to. The Pope means a transcendent personal being of limitless power who has frequently miraculously intervened in the world to suspend natural law, and who holds men and women in existence after their bodily death, whereas you and D. Z. Phillips do not mean anything remotely like this; and this difference cannot be concealed by appealing to Wittgenstein on chairs and tables.

Voice J

I am not so confident about your distinction between the Pope and so-called neo-Wittgensteinians. Take a philosopher like Richard Swinburne who assigns high probability to the truth of religious belief. This notion and the arguments he uses have nothing to do with religious belief. Belief may be inspired by awe and terror. Why speak of naturalism here, unless like Williams and Nagel, you think these terms are outdated?

Voice I

I used the term 'elitism' in connection with the religious responses you have in mind. I appreciate that it is a provocative term that raises hackles. And I could have said what I wanted to say without using it. And it does not affect the truth-or-falsity of the neo-Wittgensteinian type of philosophy of religion. But I used it because the literature does not suggest that philosophers of this school are aware that the kind of religion they are advocating is a viable option for a fortunate minority of human beings, so that if what they advocate is true religion, this is very bad news for humankind as a whole. I would expect neo-Wittgensteinian philosophers of religion frankly to acknowledge this, and to regret it, but to hold that unfortunately this is just how the universe is. Instead however J gets defensive about it, and so the point has to be pursued a little further. It doesn't help much to point out that affluence can be a handicap to spiritual and moral growth as well as dire poverty and deprivation. For if it is as hard for a rich man to enter the kingdom of heaven as for a camel to go through the eye of a needle, nevertheless, the rich man can do something about this, which is presumably why Jesus said this. But a child born into a situation of desperate poverty in a violent slum, deprived of adequate food, education, having to live by violence and dying a violent death at the age of 12 does not have the freedom to escape his situation. The idea of transcending the ego point of view and rising into a serene freedom from selfish desires and an equal acceptance of life's vicissitudes, both good and bad, requires for its realization at least a bare minimum of social justice on earth. The Buddha, who taught this nirvanic ideal more influentially than anyone else, recognized that all too often many people are so circumstanced that they will not attain the nirvanic state in their present life, but will have to continue towards it through many lives.

But – and this is where the big issue emerges – within the Buddhist picture of the universe as a vast process within which dispositional or karmic structures continue through time to find expression in a succession of lives, the goal of nirvana is not a mockery. It is ultimately open to everyone. Not only Buddhism, but also the other traditions, can say, in the words of the Christian mystic, Julian of Norwich, that in the end 'all shall be well, and all manner of thing shall be well'. But if, with philosophical naturalism, we cancel that larger picture according to which our present life is only a small part of our total existence (whether we think in terms of the Buddhist or the Christian or the Hindu or some other version of that picture) then we are left with the harsh fact that only the few who can attain to this goal in the present life can ever attain to it. For the great majority it has been and is an illusory goal. That is why I said in my paper that the naturalistic picture of the universe is profoundly pessimistic, it is bad news for humanity as a whole. And I think J should simply acknowledge that as a regrettable fact which does not however even tend to show that this dark picture is not true.

Instead J attempts *tu quoque*. He points out that there is a sense in which my own position should be called elitist. And this is true, but it is in a very different sense. Any philosophy, including J's as well as mine, can if you like be called elitist in the sense that only a small minority of human beings will accept it. In this sense every philosophy, and indeed every position in the sciences and in the humanities also, can be called elitist. I doubt, however, whether this is a useful sense of 'elitist'. But if it is, this kind of elitism is quite different from the kind I was speaking about in my paper.

Voice J

But you offer more than that. You claim to know and offer an explanation of what ordinary believers do. I don't think ordinary believers raise the issue in this way, and would not recognize it. Perhaps they refrain from the judgements you seem so confident in making.

Voice I

You may feel this because of the criticism you make in your paper of the reparation theodicy – a theodicy according to which we will receive reparation after death for the evil suffered in the present life. You say, 'A God who inflicts suffering in order later to make reparation for it is a moral criminal' and cite D. Z. Phillips as agreeing with this. I also agree with this! I blame myself for not having referred (at least in a footnote) to my book *Evil and the God of Love*, or to the many articles that I have published on the subject of theodicy over the years, in which I oppose both a reparation theodicy and also the idea that when something bad happens it is God who is causing it to happen. The Irenaean theodicy that I have advocated, based on the writings of Irenaeus in the second century and Schleiermacher in the 19th century holds that God has brought us into existence within the evolution of the universe as initially imperfect and immature creatures in an environment which includes contingency and unpredictability and of course the very important factor of human freedom; and in this developing universe we can so respond to its mixture of good and evil, including its challenges and problems and disasters, as well as its beauties and joys, as to begin to grow morally and spiritually from what Irenaeus called the image of God towards what he called the likeness of God. This process begins in the present life and continues towards its completion beyond this life. Hence the slogan 'No theodicy without eschatology'. And the basic idea is not reparation but the fulfilment of our potentialities through a long creative process.

Voice J

I accept that I is not offering a reparation theodicy and I regret the criticisms which assumed that he was. Nevertheless, certain criticisms retain their force. It is incoherent to assume that the evils that I have committed, or that have been done to me, somehow retreat into the background simply because I live on after death. If I could go back in time and were able to undo the evils committed it would be different. But I do know *now* what it is to seek forgiveness and to go on, despite what I have done, when I have received it. Nothing I says about living on shows how it can fulfill *that* role.

Voice I

J says that 'Job, in refusing to curse God, refuses to allow anything contained within a naturalistic inventory of the contents of
the world to determine the status of his relationship to God, and
so transcends all items in that inventory.' I wish we could leave
poor old Job alone. His trouble is that he is a fictional character.
He never existed. And we can establish anything by inventing a
character to illustrate it. The same applies, incidentally, to
Tolstoy's characters, who often appear in these discussions. It
would be better to talk of people who actually existed. If you *have*
to illustrate something good by inventing a story, a fiction, that is
bad news.

Voice A

But what if the story calls me to be something I am not? What if
the story is my superior?

Voice I

I am saying that it is safer if what you respond to is the lives of
saints who actually lived.

Voice K

Let me give you a clear counter-example. I was brought up in a
fundamentalist environment where I was taught that Adam and
Eve were an actual couple. It bothered me. Why should I be to
blame for something done by a person I never knew and who was
so remote from my own life in time and place? But in theological
college, by learning that they were *not* an actual couple, I came to
see how Adam could dwell in me, how the story could tell me
something about myself. The story could only make a demand on
me when I saw that it was not 'real' in the sense that I is insisting on.

Voice F

Furthermore, people's ordinary lives and the way they worship
have been informed by the arts in innumerable ways. I am not
putting forward the crude view that people have to read poetry in
order to love in a certain way, but am saying that the existence of
great love poetry, great music, great architecture, has created possibilities in people's lives which wouldn't exist otherwise.

Voice I

I don't deny that the religious character of people's lives can be illustrated by, or expressed in the arts, in the way you describe, but the primary religious sense is the one you find in people's lives.

Voice F

No, the arts I mentioned are not simply illustrating religious characters which already exist. They create possibilities, in their own medium, which would not exist otherwise. Notre Dame Cathedral is not an illustration of religious ideas, but a contribution to those ideas in architecture.

Voice G

I think it is right to emphasize what is actual, what is actually achieved in a human life. But it has to be recognized, too, as K has shown, that that achievement can have been called forth by a story which is not itself historical, but which makes a demand on us and draws us.

Voice F

What does I say about his own idea of an ultimate reality which is itself supposed to be beyond anything actual in our experience?

Voice I

I do want to speak of the concept of the Real as the ultimate reality lying beyond the scope of other than purely formal human concepts. It seems to me that this idea is required by any realist interpretation of religion in its plurality of forms. We start out from within our own tradition (Christianity) and with the faith that its particular forms of religions experience are not purely imaginative projection but are a cognitive response to a transcendent reality of some kind. We then notice that there are other streams of religious experience – Muslim, Hindu, Buddhist and so on – producing comparable moral and spiritual fruits in human life, and so we extend to them the same acceptance of them as not purely projective but at the same time responsive. What is experienced within the different traditions is always a particular God figure or a particular non-personal reality. But these cannot be the ultimate reality as it is in itself. They can however be that ultimate reality as humanly conceived and experienced in the ways provided by the different traditions. So we have the picture of the ultimate ineffable noumenal reality, the Real, and the range of its phenomenal manifestations to humankind. But it is not the case that we can say nothing about the Real in itself. We can say that it is that which there must be if human religious experience in its variety of forms is not purely projection. The difference between affirming and not affirming the transcendent Real is precisely the difference between a critical realist and a non-realist understanding of religion. And the sense in which this ineffable transcendent reality is 'benign' in relation to humanity is simply that from our human point of view it is benign or good as the ground of our highest good. It is what it is, but from our human point of view what it is answers to our human concept of good.

Voice C

You say that the Transcendent Real has no substantive qualities and you go through quite a list. It is neither good nor evil, which suggests it might be neutral. It is neither physical nor mental. It has no attributes other than those which are formal. But then you start talking of the Transcendent in ways which are substantial. You say that the Transcendent is universally present, that it affects human consciousness and that it is benign. Those are all substantial attributes. That is contradictory.

Voice I

It is a problem of how we can find a language to speak of the Transcendent. There does seem to be a formal contradiction. The Transcendent cannot have substantive attributes, yet it appears to have some. It is beyond phenomenal reality and yet affects it in a way we call benign.

Voice C

But this is to say that the Transcendent does not have substantive attributes and that it does. You go on to enumerate them.

Voice I

Isn't it a question of language?

Voice C

No, a question of coherence.

Voice I

It has no intrinsic attributes, like being good, but only relational attributes. That may be a better way of putting it.

Voice F
Perhaps it is a matter of language, but not in the way you think. There are connections between your notion of the Transcendent and what you say about ordinary concepts such as tables and altars. You want to call our perception of these examples of 'seeing as'. I may see the table as an altar. But then you say that 'This is a table' is itself an example of 'seeing as'; seeing *this* as a table. But that is confused. It treats the demonstrative pronoun as though it is the name of a thing. We can be taught the use of 'table' and 'altar' partly by saying, 'This is a table' and 'This is an altar'. But I was not taught the use of 'this' by anyone saying 'This is a this'. I am borrowing from Wittgenstein here. 'This' is not a 'something' which has formal but no substantive attributes, and the same should be said of the Transcendent. Both notions are chimeras. You are looking for something which doesn't mean anything.

Voice I
That is irrelevant. The phenomenal manifestations are not instances of 'seeing as'.

Voice F
Then I don't follow you since I thought there was an analogy between 'seeing as' and 'experiencing as' – experiencing 'the ultimately real' as God, the Brahman, the Dharmakaya or the Tao.

Voice E
A further difficulty is that I does not do justice to the way in which believers express their faith. If they say that God created heaven and earth, they are not saying that this is their *interpretation*, or that they are seeing God through their lens, they are saying that this is how God is.

Voice I
You are neglecting the distinction between God as He is, and the way we experience God.

Voice E
But believers say 'Christ is …', 'God is. …' Muslims may say different things. They can't all be true.

Voice I

But could it not be that the *same* Transcendent is revealing itself in these different ways? How God is in Himself is beyond all our concepts.

Voice G

There are religions without the Transcendent. Reincarnation is a curse in Hinduism.

Voice I

But it is a curse which leads to a further end.

Voice J

I am conscious of the fact that I am ignorant of many world religions, but I am suspicious of the search for the essence of religion in the Transcendent. You ought to take seriously the suggestion that the reason you cannot say anything about it is that it doesn't mean anything.

Voice L

We refer to 'the believer' in a superficial way. A recent survey showed that 70 per cent of USA Baptists believe in reincarnation. Arguments of philosophers of religion like Swinburne are ridiculous. But if we come across religions we don't understand, it may still be not as bad as quantum mechanics. Wittgenstein whom J appeals to is a product of Western culture. What we really need is an empirical study of religions. I don't believe in the philosophy of religion, but in philosophies of religions in which specific beliefs can be studied.

Voice M

L and J want to talk of religion in specific contexts. I wants to insist that what all religions have in common is that they're all talking about something *real*. I support that. My difficulty is that he is not pluralistic enough. I makes it look as though differences between religions aren't really important. But these are real religious disputes.

Voice I

I admit that I can't assume *a priori* that the fruits of Christianity and Buddhism are the same. I simply find that they are.

Voice F

I do not deny the importance of empirical enquiry, but philosophical puzzlement cannot be dealt with in that way. Certainly not by asking people what they believe and recording the results. In talking *about* their beliefs they would be doing a kind of philosophy. If you asked them what they were doing when they thought, you might find one house in Claremont to be Cartesian and the one next door to be physicalist. We have a deep tendency to ask the central philosophical questions. Plato is here to stay.

Voice L

I was emphasizing cultural diversity.

Voice F

Agreed.

Voice H

But how much diversity is recognized in the all too bland distinction between naturalism and religious faith? I object to the assumption that life can't be worth living without a belief in immortality. Serious naturalists are not terrified without a promise of pie in the sky. I object to the restrictive character of I's alternatives.

Voice I

I don't hold that people who do not believe in God *must* be miserable. But I do say that their satisfactions are short-term and are only available to the lucky.

Voice H

But lives have been transformed despite the tragedies in them.

Voice I

But I want to emphasize potentiality for change. God has created us with these potentialities and would not allow us to be cut off from them. Consider death in infancy. Think of the cramped potential in deprivation and slavery. What is one's conception of what is being *wasted* in them? That is the difference between religion and naturalism.

Voice H

But the values open to naturalism are not confined to those you suggest.

Voice I

I allow for what you have in mind. I quoted Russell who found plenty of satisfaction in life. But I'm looking at humanity as a whole, and suggesting that naturalism is bad news for it.

Voice H

It may be bad news for you, since if you deny God and immortality all is lost.

Voice I

No, plenty remains, but, for many, life will have been a bad story.

Voice J

I may come to conclusions about my potential, but how can you be so categorical about others? Also, if what you offer does not make sense, it is no news at all.

Voice N

That may be true, but are you too sweeping in what you say does not make sense? For example, you say that philosophical proofs have nothing to do with belief in God. D. Z. Phillips has shown how they may be related although they cannot achieve everything they promise. But to have no worth? Aquinas thought they had some importance. How much is another question. They cannot produce faith, but they may be preambles to it.

Voice J

I agree. There can be a religious interpretation of the proofs. They can be spiritual exercises. What I would be worried about is an analysis of religious belief into a 'religious' part and a 'belief' part.

Voice H

Well, you certainly can't win an argument with a Kierkegaardian because they are not arguing. Of course, they don't win either. They are making a case in a non-argumentative way. Nietzsche doesn't argue either. He and Kierkegaard are trying to reconstitute people's thinking. Can I's cosmic pessimism be avoided without re-course to religion? Nietzsche thought that there was a religion without transcendence and that Spinoza and Hegel had found it. It was more substantial than Feuerbach. Tillich counted himself among ecstatic naturalists. This is a possibility which is better than a prosaic religion, but it is religion bereft of transcendent realities.

So I set out why this is an important task: to show how the death of a transcendent religion does not have nihilistic consequences. So I offered an alternative celebratory perspective, which might be called religion in a sense. It transforms consciousness and produces creative and nurturing values. Spinoza, Hegel and Nietzsche, without transcendence, hook on to what is elemental, development-al and transfigurable. It is our task to think on these things, while admitting that there is nothing eternal in where they come from or in where they may go to.

Voice O

As H says, there is something odd in trying to follow Kierkegaard. If you teach it, you turn it into something different.

The notion of transcendence has been developed in a philosophi-cal context. Nietzsche said 'God is dead'. He meant the Christian God, but he incorporates the whole metaphysical tradition of Western philosophy. He says that there are no grounds for reli-gious belief. We should not follow the herd, but live as self-affirming human beings. But this conclusion is itself developed within a philosophical context. It led to further developments, for example, in Bataille. Derrida argued that Nietzsche is arguing for an 'opposite', a view which gets its sense from theism. So they, along with Heidegger, try to develop a language without tran-scendence, and we can pursue it impersonally.

What I wanted to do was to transpose this into a *personal* mode. If nihilism is a loss of meaning, it is a loss for *you*, so can it be treated in an impersonal way? How is the cognitive conclusion supposed to engage me? In the *Concluding Unscientific Postscript*, Climacus exposes this comically.

Wittgenstein said, also comically, that at least a sentence should look like one. And an answer to a problem must look like one. Can there be a theoretical answer? Think of Munch's 'The Scream' as a cry of despair. Are you going to say to students, 'Today's topic is the meaning of life'? Is the problem present to us? It is not like a problem in mathematics or science.

If the problem is the problem of life, it must take a first-person form. If I despaired of a relationship with someone, how would a theory help? There is no *general* question about the meaning of life with a disinterested answer. If the resolution is personal, the despair disappears. Climacus sketches different forms in which despair may occur and how it may be removed. In this context transcendence may be relocated, since delivery from despair cannot come from you. If you were delivered by love it would be seen as a gift, a grace. It has to be received in the first person. It cannot be objectified. So I want to relocate transcendence in the subjective, and ask why philosophers fly to the general and the objective. But, then, how do I communicate this? The other forms of life, the aesthetic and the ethical, involve the development of human capacities. But if my despair is total, delivery must come as a gift which is not of my making.

How can a life of self-abnegation be communicated except in the first person? So Kierkegaard's pseudonyms speak in the first person. We may recognize ourselves in them and be led to examine ourselves. That is why Kierkegaard is a religious author.

Can I stop there? I can go on in a disinterested way, but Kierkegaard never does this. I've lifted all I've said from his pseudonyms. So am I trying to do something which needs a religious context? But I can't do that, partly for personal reasons. Climacus wants to oppose philosophy's conception of its relation to religious belief. Stephen Mulhall in *Faith and Reason* suggests that philosophy must abandon its judgemental view and replace it with the task of conceptual clarification. It will clarify the grammar of different perspectives.

I have qualms about this philosophical attitude. Those who live by these perspectives do not see them as possibilities. They are driven to them. To present them as possibilities or choices is to falsify this relation. They are arranged before us without threatening us. We must present them as lived. They are presented by Kierkegaard, indirectly, from a religious point of view, via the pseudonyms who speak for themselves. So I cannot present this paper. I revoke it.

Voice D

If the question is whether there can be religions without transcendence the answer is 'Yes, we have them.' We can excise it from the Western tradition. What I can't accept is H's claim that we do not need transcendence. How is that to be established?

Voice H

I'm not saying you have to choose *the* correct way. I'm offering a possible way.

Voice O

I'm unhappy with that. There is no general way here. The issue must show a personal interest.

Voice H

How can 'truth', 'death' be drawn back into subjectivity in such a way that disinterestedness is eliminated? 'What is the meaning of my life?' That is a general question. If I have it, others may too. I don't want to limit God to my consciousness. Paradigms in religious worship tell us about what a relationship with God ought to be.

Voice O

But this presupposes what the question must mean. To say that God is a form of my consciousness would not be an act of self-abnegation.

Voice A

Is H an example of direct communication? Should he work on our emotions?

Voice O

How would you go about settling that question?

Voice A

You have to decide on the relative importance of the perspectives.

Voice O

I prefer Nietzsche when he turns from a philosophical critique of religion to describe it as a hatred of life. That is a more appropriate tone. He is appropriating the personal, not arguing from a disinterested superior position. These tendencies oscillate in Nietzsche.

Voice F

The matter is complicated in Kierkegaard. Climacus sees that part of 'the monstrous illusion' is to turn religious belief into a philosophical thesis. Hegel is attacked as an extreme example of this confusion. Hegel's system is revoked. But this is seen with philosophical clarity by Climacus, a philosopher who is not a Christian. But, now, Climacus sees that this clarity, too, is at an infinite distance from faith. If, then, he confuses them in the search for the happiness Christianity promises, philosophy must be revoked.

Voice O
But he revokes the *whole* book.

Voice F
I think that is confused. I do not have to revoke the philosophical observation that Christianity makes a certain demand of me, and that it is not a philosophical thesis. But to see this, philosophically, is not to respond to the demand.

Voice O
I hope you're right. But I think the question needs a religious position.

Voice K
People don't live monadically. What is a purely personal faith?

Voice O
Of course, the issues I raise may involve my relationships with others, but can the issue of what I am making of my life be raised professionally?

Voice H
Didn't Kierkegaard offer a kind of genealogy in *Stages on Life's Way*? He showed the dialectical relations between them like Hegel, except that, for him, the dialectic goes on within an individual. But he doesn't think this is unique to himself. It is unloaded in a mesh of possibilities. He shows us what happens if we wander down certain ways. He thinks we'll break down, but it isn't a purely subjective affair.

Voice O
What is shown is a range of particular 'I's. When you read them you feel the force of them. So you are addressed. But you are already living. He wants to disturb. In Hegel each stage is superseded in the dialectic. Hegel turns out to be God.

Voice G

We have a spiritual problem. H seems to look for a strategy or therapy to cope with it. But if I recognize values as absolute I don't choose to. I must find them for myself and no one can endow them with value for me.

Voice H

Neither for Nietzsche nor for me is the answer 'out there'. No one was more impassioned about that than Nietzsche. For him it was a tremendously personal quest. How could one recover one's bearings when what one was raised in has gone? But that doesn't mean that 'the personal' is the only way of getting this into focus. To stand back, to see how all this came about, to analyze different strategies of understanding is relevant despite the fact that the crisis is existential. If you go towards nihilism, what made you think like *that*? An appreciation of the wider context is essential. Without that you can't work your way out. So I'm not stuck in the detached mode and neither was Nietzsche.

Voice O

But you said you need a therapy.

Voice H

You may see 'death of God' not as an illness needing therapy, but as an attempt to solve a big problem.

Voice C

What would 'God' be within naturalism when transcendence has gone? The Pragmatists tried to answer this.

Voice H

I'm tempted by that way of thinking, but it tends to argue without examining the wider presuppositions I have mentioned.

Voice P

H stresses the possibility that belief in the transcendent may be the product of repression. Can such repression be found in naturalism?

Voice H

Yes, paths may go in all directions. Of course there are tensions galore in naturalism. But its essential insight is that all values are ephemeral. They will, in the end, all go with the wind. That requires as much passion as we find in Kierkegaard.

Voice Q

Surely we need criteria to determine what we are prepared to recognize as God, Kantian-like criteria.

Voice H

First we need to decide what the options are, and then to decide what we do in relation to them.

Voice N

But to recognize it as an option is already to have chosen it, in a sense. Values determine what we are prepared to call options.

Voice B

Where *everything* is an option don't we have a shallow dilettantism?

Voice H

My invitation is to consider what form of life is needed to sustain values which transcend utilitarian values. This reflection requires freedom, but not freedom abstractly conceived, but the kind which comes from involvement in artistic and other forms of creativity.

Voice L

There are certainly different senses of 'transcendence'. If God is said to be 'beyond' space, it must be in a figurative sense, otherwise he would be in another bit of space. But pluralism involves marking off religious systems of belief. We tend to concentrate on big systems, a fact which conceals the variety within each.

Voice M

Within traditions which speak of transcendence people may work out a religious perspective without it. I don't want to argue about that. What I find hard to accept, in the face of rich traditions, is that maturity of thought entails giving up the notion of transcendence. I note how a thinker like Aquinas struggles with the relation between transcendence and immanence. We are told that transcendence is beyond the natural. Does that mean that it does not exist? Can 'transcendence' be a way of avoiding talking about God?

Voice L

The major religions turn on the different emphases to be found in them.

Voice I

The trouble is with the assumption that because of these differences, one religion must be right and all the others be wrong. We need to recognize, as Kant did, that we know within restrictions. Aquinas said that things known are known in the mode of the knower. So it is reasonable to postulate the Real beyond the scope of our different systems. The different absolutes are different human responses to this ineffable reality.

Voice L

No religious or philosophical standpoint is true. In my recent book *Choosing a Faith* I recognize that many do not choose a faith. But some do. So they might as well have good criteria. Relativism is wrong, but I go some way towards it as a soft non-relativist. So as well as the Hick model we need to recognize the limits of proof. You can't prove the Koran. We have to recognize when we reach bedrock.

Voice U

I think we need to make certain distinctions when we discuss pluralism, because the mere recognition of it is often equated with tolerance, as if tolerance were entailed by the recognition of pluralism. Tolerance may be a condition for dialogue, but what you tolerate, religiously, will surely depend on the content of your belief, including your beliefs about transcendence.

Voice G

'Pluralism' can mean many things at different levels. First, there is tolerance in relation to others. Second, in scholarship there is the recognition of differences. Third, in philosophy we recognize issues of generality. Fourth, spiritually, something is revealed to me. The mode of the believer is not compatible with the other levels, because if I am serious I will want to speak of what is false or corrupt.

Voice L

The need for toleration is important politically. Settle matters by agreement, not by shooting one's opponents. But pluralism doesn't mean having to say that all religions are equal. As I have said, there is the plurality within religions. Where some see dignity, others see the need for a holy war.

Voice G

That turns everything into a phenomenon.

Voice L

What's wrong with that?

Voice G

We don't worship under that description.

Voice F

Do you agree, however, that if it were possible to clear up confusions of different kinds, leaving us with genuine religious differences, it is essential, philosophically, that we leave logical space for the possibility of saying, 'That is a false god'?

Voice M

Absolutely.

Voice E

The difficulty I find with Hick's notion of transcendence is that it seems like Nagel's 'view from nowhere'. Religions have organic connections within them and between them. Oppositions often account for their genesis. But from what culture does Hick's Transcendent Real come? What status does it have? In Aquinas God's simpleness is that of the Creator in Christianity. It is not a metaphysical explanation.

Voice I

Let disputes within religions flourish. As for relations between religions, there is no contradiction in saying that the same God is experienced in different ways. The idea of an 'ultimate reality' is arrived at inductively. We see that the fruits of different religions are comparable with those of Christianity. By extending to them an intellectual golden rule, we recognize them. So whereas I agree with G that one starts, spiritually, in one's own religions, that creates a philosophical problem. So we conclude that there is a transcendent being who is experienced in different ways. This is not a 'view from nowhere', but, inductively, the best explanation.

Voice M

It is often assumed that a readiness to enter a dialogue is an indication of loss of faith. Some Rabbis pointed out to me that in orthodoxy of a certain kind there is a prohibition against dialogue. Dialogue tends to recur at the margins of faith.

Voice L

Dialogue, when it occurs, is not primarily philosophical. It happens between people who discover affinities. Dialogue is not between conservatives, and authority is often opposed to it. There was less dialogue pre-Vatican II than there was after it.

Voice A

But M *was* calling for a philosophical dialogue. What would be the result?

Voice M

In the past it has been thought that philosophy could *show* the superiority of one religion over others. But I make no such prediction. The outcome is yet to be realized. But we need tolerance to govern our conduct with respect to those with whom we disagree. Differences can be appreciated without undermining respect.

Voice L

There is a need to understand others. That is why I went over to Religious Studies. Value judgements must be abandoned while empirical studies are completed. Description is not dialogue. Informed empathy precedes dialogue.

Voice I

I don't think 'tolerance' is a good word. To tolerate others is to put up with them, and that is condescension. There will be aspects of one's own and other religions which one will find intolerable. I find the activities of some Right-wing Christians intolerable. But what I have found in the Christian–Buddhist dialogues which began at Claremont is that one came to see something of the point of their practice. We were fascinated by ideas so very different from our own. No one was converted, but we strove to understand each other's point of view.

Voice E

But I still want to insist that I may understand something and say of it, 'No, that's not God.' I'd reject rituals involving child sacrifice for example.

Voice R

But how is one to decide? If you say that the torture of children is wrong, don't we need, in practical terms, something that underlines that judgement? And where can we find it if there is no transcendent?

Voice H

But why assume that you have no values if you do not believe in God? Are we to frighten people into their values with religious threats? Practical ethics must depend on reflection, but it need not take a metaphysical form.

Voice B

But you are asking for something which can only be answered in the first person as O emphasized.

Voice H

I don't need to do philosophy to know that it's wrong to torture children.

Voice G

But, then, the same may be true of religious belief. There need be no ulterior motives.

Voice C

I'm assuming that one thing religious belief offers is false: there is no survival of, or resuscitation from, complete physical death. In discussing the badness of death it is useful to use the distinction between intrinsic and extrinsic value. I concluded that death, though inevitable, is not intrinsically bad. Death at a certain time may be extrinsically bad or extrinsically good. Death at a certain time is not always inevitable; it is sometimes avoidable. Fear of death is intrinsically bad and may be unavoidable, but we may be able to diminish it to some degree.

The concepts of intrinsically good and intrinsically bad are not *subjective* concepts – whether something is intrinsically good or bad is not a matter of whether we like or dislike it, or approve or disprove of it. If something is intrinsically good or bad it is necessarily so. If something is intrinsically good or bad, there are no circumstances in which it is not intrinsically good or bad. The greatest intrinsic goods and intrinsic evils contain some degree of consciousness. There is a stronger connection between consciousness and something being intrinsically good or intrinsically bad *for a certain person*. A state of affairs is intrinsically bad for me provided it consists in my being in some conscious state that is intrinsically bad, for example, my being sad.

E claims that I can only show that my being dead cannot be intrinsically bad for me when *I am dead*. He says I can't show this before I am dead. The bearer of intrinsic badness must be an actual state of affairs. But since my actual death cannot be a state of affairs for me, it cannot be intrinsically bad for me. All this is consistent with *my fearing my being* dead being, when actual, intrinsically bad for me.

E asks whether my wife's being murdered can be intrinsically bad for me. The answer is no, because even when it is actual it does not consist in my being in some conscious state. It can only be extrinsically bad *for me*, even though it itself is no doubt intrinsically bad. E suggest that it follows that I cannot rationally fear her death while she is travelling in a bandit-ridden land, unless I fear it because I think it will cause me to have bad experiences. Having drawn this inference E suggests that my view is that of an egoist. All I really care about is my good and bad experiences. I view other things as good or bad only so far as they cause me to have good or bad experiences.

E's inference is logically fallacious. But perhaps it is my fault that he made it. I linked intrinsic goodness for me with consciousness, but did not explicitly say that any state of affairs that is intrinsically good for me involves a conscious state on my part. Once the link is made, we see that E's inference is fallacious. To say that my wife's being murdered is not intrinsically bad for me is merely to note that it does not consist in my being in some conscious state that is intrinsically bad. It is not to say that I love my wife only for her dowry, what she can do for me, and do not love her for what she is in herself. My fearing that my wife will be murdered in a bandit-ridden land is a state of affairs which, when actual, is intrinsically bad for me. Do I fear the actualization of the object of my fear only because of the bad experiences it may cause me to have? Of course not! I fear it because it is intrinsically bad and involves someone I deeply love and care about.

E discusses what he takes to be a more fundamental problem with my whole argument, namely, my linking intrinsic good or bad with consciousness. After introducing a subjective account of value – x is bad for a person if that person thinks x is bad – E links his subjective account with value. As a piece of legislation E is entitled to do this, but what mystifies me is the conclusions he then arrives at concerning my views. Here are three quotations that attribute to me views which are foreign to me and my paper.

'It appears to be a tacit assumption of [C's] argument that, for the person contemplating his own death, his own well-being has positive value, and further that this value is the greatest and most important of all his values.' We are not given a hint as to where the 'tacit assumption' is made in my argument.

'On [C's] account I can rationally fear the occurrence of x only if it is possible that I may experience x and if I believe the experience of x would be a bad experience.'

'[C] holds that we can rationally fear x only if the occurrence of x would be a bad experience for us or cause us to have bad experiences.'

We are not given a hint as to where my account even suggests such naive and morally repugnant views as these. Only the crudest of egoists could hold the views that I am here unequivocally asserted to hold. I would be grateful for chapter and verse from my paper to support these assertions as to what my account implies.

Voice E

My argument is not that C is an egoist, but that egoism is implied in his *arguments*.

We are discussing this issue for a real reason. We are all going to die. The subject is close to the subject of O's paper. The link of 'value' and 'experience' in C's paper is problematic. For example, we value far more than we experience. Again it is not true that 'being sad' is always bad for me. This is not true of 'pain' either.

If I were to talk of death I wouldn't start from here. Christianity takes death seriously, but it doesn't talk in terms of resuscitation. Its talk is not straightforward. Jesus is raised on the third day, but he also says to the thief on the cross, 'Today thou shalt be with me in paradise.'

Talk of survival after death is problematic. I can't talk with them, look into their eyes. So survival can't do the job we want it to perform. C and I agree on that.

We value being active in the world, but we are passive when death comes. Inmates on Death Row try to kill themselves. They want to be active, to take control of their deaths. Death is an enemy.

But there are other attitudes to death. It can be seen as a friend. To be cradled is to be passive. We give ourselves in trust to be cradled. If you believe that your death is in the hands of a personal God, you will react differently from a reaction to an impersonal transcendent, or no transcendent at all. For example, death may be linked with judgement. It is too late to do something about a relationship when the person has died, but you may believe it will be sorted out in heaven.

Religiously life is a gift. The attitude to it is gratitude. Learning to die is learning to give back this gift.

Voice F

We need to look at what might be meant by the reality of the dead. If I say 'My dead father watches over me' the sense of that depends on my father being *dead*, not on his having survived death. The will of the dead is fixed. We either come to terms with it or not. That is why I wouldn't myself speak of things being 'sorted out'.

Voice C

I haven't considered whether the dead can be said to be real. They certainly have no conscious experiences. We may regret that, but that's the way it is. But death isn't always the worst thing.

Voice D

If you link goodness and badness with actuality, what happens to past events? Do I not regret that Hitler murdered six million Jews?

Voice C

My having been born is an actual state of affairs, but I cannot say that of my death before it occurs.

Voice D

But, on your view, if a wicked tyrant is dead, he has no chance to change.

Voice C

Perhaps it's better that he's dead.

Voice H

What is intrinsic badness? Because my death is in the future for me, you say that it is my fearing it that is intrinsically bad. But isn't this artificial? Heidegger speaks of 'my being towards death'. It can't be assimilated to other cases of fear and distress – it is fear towards death. I remember saying at the APA that what we feared was 'having to die' but not death itself. Nagel replied that he wouldn't mind 'having to die' if he did not end up being dead. That kind of shut me up.

The fear isn't always bad. The Good Book says that the fear of the Lord is the beginning of wisdom. Fear has an intentional object. This cannot be avoided when you discuss death. Responses to it vary.

Voice C

It may be that my death is good in certain circumstances. I may be terminally ill, in agony, and so on. So having to die may be extrinsically good, but it is not intrinsically good. Similarly, pleasure is intrinsically good, but when I am pleased at a contemptible deed it is not good. What is good is my being displeased at it. The wider context makes a difference to the pleasure. And the same is true of fear.

Voice E

But if I am distressed at the suffering of a child, what is bad is not my distress, but the suffering of a child.

Voice C

But the complex state of affairs still contains what is intrinsically bad. The wider context is not the sum of the values of its parts.

Voice S

What is the difference between 'feeling sad' and 'fearing death'?

Voice C

Hume talks of the horror of annihilation and says he was without it. But most people when they reflect do have this fear.

Voice G

What we have here is less a thought than a force. We dread the end of life.

Voice E

This is true when I want to hold on, come what may. My life may lose its shape. And I still want to go on. Isn't there something despicable in this?

Voice C

There may come a time when there is little point in clinging on to life. One is better off dead. Whether that is despicable or not I don't know. I don't want to judge it. A fear of death is neither rational or irrational. It is a kind of natural fear, so I don't want to judge it.

Voice T

My difficulty is with your notion of intrinsic goodness and badness. This seems to be isolated from the actual reactions to death.

Voice C

G. E. Moore's method of treating intrinsic goodness was to imagine the state of affairs in isolation in the universe. He then asked whether it is better that this should exist or not. Reflection would show it was. If someone disagreed he would be wrong.

Voice F

But there are difficulties in Moore's view. As a matter of fact he was assuming a background without realizing it. The 'thing' in isolation is like a Ming vase in isolation in an art gallery. It is an artistically determined space. 'Alone in the universe' doesn't mean anything. No judgement would make sense. Further, as John Anderson points out, Moore slides from treating 'good' as a property to treating it as a relation. He smuggles into the analysis of the property the relation in which we stand to it. And that is what C seems to be doing. He wants to determine what is intrinsically good independent of any perspective.

Voice T

That is why, philosophically, we must remain at the level of different moral and religious perspectives.

Voice C

But isn't there a fact of the matter? All the perspectives show whether death is extrinsically good or bad for those who hold them. But they could be wrong.

Voice T

Of course they could, but ask yourself how they come to see this. Not by divorcing themselves from all moral judgements but by coming to some other moral judgement in the light of which they give up their previous one. But that judgement – 'that it's wrong' – has no sense apart from *some* moral judgement and that involves some perspective or other. 'Intrinsically good' or 'intrinsically bad' are not monadic terms cut off from the context of moral and religious perspectives and the specific judgements we make.

Voice G

How does 'transcendence' enter into these judgements? In what mode is it to be recognized? If we think of intentionality we can ask what kind of response is involved in desire for the transcendent. We need to get away from certain dominant models in the distinction between theoretical and practical philosophy. The good is thought of as something we pursue. Aristotle is positive and Kant negative in relation to this view. Martha Nussbaum suggests that religion is a pursuit – an attempt to go beyond the human, beyond old age, suffering, and death itself. She concludes it is meaningless. Life beyond the human would be boring and she illustrates it in terms of life with Calypso, and Odysseus' relation to Calypso. But this is a straw target. She says that the human has limits, so to attempt to go beyond them is nonsense.

But what if, unlike Aristotle, we say that the good is not an object of desire? It is not possessed. You have everything, and then you are bored.

But the desire is the recognition of perfection and, hence, of a distance. We are at a distance from goodness. The divine is not given in experience. What we experience is imperfection. Aristotle says that whatever is actual is possible, but when I experience myself as evil I experience something which must not be. As long as our thinking is in terms of means and ends we will find it difficult to appreciate a good which draws us without being something we can possess. This, I suggest, can be appreciated in terms of our being drawn by the beautiful.

Voice S

I accept what G says about 'the beautiful' and its power to draw and inspire. But Nietzsche wants to examine these concepts in a genealogical way. He ask what historical conditions give rise to these values. Kierkegaard would not agree with the analysis. In this way the experience is recontextualized. Imagine a field of daffodils. You are impressed aesthetically, but I tell you not to waste your time and get on with writing your philosophy paper. So the aesthetic or the ethical is criticized from a practical point of view. The idea that this clash can be settled from a neutral point of view is an illusion.

Voice G

Sometimes, the prudential standpoint does not recognize any other. Can we recognize other perspectives philosophically?

Voice P

We must ask what it is about finite creatures which leads them to the transcendent.

Voice G

Kant would say that it is because they are rational creatures. I do not want to say that. I don't know what kind of answer is being looked for. I simply note that the response takes place. I tried to elucidate the response without appeal to God to see how far one can get, and partly for personal reasons. The response I am talking about in response to beauty is one of gladness. I want to say that this is true with other examples.

Voice S

Would you say this about any value?

Voice G

Any absolute value.

Voice F

Go back to the example of a field of flowers. St Francis said that the way they gave praise to God put him to shame. On the other hand, Spandrell, in Aldous Huxley's *Point Counter Point*, slashes them with a stick saying, 'Damn your insolence.' It is philosophically important to see the possibility of these radically different reactions.

Voice G

You and H seem to assume that you can occupy a position, philosophically, which enables you to say how things really are. But the essence of O's point of view is that this is a first-person matter and that its character changes when viewed philosophically. It's like taking pebbles out of water.

Voice S

So a genealogy of morals is misplaced.

Voice G

Yes.

Voice V

Don't we have to admit that even in philosophical discussions the offering of an example has persuasive force? Doesn't it invite you to go along with it?

Voice F

You'd better be careful here, otherwise one will end up saying that one can give a perspicuous description only of one's own perspective. 'Go along with it' is ambiguous. It may mean 'personally agree with' or simply 'acknowledge'.

Voice H

And that is why we need first-person and third-person perspectives. They must be brought together. Unlike F, I conclude that you can talk of the transcendent without talking of absolutes. So our choice is not between absolutes or meaninglessness. We can't speak of 'the human' in the void. In music, for example, Beethoven transformed what was possible before him.

Voice G

Of course I am not denying the things that people may value; various vocations, for example. I am interested in bringing out what might be meant by being drawn by an absolute value.

Voice O

The first-person perspective is important. Suppose I see two people responding to a field of flowers, one religiously and the other aesthetically. I note the differences. But, notice, thus far *I* have said nothing. For example, do I marvel at one and not the other? When I have a first-person perspective I am speaking out of it.

Voice F

But is that the only way of speaking? And in philosophy isn't the need to teach differences important in avoiding certain confusions; for example, the confusions of talking metaphysically of the ultimately real?

Voice G

I am talking about a beauty which beckons. In wanting to be clear about it I have to have a respect for truth. For Descartes, truth and perfection come together, as do doubt and imperfection.

I was referring to this when I said that the beautiful reveals my imperfection, my distance from it. That is why I said also, in contrast to Aristotle who said that the actual was possible, that my resistance to beauty, my violation of it, though actual, is something which cannot, should not, be.

Voice H

Surely, what Aristotle meant when he said that the actual was possible was that it can happen. You may say, 'It must not be.' Aristotle is saying that unless it *can* be it can't be. You may say it must not happen, but it's sure happening.

Voice E

But G is showing us examples which it is difficult to leave at a third-person level of appreciation. You are invited to share them. You are asked: can you do anything with them?

Voice S

Wittgenstein tries to get us to see the possibility of seeing things in a certain way, but you can still walk away.

Voice F

Certainly, Wittgenstein says that if a way of looking at things does you harm, drop it, though it may harm many people. On the other hand, if you *can* see it in that way, you may still not appropriate it personally. That can be true where religious notions of transcendence are concerned.

The differences in this conference lie between those who want to identify transcendence with the ultimately real which is said to be religious in character; those who think this notion of transcendence does not do justice to religious notions; those who think that certain religious possibilities can be appreciated only if they are felt to make a personal demand on one; those who think that the religious ideas are suspect, but offer different conceptions of transcending what is banal and purely prudential in human life; and those who think that philosophy's task is the descriptive one of bringing out the character of different perspectives, religious and secular, descriptions made necessary, not simply by our tendencies to generalize, but by our tendencies to misunderstand and falsify the heterogeneity of perspectives in human life. These discussions began by considering, whether, if we abandon metaphysical conceptions of Transcendence and Truth, ordinary conceptions of transcendence and truth are rescued from philosophical distortions of them.

Index

Absolute, the, 7, 13, 25, 29, 57, 241,
  242
action, 178, 183, 192, 193, 196, 198,
  210, 212, 214, 215–16, 221, 226
Aischylos, 221
Allen, Barry, 1, 2, 25, 26, 30, 32, 33,
  36, 37
Allen, Woody, 142
Anderson, John, 282
Aquinas, St Thomas, 51, 59, 125,
  128, 140, 267, 273, 274, 275
Aristophanes, 215, 216, 232
Aristotle, 31, 183, 205–6, 220–2, 223,
  227, 283, 286
art, 20, 90–1, 96, 229, 235–6, 239,
  261–2, 273
artifact, 2, 11, 15, 16, 20, 252
aspazdesthai, 211–16, 218, 230–1, 232,
  238
autonomy, 197–9, 201, 204, 212, 225
Ayer, A. J., 9, 23

Barabas, Marina, 3, 233–4, 236–43,
  246
beauty, 4, 209–18, 221, 233, 235,
  236–40, 242–3, 246, 283, 284, 286
Bentham, Jeremy, 223
Boyle, Robert, 13
Brandom, Robert, 23
Brooke, Rupert, 54, 59
Buber, Martin, 226–7
Buddhism, 114, 117–18, 119, 120,
  123, 259
Burden, Chris, 238–9

Calypso, 179, 180–3, 184, 220–1, 283
Christian, William, 127, 129
Climacus, Johannes, 98–102, 103,
  104, 105, 107–8, 268–9, 270–1
Conant, James, 246
concept formation, 237–8
contingency, 7, 15, 18, 19, 28, 33–4,
  35, 91, 242–4, 247
Cupitt, Don, 44

death, 3, 50–1, 82, 133–47, 149–73,
  179, 188, 277–82: vs. dying, 135,
  140–1, 143
Derrida, Jacques, 97, 102, 103,
  268
Descartes, René, 13, 187, 188, 193,
  194, 224, 229, 286
desire, 165, 170–1, 179, 183, 185,
  193, 196, 203, 206, 214–15, 283
Devil, the, 35
dialogue, 3, 216, 276
Diamond, Cora, 246
Di Noia, J. A., 3
Diotima, 181, 217, 231–2
disinterestedness, 12, 13, 14, 34–5,
  98, 99, 100, 105–6, 269–70
divine, the, 76, 79, 80–2, 86, 89, 91,
  178, 179, 180–2, 186, 187, 188, 195,
  214, 221, 244, 251, 283
dualism, 18, 56, 192, 199, 201, 233,
  236, 247
Dubos, Rene, 46
Dupré, Louis, 124

Einstein, Albert, 79
elenchos, 178
elitism, 60–2, 258–9
ephiesthai, 183, 186, 188–90, 194, 198,
  205–6, 208, 210, 213–16, 218, 221,
  222, 223, 231
Epicurus, 137–8, 139, 141, 144, 147,
  153, 158, 164, 169, 171
epistemology, 16, 27, 28, 52, 54, 68
Eryximachos, 215
eschatology, 48, 50, 65, 67, 69,
  260
eternal life, *see* immortality
eternity, 50
ethics, 8, 22, 193, 196, 213, 226, 233,
  236, 238, 277
evil, 45, 46, 61, 62, 152, 159, 161,
  186, 188, 190, 200, 227, 260, 283
evolution, 14, 15
existentialism, 229

288

DATE DUE
